The Dramas of Life . . .

Botsotso 20

First published by Botsotso in 2019

Box 30952 Braamfontein 2017
Email: botsotso@artslink.co.za
Website: www.botsotso.org.za

the plays©the playwrights themselves
the visuals©the playwrights themselves

ISBN 978-0-9947081-5-1

Editorial board: Allan Kolski Horwitz, Siphiwe ka Ngwenya, Ike Mboneni Muila
Design, layout and make up: Vivienne Preston

CONTENTS

THE DRAMAS OF LIFE...

Examining the state of playwriting in South Africa over the past fifteen years, one is not surprised to find that those writers who wish to engage with the wider socal realities, provide reflections of a society in crisis – the first bloom of liberation in the 1990's having quickly dissipated and the contradictions of apartheid capitalism, which the 1994 political settlement had not honestly and adequately addressed, becoming more and more apparent.

And so racism [as addressed in *Isithunzi]* continues to bedevil us; patriarchy and the broader imbalances of gender relations [as explored in *Sleeping Dogs* and *Finding Me*] still haunt relations between men and women of all cultures, both the secular 'western' and the tribal; the spectre of homophobic attitudes [as represented in *The Couch]*, despite legal freedom, still taints contact beween the gay and straight worlds; issues of corruption and misgovernance [as dealt with in *The Good Candidate* and *Shoes and Coups]* increasingly bleed our scarce public resources so that the majority are trapped in poverty; the education system [as highlighted in *Iziyalo Zikamama]* badly fails working class youth, condemning them to a vicious cycle of few skills and great need; and, finally, the *burnout/ sellout* of the seeming 'progressives' of the 1980's, continues to spawn violence and mistrust [as dissected in *Book Marks]*.

As such, the overall picture is not edifying. But in noting these depressing truths, it is encouraging that playwrights are, firstly, not shying away from raising them; and secondly, that they are doing so in original and thought provoking ways so that engaging and absorbing theatre is made and not just despairing propaganda. And in so doing, even, if at bottom, the picture is negative, they plant proverbial 'seeds of change' – for surely, we all must hope that a new generation can reverse the self-destructive patterns of behaviour that drive both the old white economic and social structures and the new black elite.

One must also comment on the technical proficiency of the playwrights. While most follow a conventional structure of linked scenes setting out a narrative, there are also more experimental approachs which mix styles and collapse different structures into new wholes. For example, the three largely work-shopped plays [*Iziyalo Zikamama, Finding Me* and *The Couch]* use contrasting techniques to drive themselves: *Iziyalo* creates a chain of independent characters and situations/scenes which taken together give a grand picture illuminating its theme of reading as a critical skill/activity; *Finding Me* follows a similar pattern in developing its situations depicting contemporary gender relations but two main characters, who witness a series of over-lapping conflicts, anchor the piece giving it a more Brechtian feel; *The Couch* triggers its action with key monologues delivered by each of the characters whose inner 'devils' thereafter reveal themselves. Interestingly, *Book Marks* also uses monologues to launch itself but after introducing all the characters, allows them to withdraw and then return, one by one, before everyone is finally present and participates in its violent climax.

Overall, the plays create strong, memorable figures:- from the two brothers pitted against one another and their humiliated mother in *Isithunzi;* to the unhappy husband and wife whose childlessness causes much pain and confusion in *Sleeping Dogs;* to the poor township coffin maker, his prostitute lover, the thuggish soldiers and other inhabitants of a mythical African republic who struggle for salvation in *The Good Candidate;* to the hyped up caricatures of the two 'super women' who contest for power in *Shoes and Coups;* to the listless, conforming students who share digs but whose intimacy is blown apart in *The Couch* — all these and more give life to the different personalities and language rhythms that fill the spaces of our ghettoised, pressured society.

While more commercial plays [that have a middle class suburban audience] and stand up comedy dominate the performing arts, the type of committed theatre represented in this anthology demands critical responses from the audience. Sadly it is under threat because of severe financial restraints and limited audiences and, like poetry, is viewed as an incidental art form so that its practitioners struggle to mount productions. But on the strength of these plays, one can see that the inspiration and soul-searching that live theatre offers will not easily be suppressed.

ALLAN KOLSKI HORWITZ
JOHANNESBURG

THE MARKET THEATRE

The Market Theatre present's "Isithunzi" a DAC Incubator Project

ISITHUNZI

26 MAY - 18 JUN 2017

Author: Sipho Zakwe | Director: Luthando Mngomezulu

ZWAKALA
FESTIVAL
2016 Winner

arts & culture
Department:
Arts and Culture
REPUBLIC OF SOUTH AFRICA

#MarketTheatre
f ⓨ ⓟ in g+

BOOK AT **WWW.MARKETTHEATRE.CO.ZA**

WRITER'S NOTES

The writing of ISITHUNZI was influenced by a gruesome video which went viral in January of 2007. This video saw five black cleaners [4 females and 1 male] being forced to eat food which had been urinated on, after which they were made to perform demeaning activities on University premises [the University of Free State]. The people responsible for carrying out these activities were four white male students from the University who justified making the video by claiming that it was for a school project – a claim which was later found to be untrue. The play follows the lives of two brothers, uScelo and uMuzi, sons of one of the ladies humiliated in the video. Muzi and Scelo are at two opposite ends of the stick but each, in his own way, faces up to and wrestles with the task of reclaiming their family's dignity.

As a black male, originally from KwaZulu-Natal [a province which prides itself on its moral teachings], the video struck a nerve so intense that the complexities of this incident, and its dynamics within the South African context, demanded that they be explored and expressed in a body of work. Along with the racial tension which the actions/violations perpetuated – not only in the University but in the country as a whole – issues of morality, mercy and respect also called for examination. Loosely translated as 'shadow' in its singular form, ISITHUNZI explores themes of dignity, respect and reconciliation with both self and other. As such, it is a piece which allows for individual introspection as well as for dialogue to take place with regard to the big 'elephant in the room': the overt racism which we tend to shrug off as part of history but which always seems to slip through the cracks and unveil its commanding presence.

Essentially, ISITHUNZI's core message, which is embedded in its text, is to illustrate to people of colour that reconciliation with oneself and with each other is a vital component in defeating racism and healing the black community. Hence the play's ending which sees the brothers, Scelo and Muzi, moving towards reconciliation. It creates a warmth and tenderness which leaves us with a sense of hope and optimism with regard to their particular relationship and to the general social detoxing of all the damage that racism causes.

HISTORY

ISITHUNZI [previously entitled *The Cleaners*] was first performed by Duma Ndlovu Academy graduates Sipho Zakwe and Lungani Mabaso under the direction of Luthando Mngomezulu on 16 June, 2016 at Space.com [Joburg Theatre]. As recent graduates from DUT at the time, Sipho and Lungani knew that they had to create their own work in the industry in order to maintain and hone their skills. Shortly after this run at Joburg Theatre, the pair entered the 2016 annual Market Theatre Zwakala Festival, under the mentorship of Omphile Molusi, resident writer of the local soapie, *Scandal.*

The play won first place at the festival and was awarded a full three week run at The Market in 2017 [sponsored by the National Arts Council]. After being produced by The Market, it was selected to represent that theatre at the first ever NAC 'Trade Fair'– a one-week festival which saw plays from all around South Africa compete against each other. ISITHUNZI won Best Direction [Luthando Mngomezulu] and Best Production respectively. Thereafter, it became part of the 'Troubling Seasons of Hate' Conference organized and held by WITS University.

ABBREVIATIONS

a. FX: Special effect
b. US: Up stage
c. USL: Up stage Left
d. CSL: Centre stage left
e. CSR: Centre stage right
f. SFX: Special effects
g. USC: Up stage centre
h. DSC: Down stage centre
i. AV: Audio visual

PREFACE

USC are blinds which are used to project visuals and for shadow puppetry. They are also used for costume and scene changes. The character of SCHALK is played by MUZI.

SCENE 1

SCELO and MUZI stand at CSL and CSR. A spotlight shines on each of them. SCELO, who is neatly dressed, well-groomed, wears a jersey around his shoulders and a digital watch on his wrist. He is walking to squash practise in an upright posture and happy manner; he carries a duffle bag which accommodates his sporting gear. MUZI on the opposite side wears the cleaner's uniform and a 'spoti' hat on his head. He sweeps in a joyful manner. MUZI receives a phone call from his mother who is audible through the sound system. MUZI answers the phone.

MUZI: Hello oledi.

Silence.

MUZI: Hello . . .?

[FX] MA: Ja Muzi . . . *[Hello Muzi]*

MUZI: Ja oledi . . . yonkinto ihamba kahle? *[Is everything alright?]*

Silence.

MUZI: Oledi . . . ? *[Mom]*

[FX] MA: Yonke into ihamba kahle mntanami. *[Everything is alright my child]*

MUZI: Usunjani kodwa wena lapho ekhaya? Uyalulama? *[How are things at home? Are you feeling better?]*

[FX] MA: I'm getting better my child . . . I just . . .

Pause.

[FX] MUZI: Khuluma oledi . . . *[Speak Mom . . .]*

Pause.

[FX] MA: I just called to tell you that . . .

MUZI: To tell me what?

Pause.

[FX] MA: That I love you.

MUZI is not sure how to respond.

[FX] MA: Not at any given point do I want you to question the love I have for you and your brother uScelo. Whatever evil this world throws at you, I need you to promise me that you will not retaliate and act out of anger. Such battles are not for us to fight, but they are that of the Lord. Act in a way that shows your morals and how you were raised. Walk a different path to the one taken by your father because we cannot afford to lose another member of the family. Nguwe inhloko yalelikhaya manje. Kumele ube isibonelo kumfowenu. Uma singashiwa nguwe ubani ozomusiza ekuqhubezeni izifundo zakhe? So promise me mnt'anami, that you will try your best to do good in every given circumstance. It is the only way that a person can fight a battle without the risk of losing their dignity in the process [. . .You are the head of this house now. You need to set a good example for your brother. If we had to lose you who would help me in furthering his studies?]

MUZI: [Confused] Oledi iqhamukaphi yonke lento? [Mom, where is this all coming from?]

[FX] MA: Muzi . . .promise me.

MUZI: Are you sure everything is okay?

[FX] MA: Ngithembise mnt'anami. [Promise me my child]

Pause.

MUZI: Ngiyakuthembisa Oledi . . . ngyakuthembisa. [I promise Mom, I promise]

MUZI'S mother drops the phone. MUZI is left curious and confused. Shortly after, SCELO and MUZI simultaneously receive messages on their cell phones. The 'Reitz Four' video is projected on to the blinds USC.

MUZI: Schalk!

SCELO: Jou moer!

They both dial on their cell phones. They speak simultaneously.

MUZI: Oledi . . .

SCELO: Schalk . . . !

MUZI: [Angry] Indaba ungangitshelanga ngalento sonke lesi sikhathi? [Why did you not tell me about this?]

SCELO: Why did you do that to my mother?

MUZI: iProjecti?

SCELO: A project? That doesn't give you the right to treat them like that Schalk.

MUZI: Lokho akubaniki imvume yokuthi beniphathe noma ikanjani. [That does not give them the right to treat you like that]

11

MUZI: Akubalulekile ukuthi ivideo ngiyibone kanjani! Ubugula sonke lesi sikhathi ngenxa yaleya mgulukudu! *[It does not matter how I saw the video! This whole time you have been sick, it was because of those scum]*

SCELO: Oh, that's really petty of you Scalk.

> *Pause*

MUZI + SCELO: Yes, it is!

> *The simultaneous conversations stop.*

MUZI: Ngiyeza ekhaya manje ngizokubona . . . *[I am coming home, now]*

> *MUZI turns to leave but stops abruptly.*

SCELO: Yes! That is exactly what I think of you right now, petty and insensitive.

MUZI: If I stay here, I will see Schalk and his friends and I will just go . . .

SCELO: . . . crazy!? How am I crazy? You are insane for even thinking about treating vulnerable old ladies like that!

MUZI: Kulungile Oledi ngizosala la emsebenzini. Ngeke ngimenze lutho uSchalk. *[Alright, I will stay here at work . . . I won't do anything to SCHALK].* MUZI drops the phone. He gasps angrily in thought for a moment.

MUZI: Schalk!

> *Furious, he begins looking for SCHALK.*

SCENE 2

SCELO and SCHALK carry squash rackets. A squash court is projected onto the blinds USC. SCHALK is very warm, friendly and caring towards SCELO.

SCHALK: You know Skhelo, I've been thinking about ways of getting our games to move faster. I'm not saying that your style is slow or anything like that, I mean, defence is a strong component of the game. But we need to move on to like . . . the exciting stuff now, offensive play . . .

SCELO: Small talk won't wipe that video off the internet jou blerrie fok!

SCHALK: Geez Skhelo, calm down.

SCELO: What were you all thinking doing the "power grub" on them?

SCHALK: *[Playfully]* Agh we were just having fun with the Skwizas. We did not know that the video would go viral.

SCELO: But why with the cleaning staff, Schalk? With my mother?

SCHALK: It was funny man; did you see? The Skwizas were having the time of their lives.

SCELO: Bet you wouldn't be laughing if I made your mother eat my shit.

SCHALK: *[Offended]* Skhelo, don't be like that now, boytjie.

SCELO: Schalk, you're the one that peed in that damn stew!!!

Pause. SCELO'S outbreak sparks a tense moment.

SCHALK: *[Bursts into laughter]* With all this screaming and shouting do you know what you sound like? An APE! *[Making monkey noises]*

Silence

SCELO: *[Disappointed]* I'm glad you find this funny Schalk.

Pause. SCHALK notices SCELO'S genuine disappointment.

SCHALK: Okay, here is what we will do . . .

He pulls out his wallet and takes out a R50 note.

SCHALK: . . . You are going to take this and you are going to buy your mother some flowers from the florist down the road. It's the least I can do Skhelo. I wouldn't want to jeopardise the friendship between me and you.

SCELO: I was thinking that maybe you guys could come over to my house for a formal apology over the weekend.

SCHALK: By the township?

SCELO: Yeah.

SCHALK shrugs.

SCELO: Come on Schalk! Meet me half way. This is my mother we are talking about. Come over and apologise to her in person if you really don't want to jeopardise our friendship.

Pause. SCHALK takes a moment to think things through.

SCHALK: I will speak to the gents and see what they say.

SCELO: *[Smiling]* How about this Saturday?

SCHALK: I can't promise anything hey, I don't know if the gents will agree to come so don't get your hopes up buddy.

SCELO: *[Smiling]* Great, see you and the gents this Saturday.

For a moment, SCHALK is uneasy. But his energy quickly picks up again.

SCHALK: Enough with this chit chat. Let's play now Skhelo.

SCELO: Now what were you saying about my playing style earlier?

SCELO serves. SCHALK and SCELO play a game of squash facing the audience.

SCHALK: You need to attack more!

SCELO: You need to DEFEND first!

SCHALK: ATTACK!

SCELO: DEFEND first!

SCHALK: ATTACK!

SCELO: And then finally you . . . ATTACK!

*SCELO wins the round by defeating SCHALK; he shows great excitement.
The two play out the end of scene.*

SCENE 3

*MUZI walks home in fury. SCELO walks home still dressed in his squash gear.
He carries flowers in his hand.*

MUZI: What gives them the nerve to treat my mother like that? Do they
know how hard she has worked to keep the dignity of this family? Now
they think they can just come and take that away from us, not this time
Schalk. Umthetho wenu niyafana nonke, ukubona umuntu omnyama
ehlukumezeka kunijabulisa ngendlela eyisimanga. Nami ngizojabula
ngendlela eyisimanga mhla sihlangana. *[You are all the same, you enjoy
seeing black people suffer. Well, I will also get my fair share when we meet
Schalk . . . I will skin you alive]* I will not rest until I find you and your
friends Schalk, and when I do, I will slaughter you like a goat in the
butchery. Ngizonihlahlela bafana bami!

SCELO: What Schalk and the gents did was unacceptable! It was absolutely
normal for me to react like that, I mean my mother was humiliated – how
else was I supposed to react? I sure as hell did not react like an ape. I am
not an ape. Yeah, I am not an ape. Hey Schalk! I AM NOT A FUCKING
APE! How can apes beat you at your own game, Schalk? Fuck you and
your ape talk! Fuck you, fuck you and fuck you for ever calling me that!

MUZI: No, no, no! I cannot go against iOledi. I promised her that I would
not react this way. Angikwazi ukuphinda lento eyenziwa itimer, lokho
kuzosiphindisela emuva, nami ngizofela estok'sini njengaye. Kodwa
uyazi wafela iqiniso, asikwazi ukuyekela abelungu ukuthi besixhaphaze
noma ikanjani. Sekwanele manje! . . . Cha Muzi, khuzeka. Ubani ozosala
ebe yinhloko yalomuzi? Who will help Scelo with his fees at school?
Ngizoshiya iOledi ukuthi lihlupheke lodwa? Cha nsizwa, yehlisa umoya,
uzolithola icebo. *[. . . I cannot repeat what my father did, that will set us
back. I will rot in jail just as he did. But he died for the truth. We cannot
allow whites to keep treating us in this manner. Enough is enough. No Muzi,
you cannot do this! Who will be the head of the house? I will leave Mom to*

suffer by herself? No, Muzi, keep calm. You will find a solution to all of this]
SCELO: No, no, no! I cannot say that to Schalk. He is the only white friend I
have. Besides, he gives me lunch money when Muzi can't. His father helps
us with food from his farm and plus he just makes me look cool in front of
everybody. He brings me dignity. I don't want to lose all of that. Schalk just
needs to speak to the gents, they come over for dinner, and they apologise.
The only way we can get through this is if we reconcile, set our differences
aside, and put all of this behind us.

SCENE 4

*A stressed and depressed looking MUZI is seated; he speaks to Ma who is
represented by the audience. Ma's voice is heard through SFX as her face is
projected onto the blinds CS.*

MUZI: Ngiyakuzwa Oledi, ukuxola yikho okusiza ukuthi umuntu engabi
nosizi uma oniwe, kepha kunzima ukuhlala nalolusizi, nalentukuthelo
evuthayo ngaphakathi kwami, sibe sazi ukuthi baziphilela kamunandi le
emajalidini labafana. *[I hear you, Mom. Forgiveness is the only way that a
person's heart can be at peace when one has been wronged. But it is hard to
live with this pain knowing very well that Schalk and his friends are living
peacefully in the suburbs]*
Enter SCELO.
SCELO: Sorry I left my clothes on the floor this morning Mom. I was late for
school. It won't happen again . . . howzit bro.
*SCELO approaches MUZI with a fist bump but MUZI gives him the cold
shoulder. SCELO is disappointed.*
Pause.
SCELO: You saw the video?
Pause.
MUZI: You got those for her?
SCELO: Well, actually they're fr . . .
Pause.
SCELO: Yeah . . . flowers are a good way of showing someone that you care.
[Shouts out] They're for you, Mom.
MUZI: If you cared then she would have been the first person you attended to.
SCELO: I had practise.
MUZI: Then you prioritise Scelo! iOledi has locked herself in her room for

the past couple of days. Have you even thought about checking up on her, seeing if she's okay?

SCELO: I was going to.

MUZI: Nini?

SCELO: When I come back from squash practise.

SCELO appears to be disappointed in himself. So is MUZI.

MUZI: You need to stay away from them.

SCELO: But they are my friends.

MUZI: You'll make new friends. Baningi ontanga bakho la elokshini. *[. . . there are many boys your age here in the township]*

SCELO: I can't have friends here in the township. My mind-set is way different from theirs. What would we even talk about?

MUZI: I don't care what you talk about. We have become a big joke in this community because of them. Now stay away from them.

SCELO: No!

MUZI: No?

SCELO: No! Muzi I'm old enough to make my own decisions. I'll be friends with whoever I want to be.

MUZI: Oh, so you are old enough? Well then I guess you are old enough to buy your own clothes. I guess you are old enough to provide transport and pocket money for yourself.

SCELO: I didn't mean it like that.

MUZI: No? Then tell me what else you are old enough for so that I can stop wasting my time giving it to you. I guess you are old enough to pay your own tuition fees.

SCELO: That's not what I said.

MUZI: That's what it sounds like Scelo!

SCELO: Look Muzi, I know that you and mom have made a lot of sacrifices for me, and I appreciate that. But is it my fault that I have all these opportunities? That I go to that university? Is it my fault I can have white friends and you can't because of your selfish sentiments?

MUZI: There is nothing selfish about protecting my family. You know damn well what their kind has done to people like us over the years – yet you call me selfish for protecting you against them?

SCELO: Their kind? It is people with this kind of race ridden mentality that prevent this country from moving forward.

MUZI: I don't care about the rest of the country! I care about what goes on in this household.

SCELO: What's the difference?

MUZI: The difference is that I don't bury my head inside smelly trashcans just so that I can make this country a better place. I don't tolerate cleaning after everyone's mess just so that this country can move forward. I don't sacrifice my dignity for this country. I do it because I owe it to iOledi. It is my responsibility to look after this household. It is my responsibility to take care of you. Do you think I enjoy seeing guys my age building their future while I work trying to build yours? I also have dreams Scelo. I also want to receive an education just like you but I can't because I have the burden of taking care of you . . .

MA: Sekwanele! Bo Mnguni! Bo Qwabe bo Yeyeye! Bafana bami yekani ukulwa. You know how this has affected me, how it has affected the cleaners and the family. Muzi, Uma ufuna ukungisekela ekuphatheni lomuzi kuzomele wehlise ulaka, ungafani noyihlo. Nawe Scelo, ungasukuba nenkani mfana wami, qala ngoku lalela ukuthi omunye umuntu uthini ngaphambi kokuthi uphendule. Kuyangithokozisa ukuthi sengikhulise amadoda anemibono yabo, ngiyathokoza futhi ukuthi lamadoda engenza noma yini ukuvikela uMama wabo, lokho kutshengisa ukuthi niyangithanda. Ngiyanithanda name bafana bami, kepha musani ukulwa. Ingalo yomthetho izokuxazulula lokhu okwenzekileyo. Thina kumele sihlale emkhulekweni, qha! *[Enough! Mnguni, Qwabe, Yeyeye. Boys, please stop fighting . . . Muzi, if you want to help me in running this household, you will have to lose the aggression – do not be like your father. And you, Scelo, do not be hard headed, listen to what the other person is saying before you make your point. I am glad that I have raised two men who have their own views, who strive to protect their mother at all cost. That shows that you love me. I love you too. But we have to have to let the law take its course. The only thing we should dwell upon is prayer.]*
    Pause.

SCELO: Yes Mom, we can't fight violence with violence – that only ends in turmoil, history has taught us that. Forgiveness is our only option. They're coming over this weekend.

MUZI: Ini?! *[What?]*
    Slight pause.

SCELO: They said that they want to apologise to you, Mom.

Great disappointment fills MUZI'S face

MUZI: He is bringing the enemy into our home . . . Ma?

Pause. MUZI waits for Ma's response, it does not come. MUZI attempts to leave.

MAH: Muzi! *[Uneasy]* Whatever you do, stick together bafana bami.

MUZI exits. As SCELO attempts to give his mother the flowers, the image on the blinds abruptly disappears; SCELO is saddened.

SCENE 5

FEMALE REPORTER: We are here at the University of the Free State where a video went viral, a video that saw four black female cleaners and one male cleaner being forced to eat what was a very unappetizing mixture by four white university students. I have with me here a student who has seen the video. Tell us, sir, what was your reaction when you first saw the video?

TEBZA: I was sitting there by the cafeteria then I hear lots of noise coming from this side and other students laughing. Me, too, I think I also want to laugh, so I go there and look to the phone and I say "yo," I say "yo, yo, yo . . ." because it's not nice what I see them do to our mothers.

REPORTER: How is the atmosphere in the university following this incident?

TEBZA: How must atmosphere be like? Because is usual this thing here. They treat us like dirt these people. The ANC Youth League toyi-toyi one week, and then do press conference, and then nothing happen after that, even them they have failed us. This thing it never stops.

REPORTER: So you think this was an act of racism?

TEBZA: This is UFS, my madam. Of course it was racist!

SWITCH TO:

REPORTER 2: Thank you, Natasha. I am standing here with one of the cleaners from the University. How does it feel to have your colleagues treated in that manner?

MUZI: uMa'wami loya.

REPORTER 2: Oh, really! *[Turns to camera]* One of the ladies in that video was actually his mother. If I may ask, how is your mother coping after this unfortunate incident?

MUZI: *[To camera]* Into engingayisho ukuthi inhlonipho into engakhuliswa ngayo. Uma labafana bekwazi ukwenza into ebuhlungu kanje kwabazali

18

bethu, kutshengisa khona ukuthi bakhula kwimizi engena nhlonipho futhi engena engenamfundiso ekutheni umuntu om'dala uphathwa kanjani. *[All I want to say is that respect is a principle that I was raised by. If these boys can do something like this to our mothers, that goes to show that they were raised in households which have no teaching of respect and how elders are meant to be treated.]*

REPORTER 2: What is your way forward from this point onwards? Are you taking legal action?

MUZI: Wena ubungenza njani? *[What would you do?]*

SCENE 6

uBaba uMPUNGOSE is sweeping in the toilets. He seems calm and at peace with all that is happening around him. MUZI sets up his work station by emptying his bucket which reveals a number of cleaning liquids. He picks up one of these and begins to open it.

MPUNGOSE: Hayi Muzi! Awusazivikeli manje? Ufuna ukulimala? *[Muzi, do you not protect yourself anymore? Do you want to get hurt?]*

   MUZI pulls out gloves from his pockets and puts them on before picking up the chemical substance.

MUZI: Ewu, umqondo wami awukho la Baba uMpungose. *[My mind is elsewhere Baba uMpungose]*

   Slight pause.

MPUNGOSE: *[Concerned]* Ungasukucabanga kakhulu mfana wami, konke lokhu okwenzekile kuzodlula. Thula wena ubheke. *[Do not think too much my child. All that has happened shall pass. Watch and see]*

   MUSI examining the cleaning liquid.

MUZI: With all that is happening right now, I wouldn't mind washing my lunch down with a bottle of this today. Ngikhohlwe nya ngayoyonke lento. *[So that I may forget about all of this]*

MPUNGOSE: Hayi Muzi! Ungasukukhuluma kanjalo mfana wami, we will all get through this together. There is no need to bring death into this, death has no place here. *[No Muzi! Do not speak like that my child . . .]*

MUZI: Well, I have had enough. Ontanga bami bashayela izimoto zikanokusho, bathenga izindlu, mina ngiyasebenza la, ngizama ukwakha ikusasa lika mfowethu uScelo, kepha wake weza kumina ezongibonga?

Cha. Kunalokho uvumela labelungu ukuthi bemudonse ngekhala . . .
*[People who are my age are driving luxurious cars and buying houses while
I work tirelessly trying to build Scelo's future. But has he ever thanked me for
that? No. Instead, he allows Schalk and his friends to control him.]*
MPUNGOSE: Uyabona lokhu okwenzayo Muzi, ubudoda. Indoda inakekela
umndeni wayo ngasosonke isikhathi. *[See, what you are doing Muzi, it is
called being a man. A man takes care of his family at all times.]*
MUZI: Kepha ubani onakekela mina? *[But who is there to take care of me?]*
MPUNGOSE: Ngiyezwa ukuthi uthukuthele kepha ungasukulibuka ngeso
elibi loludaba. Ngokuhamba kwesikhathi inhliziyo yakho izogculiseka,
ithole ukuthula ngoba uzobe wazi ukuthi ubunomthelela kwimpumelelo
yomfowenu uScelo. *[I can tell that you are angry my child, but please do
not look at this situation in a negative way. As time passes, your heart will be
filled with joy and happiness because you will know that you played a vital
role in Scelo's success.]*
MUZI: Angisafune lutho oluzongihlanganisa noScelo mina. Kusukela
namuhlanje ukulamana kwethu ngokwegazi kuphela, hayi ngokomlomo.
*[I do not want anything to do with Scelo. From today onwards we are only
brothers by blood.]*
MPUNGOSE: Ulahla umfowenu? Igazi lakho? Akusizo izenzo zendoda lezo
mfana wami. *[You are disowning your own brother? Those are not the doings
of a man.]*
MUZI: *[Angrily]* Wazini wena ngokuba indoda?! Ukube ubuyindoda
ubuzovikela oMama mhla behlazwa ilabafana ngalola suku, kepha
awenzanga lutho! *[What do you know about being a man? If you were
truly a man you would have protected my mother that day, but you didn't!]*
[Regretting his outburst] Ngiyaxolisa baba. *[I am sorry.]*
MPUNGOSE: Empilweni yensizwa kuke kufike isikhathi la okumele
ehlise khona umoya, ekhophozele eze eguqe phansi ngamadolo omabili.
Lezenzo azichazi ukuthi lowomuntu akasiyo indoda, ngoba indoda
awuyiboni ngamandla ayo, kepha uyibona ngobuhlakani nezenzo zayo.
Uyibona ngokuthi ikwazi ukudlula kubobonke ubunzima emhlabeni
ukuze inakekele umndeni wayo. Ngiyafisa ukuthi ngabe kukhona
ebengingakwenza ngalolasuku ukusivikela kulaba bafana, kepha isimo
sasingangivumeli. Kwakubalulekile ukuthi ngizehlise, ngicabangele ikusasa
labantwana bami. Angazi ukuthi ngingenzenjani uma ngingalahlekelwa

ilom'sebenzi ngoba yiwo owondla umndeni wami. Indoda uyibona ngokuzimisela kwayo ekwenzeni noma ikuphi okudinga ukwenziwa ukuze ivikele umndeni wayo. Nami ke ngangenza lokho ngalola suku, ngangivikela umndeni wami, njengendoda. *[There comes a time in a man's life when he needs to be calm and submissive. That does not mean that he is less of a man because you do not see if a man is a man simply by his physical strength, but you see a man by his actions and wisdom. You see a man by his ability to be able to go to the ends of the earth in order to take care of his family. I do wish there was something I could have done that day to protect us from those boys but my situation did not allow it. It was important that I submit to those boys because this job is all that I have, it is what allows me to take care of my children. You see a man by his willingness to endure all hardships in order to be able to take care of his family. That is what I was doing that day. As a man I was willing to protect my family by all means.]*

Baba uMPUNGOSE exits with a sense of relief. Spotlight on MUZI as he holds the chemical substance in his hand and looks at it thoughtfully. This scene is underscored by suspense evoking music. The stage is flooded with red light.

MUZI: Ngiyindoda.

He hurriedly exits carrying the chemical substance.

SWITCH TO:

We see SCELO at the Reitz residence frantically looking for SCHALK. He has difficulty fulfilling this task as other white students at the residence urge him to leave.

SCELO: Schalk! Schalk! Schalk! Howzit, have you guys seen Schalk? Come on gents, I just want to talk to Schalk quickly. Schalk! I just want to have a word with him and then I'm gone, you won't even remember I was here . . . Schalk!

SCELO gets pushed further upstage by the white students of the residence

SCELO: Come on gents! Don't do this, it's me, Scelo! . . . Schalk!! There he is, Schalk! Are you still coming tonight? . . . to apologise, to my mother . . . alright, cool buddy, I'll see you at 6pm. I'm so sorry gents.

SCELO exits hurriedly.

SCENE 7

SCELO arrives back home. MUZI sits USL. There is immense tension between the two brothers. The two stand in silent tension for a moment.

MUZI: Bathe bazofika ngasiphi isikhathi? *[What time are they coming?]*

SCELO: At six o'clock.

Tension leaves MUZI'S face as it is replaced by a generous smile. SCELO slowly returns the smile. We get the sense that the two brothers have reached a consensus. They embrace.

MUZI: Uyazi Scelo wangikhumbuza lenganekwane eyayixoxwa iOledi.

[You remind me of the tale that Mom used to tell us]

SCELO: The one that Mom used to tell us.

The two brothers kneel CS facing each other while using elaborate hand gestures to tell the story as they reminisce. Their gestures are captured in shadows by the blinds USC as assisted by lights to achieve a shadow effect. As they reminisce, SCELO translates the story in English alongside his brother. They speak simultaneously.

MUZI: Kwasukasukela . . . *[Once upon a time]*

SCELO: Cosi . . .

MUZI: Kwakukhona uNogwaja, noFudu. UNogwaja noFudu babekukhonzile ukuqhudelana. Wabe esesukile ke uNogwaja nokuhlakanipha kwakhe. Wagijima uNogwaja, wathi esemaphakathi nomqhudelwano, wathi ngoba lusa thothobala uFudu, ake ngithi ukuphumula kancane. Wabe esezumeka uNogwaja . . . uFudu lona lwabe liyincenga indlela kancane kancane lwaze lwafinyelela emphelandaba. Wathi uma ephaphama uNogwaja, wazibuza ukuthi "sekudlule isikhathi esingakanani ngilele? Ake ngiqhubeke ngigijime." Wabe esegijima uNogwaja, uma esefinyelela emphelandaba waba nokukhulu ukudumala ngokubona ukuthi ufudu lufinyelele emphelandaba kuqala kunaye . . . cosi cosi iyaphela.

SCELO: Once upon a time there was a rabbit and a tortoise and they were very good friends. And one day they got involved in a race. The rabbit set off with tremendous speed leaving the slow tortoise behind. But when he got to the middle of the race, the rabbit was very tired and decided to rest for a while. The tortoise on the other hand kept striding along making slow but steady progress. When the rabbit finally woke up, he asked himself, "How long have I been sleeping? I had better get going!" So he jumped up and ran as fast as he could but by the time he reached the last stretch, he saw the tortoise up ahead crossing the finishing line. Yes, the slow old tortoise had won the race.

MUZI: Uyazi Scelo iOledi laliqinisile. Kumele sibayeke oNogwaja bephaphe, kodwa thina sizithobe njengoFudu, size sinqobe! *[Mom was always right. We should let the rabbits flourish and be merry, but we should keep humble, composed and tactical until we conquer]*

MUZI smiles; a big smile fills SCELO'S face. SCELO exits.

MUZI looks to see if he is the only one in the room; his smile changes into a grin. He now has urgency and purpose in his step. He prepares a table with food; we see him lacing the food with the poisonous chemical he had taken from his work place.

SCENE 8

A dinner table is set in preparation for the arrival of SCHALK and co. MUZI wears a fancy shirt, a 'look' we would not immediately associate with his character. MUZI and SCELO are both anxiously moving about. SCELO makes a phone call. SFX: Cell phone ringing

SCELO: Pick up, pick up, pick up . . .

SCELO: *[Whispering]* Damn it, Schalk, where are you!? Don't let me down now, I'm counting on you. Even Muzi has decided to give you a chance. Just this once, please! Don't disappoint me.

SFX: Voicemail tone.

SCELO: Damn it!

Pause.

MUZI: *[Anxious]* And then?

SCELO: Nothing.

MUZI: Awubazame futhi. *[Try them again]*

SCELO: Muzi, I'm sure he'll see my missed calls and get back to me. *[Slight pause]* That was like the 10th time this evening.

MUZI: Maybe the 11th will be the one. Isn't 11 your lucky number?

SCELO: *[Smiling]* You remembered! You know, in a game of squash the first person to reach 11 points wins. And it's all about DEFENCE, DEFENCE, DEFENCE – not because you are a coward, but to enable you to stay in the game long enough to counter your opponent and attack when they least expect it. It's what I always tell Schalk, DEFENCE, DEFENCE . . .

MUZI: Jah jah jah! Defence defence defence. Awubazame futhi. iOledi lilele manje Scelo. *[. . . Try them again Scelo, Mom is falling asleep]*

SCELO: I'm sure he's driving at the moment, he'll see my calls. Let's give them a bit more time.

MUZI: Asithembe kanjalo. Phela nami leli shirt ngilibolekwe uBaba uNxumalo next door, liyangifanela kodwa? *[Let us hope so. I borrowed this shirt from uBaba uNxumalo next door. Does it look good on me?]*

> *SCELO does not respond.*

MUZI: Hayi, wothi ngiyobaqalaza la ngaphandle labafana, nakhu bengafiki. *[Let me have a look outside, see if they're coming]*

> *MUZI exits*

SCELO: *[Worriedly]* Don't worry, Muzi, they are on their way, Schalk never lets me down.

> *Then, noticing the different foods on the table, in a sly manner, starts eating from one of the plates. At first he seems to enjoy the taste but suddenly feeling nauseous, coughs and falls to the ground.*

SCELO: Muzi! Muzi! Muzi!

> *Enter MUZI; he sees his brother on the ground gasping for air, notices that the food on the table has been tampered with. He is devastated as he tries to aid his brother.*

MUZI: Scelo! Scelo mfowethu, phefumula Scelo! Ma! Bab' uNxumalo! Sizani bo! Scelo! *[Scelo! Scelo! Breathe . . . Ma! Bab' Nxumalo! Help!]*

> *Black out.*

SCENE 9

Similar to scene 5, MUZI sits facing the audience. He speaks to the audience as though he were seeing SCELO on the hospital bed. SFX: hospital machinery

MUZI: Ngiyazi ukuthi ngikuphoxile. Angibanga umfowenu omdala obekumele ngibe uyena. Cishe ngakubulala mfowethu. Cishe ngabulala ithemba lalomndeni . . . Sengiyabona manje ukuthi bekungamele ngivumele labafana ukuthi bengene ngaphakathi kwethu. Yimi wonke lo . . . esikhundleni sokuba ngisivikele isithunzi salomndeni, yimi oqhubeza ukushabalala kwaso. Ngixolele Mnguni . . . *[I know I have let you down. I have not been the older brother that I was meant to be. I almost killed the hope of this family. I now see that I was not meant to allow those boys to come between us, this is all my fault. Instead of protecting our dignity as a family I have made matters worse]*

SCELO: Muzi why don't you ever listen to me? Why do you always have to retaliate with violence? Do you enjoy seeing Mom hurting?

MUZI: Cha.

SCELO: Then why do you continue to use violence as a way of resolving things? From now on we are going to do things the right way. We will wait and see what happens at the press conference. Oh, they will get what they deserve and we will regain our dignity, but that does not mean that my friendship with Schalk has to suffer. Everything will get back to normal. We need to have faith Muzi.

MUZI: Ngiyakuzwa mfowethu, kodwa uma lendaba ingaxazululeki ngendlela efanele ... ngeke ngikuthembise lutho. Asilinde sibone ukuthi kuzokwenzakalani kwi Press Conference. *[I hear you brother, but if this matter is not dealt with accordingly ... I cannot promise anything]*

Silence. Lights slowly fade to black.

SCENE 10

All students living at the Reitz residence are gathered in the AV room of the residence. A specific badge, symbol, or coat-of-arms is projected onto the blinds to represent the tight brotherhood of the Reitz residence. A spotlight shines on SCHALK DSC as he addresses the audience as though he were addressing his fellow dorm mates. He carries a dumpy beer bottle in his right hand and a pocket book on his left. His lack of balance suggests that he has had one too many. There is a strong sense of pride in SCHALK'S tone of voice. While he does so, we see SCELO further US with his textbooks scattered on the floor. He is busy with his school work.

SCHALK: Who ... who ... who are we!? Who ... who ... who are we!? Ja, gentlemen, julle is die chosen mense. Everybody must bow down to you. Julle is die mooiste ras in die hele wereld. You are the superiors made in the image of the Almighty. It is not me who says this, but our father in the heavens. So if you are die chosen mense, then you have the right to choose who sets foot on your territory. You have the right to say that you do not want integration in the Reitz residence. You are simply protecting your dignity, your security and your culture from being contaminated. Because who ... who ... who are we!? Ja, julle is die top of die pops. *[Clears his*

25

throat] Revelations 8, verse 2, right here in Reitz's old bible . . . *[He reads from his book]* "They will try to shove rainbow nation down your throat but you had better refuse to swallow, for if you do swallow, your shit will stink until the second coming". So I ask you broers of the Reitz nation, do you swallow and face the stink? If you do, then voetsek to your rainbow nation, but if you spit, then sit your wit ass down. I'll wait . . .

SCHALK drinks from his beer bottle. Enter SCELO US looking for SCHALK.
SCELO: Schalk! Schalk!

SCELO stands on a platform only to see SCHALK addressing his dorm mates.
SCHALK: Ah, so you have all remained seated, good, because you have been sold a lie. There is no white in the rainbow. But when you mix all the colours of the rainbow, Johnny *[Pointing to audience member]* jou slim kop, what colour do you get? BLACK! So this nation of the rainbow was never meant for you. Nee, boetie, we have been sold a lie. If they want to protest at the press conference tomorrow, they must come with their pangas and we will come with the mighty force of the LAW! Who . . . who . . . who are we? Die top of die pops! If you look to your left, there is not a single darkie on this premises, and it should stay that way, and if you look to your right . . .

SCHALK'S eyes lock onto SCELO'S; tears run down SCELO'S cheeks; the two share a moment as SCHALK is frozen in shock, this sobers him; SCELO'S rushes off. SCHALK has a moment to himself where he tries to comprehend what has just happened. It is as though he is trying to decide whether to chase after SCELO or not. When his moment of contemplation passes, he downs his beer and lifts his empty bottle victoriously into the air.
SCHALK: REITZ forever!!!

SCENE 11

News reporters interview students. This is just before the press conference.

REPORTER: As we can see, the police are being very vigilant on this day of the press conference as rumours of war between the students at Reitz residence and the ANC student organization have been doing the rounds. Let us speak to the students to get their thoughts.

STUDENT 1: Absolutely nothing wrong with the video. The students were just expressing how they felt about the integration policy that the university has been trying to implement. Ain't nothing wrong with expressing yourself.

STUDENT 2: Ja, I heard they cooked a stew or something, and then they added chunks of garlic and protein powder or something like that. I mean how do you eat that?

STUDENT 3: There are rumours going around that students from the black res's and the ANC student organisation are planning on invading the press conference, that's why I got my camera on standby should anything go down today.

STUDENT 4: Well, I do think it's an act of racism, I mean, I doubt they would have done this to their own mothers, let alone to women of their own race.

STUDENT 5: I saw absolutely nothing wrong with the video. Those ladies looked like they were having the time of their lives.

SCENE 12

Press conference; a typical press conference table with microphones is projected onto the blinds. Reserved seats are labelled as follows: Advocate Kemp J Kemp, Professor Jonathen Jansen, Officer Johan Kruger. One actor sits in the audience while the other remains hidden behind the blinds and does Voiceovers for the other characters [dignitaries].

JEFFERY: Good day, ladies and gentlemen. For those who have just walked in, we have just heard statements from our dignitaries regarding this matter. Without any further delay, I would like to open the floor to the media for any questions you might have.

JACKSON: Hi, my name is Jackson from Morning Live. Mr Kemp in your statement you said that the workers voluntarily took part in this initiation ceremony. How did you come to the conclusion that they volunteered?

MR KEMP: Well, when one watches the video without any preconceived influence, you begin to see that all those involved seemed to be enjoying themselves. So to come to the conclusion that there was mockery and degradation would be totally inaccurate.

SIZWE: Good day, my name is Sizwe from SABC NEWS, and my question is directed to the accused. Many people whom I have interviewed have labelled you all as racists, how would you respond to this?

MR KEMP: There is no clear evidence that supports that judgement . . .

SIZWE: Mr Kemp, if the students could answer for themselves please.

SCHALK: I erm . . . I have also heard those rumours but erm . . . I could never be racist, hey. On a daily basis I interact with people who are not the same race as me. I offer what I can to the needy, I play my part, we have tons of black friends so . . . racism is definitely not in our hearts.

SFX: Chaos.

JEFFERY: Can we keep it down please! Order! Can we keep it down please.

Chaos dies down.

JEFFERY: Yes sir, go ahead.

MUZI: What measures have been taken by the university in order to ensure that this matter is dealt with accordingly?

MR KEMP: *[Clears throat]* We have proposed to the Vice Chancellor that the students each be given a R5,000 penalty fine in order to compensate for the alleged misconceptions.

MUZI stands up

MUZI: 5 000!? Ningitshela ukuthi impilo ye Oledi lami ingango 5 000? Ninyile! Niyazi ukuthi umndeni wami usuhlukumezeke kanjani ngenxa yalemigulukudu!? Izimpilo zabantu abamnyama zibalulekile nazo. Nizoyithola into eniyifunayo . . . *[R5,000? Are you telling me that my mother's dignity is worth R5,000? Do you know how our families have suffered because of the shame that those boys have imposed? Black people's lives also matter . . .]*

SFX: Riot sound in the distance begins to build up as though it is edging closer and closer. "Dubula dubula! [shoot shoot] Dubula Dubula!" Protesters enter singing protest song and carrying sticks, phangas, knobkerries etc

JABU: Bakephi labelungu!? Where are these racists! *[He sees Schalk and his friends attempting to escape]* Vimba! *[Obstruct them!]*

Smoke is dispersed from the smoke machine. A chaotic atmosphere is created. We hear a gunshot as Jabu falls to the ground.

SWITCH TO:

SCELO: Schalk! Schalk wait!

SCHALK: Wat!?

The two lock eyes. SCHALK has a look of anger; SCELO has a look of confusion and despair. SCELO tries to speak but no words come out.

SCHALK: You are wasting my time, man. Go back to your broer!

SCELO: Schalk, why?

SCHALK: Why what?

SCELO: Tell me you did not mean what you said.

SCHALK: I don't know what you're talking about!

SCELO: Back at res, when you were talking to the gents, tell me you did not mean what you said.

SCHALK: Skhelo just go back to your broer and leave me alone!

SCELO: Schalk please!!

SCHALK: Hey, Skhelo, man, stop acting like a . . .

SCELO: It's not Skhelo! Or Scales . . . It's Scelo!

SCHALK: Skhe . . . Skhe . . . Fok man!

SCHALK attempts to leave but SCELO holds him back.

SCELO: SCHALK!!!

SCHALK turns around and knees SCELO in the groin area.

SCHALK has a moment of realisation as to what he has done before rushing off. SCELO falls to the ground and cries in agony.

SCENE 13

Lights fade. The Reitz Four video is projected onto the blinds, now distorted and unclear. The video is underscored by SFX; flash-backs of moments in SCELO's journey.

- SCELO: You need to stay away from them.
- SCHALK: Ag, we were just having fun with the Skwizas. We did not know that the video would go viral.
- MUZI: It is my responsibility to look after this household. It is my responsibility to take care of you. Do you think I enjoy seeing guys my age building their future while I work tirelessly trying to build yours?
- SCHALK: With all this screaming and shouting, do you know what you sound like? An APE!
- MA: Whatever you do, stick together bafana bami.

SCELO screams and moans with great distress. He lets out a piercing cry and rolls on the ground. The aesthetics of this scene are representative of his internal transformation and emerging self-awareness.

SCELO: Fuck you Schalk! Fuck you! How could I let you come between me and my brother? How could I let you do that to my mother? How could I allow you to break me like that? You will never do this to my family again – do you hear me!? Fuck you and your disrespect! Fuck you for all the names you call me! You will never get away with this do you hear me!? SCHALK!!!!!!!!

After catching his breath, SCELO finally finds his feet.

SCELO: I am not skhelo! I am not Scales! I am SCELO GUMEDE!

Enter MUZI.

MUZI: UMnguni, uYeyeye, uPhakathwayo, uQwabe, uGumede! Osidla behlezi . . . asambe mfowethu. *[He recites their clan names; . . . let us leave brother]*

SCELO: No, no, no, no Muzi! We cannot just leave like that. We have to bring back the dignity of our family. It is what you always wanted, it's what Mom always wanted. Let us do it for her, let us do it together.

MUZI is lost in contemplation for a moment.

MUZI: Ngilandele. *[Follow me]*

MUZI exits; he is followed by SCELO. The two emerge with containers filled with flammable cleaning chemicals. They empty the contents around the auditorium with great satisfaction before meeting back on stage. They embrace. MUZI pulls out a cigarette and lights it. He hands the matches over to SCELO.

MUZI: Kwasukasukela . . . *[Once upon a time]*

SCELO: Cosi . . . *[I am all ears]*

SCELO lights a match.

The flame burns until lights fade.

END

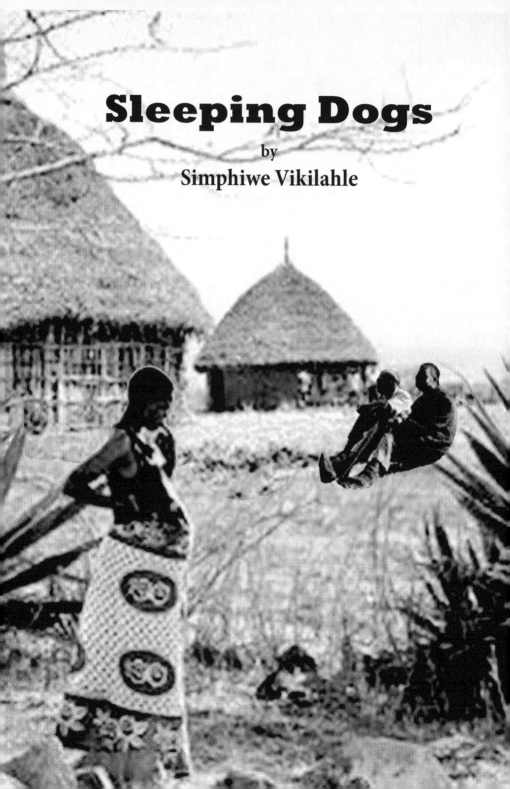

Set in Ndamase Village in the Eastern Cape, testing established tradition, the play revolves around the expected role of a woman to bear an heir and continue the family line – and a challenge to those assumptions. Overall, love and romance at Mlangeni's house are disturbed by a darkness that kills all his dreams.

'Sleeping Dogs' premiered in Port Elizabeth at the Iphulo Drama Festival in 2012. Thereafter, Vikilahle's talent was spotted by the UK-based Swallows Foundation for his highly acclaimed play 'The Journey' which has also been selected for a season at the Market Theatre.

CHARACTERS

MLANGENI: A gardener   Ziyanda Qwane

NOVUSUMZI: Mlangeni's wife   Lonwabo Xatasi

SIZWE: Mlangeni's friend   Anele Peni

BAWO uKHOVU: Old man of the village   Kanyile Mngqwamnci

SITHINI MAHOLA: Singer and woman of the village   Sithini Mahola

While the audience is entering, SIZWE is holding an umbrella; NOVUSUMZI is under the same umbrella. There are many cloths hanging from the umbrella and there is a zinc cup lying on the floor. Both SIZWE and NOVUSUMZI are talking to the audience but in an incoherent mumble. While doing so, they take turns to drink from the zinc cup.

NOVUSUMZI then moves to the far side of the stage. There we find her house, a modest rural hut in which a cooking stove is used as a heater; on top of it is a pot of uMphokoqo. In the centre of the hut, there is a table and a bunk stool. NOVUSUMZI is sitting on a straw-mat sewing her husband's trousers. SIZWE is left sitting under a tree, enjoying the shade.

MLANGENI enters excitedly; he is drunk. He approaches NOVUSUMZI.

MLANGENI: Mafumbatha kaSiwela, uNgcayimili, uNgqinib' ayibotshw' ingenanxeba. Fumb'i today is a special day, true or false? You see, Mlangeni met with Mr Simpson today.

NOVUSUMZI: *[Little laugh]* False.

MLANGENI: Rhaa! *[Giving her a paper]* What's this?

NOVUSUMZI: *[Novusumzi examining the paper]* A house.

MLANGENI: Who owns it?

NOVUSUMZI: It's Mr Simpson's house. Why are you so happy?

MLANGENI: He is selling it.

NOVUSUMZI: You will never be able to afford this house Mlangeni! You are dreaming.

MLANGENI: Novusumzi, you are right but wrong. Not even one person in this entire village will be able to afford that house, but your husband, your beautiful husband, has a plan.

NOVUSUMZI: And what is the plan?

MLANGENI: I was doing my garden this morning when a good plan came to me. I then went straight to Sizwe. I told him about my plan. He then told me that this season he won't be using his garden. Then after that I went straight to Mr Simpson.

NOVUSUMZI: You went there drunk?

MLANGENI: Hayi, Novusumzi! I had not been to the horses yet, the beers were the second on my list for today. Kaloku Novusumzi I only wear this suit on special occasion, yhaaazi when I got to his house Mr Simpson was standing there and he greeted me with that English ascent, "Greetings

Mlangeni" then we went inside. Rhaa Novusumzi sithe singekahlali naphantsi, I managed to get myself two muffins, ndazithi. Haa, haa, that's when he showed me around the house. What a big house Novusumzi, that house it's so huge – big walls, many rooms, and so many toilets! Uyabona ke Novusumzi in that big house, there's a field there. I can plant my watermelons, tomatoes, pumpkins . . .

NOVUSUMZI: Kodwa what was the cause of your visit?

MLANGENI: Yima ke mfazi wam, bendicimb' akuzubuza, I want Mr Simpson to buy his mealies directly from me starting from this season and he agreed.

NOVUSUMZI: *[Excitedly]* Uvumile, hlala phantsi tata naku ukutya . . .

MLANGENI: Wait, what do you have in the kitchen?

NOVUSUMZI: Spinach with mash potato.

MLANGENI: Bring them to the table. Let's celebrate my wife!

NOVUSUMZI: *[Like a TV presenter]* Tell our listeners about your deal with Mr Simpson.

MLANGENI: He showed me this paper, telling me about the history of the house. I want more from Mr Simpson, ngcayimili, to teach me about the business side of things so that when our first child comes, my son, we are already rich. Khangela, he will sleep in his own room, we will paint it with colours, beautiful bright colours, there will be toys everywhere – Superman, Spiderman Batman . . . no, Vusumzi, uyamaz' u Ben Ten, uzabelapho, then we will sleep in our room, upstairs. In this big house, ngcayimili, we can even employ a maid abasisi bancedisayo – not one but many. Some will look after my boy, some will cook, some will clean, some will look after you, my princess. And before they bring food, they will all ask at once, "Can we bring food, Mr & Mrs Ntaba?" And what will be your response?

NOVUSUMZI: "Yes – before it gets cold!" *[Laughing, in a playful mood. Going to the phone]* "Mrs Ntaba on the phone. Yes, your phone Mr Ntaba, Mr Simpson's on the line."

MLANGENI: Soon they will buy everything from me, there at Mlangeni's general dealer. Novusumzi please don't tell anyone about my plan but if uSizwe asks you can tell him. *[Smiling]* Before I forget, I went past the market. *[He takes out a present and gives it to her. But on opening it, she is not very pleased]* Yivule yeyakho, injanii, you know, Novusumzi, all this time you've made me very happy, the only thing we need to do now is to fulfil my mother's wishes of having uMzukulwana. Then you my wife will be caring for my first born child uvusumzi kaNtaba. *[Slight pause]* You know my first wife never made me this happy.

NOVUSUMZI: *[With anger]* Your mother was here.

MLANGENI: Don't tell me she asked about a child again.

NOVUSUMZI: She asked me if I had finished the bottle she gave me. I said yes. Then she commanded me to take off my clothes, I stood in front of her naked and she stood there staring straight at my stomach. Then she asked me, usahlamba? I said yes, I last had my periods two weeks back. Then she threatened me that you will have to take a second wife. She told me I'm not worthy to be in your family, she insulted me, she said I am barren. I don't know what more she wants from me Mlangeni. I've tried everything – just last month there was the ceremony of Itsiki here.

MLANGENI: Don't worry yourself Ngcayimili, She is getting old, but uyakuthanda.

NOVUSUMZI: I think we need to give your mother what she wants.

MLANGENI: The time will come.

NOVUSUMZI: And no more gambling for you! We have to start a family.

MLANGENI: Yes, we need that money.

NOVUSUMZI: The men you gamble with are not even married, hayi tata. When you loose akubikho mnandi aphe ndlini. . . you don't even touch me.

MLANGENI: I don't lose every day. Like I said, everything is seasonal. There is a season to sow and a season to reap, a season to win at gambling and a season for you, my wife, to get pregnant. *[Laughs]* Hey, we will even donate some of the money to this village, uSibonda uSithwakumbana, to build roads for my new BMW, khangela ndikhwele nawe qha baby ukwi front seat. Pooo, pooo . . . ndakugila mna ukuba akunangqondo.

SIZWE: *[From under the tree]* Ahh! Thul' alinyathelwa, Nkung' enamadla.

MLANGENI: Ngena ba-akuzangakulala.

NOVUSUMZI exits.

SIZWE: *[Entering and shaking hands with MLANGENI]* Nkunzi kaNtaba.

MLANGENI: Ngutata lowo, kwedini, ngutata lowo.

SIZWE: Come and see! *[Showing him something at the window]* Hee kwekwe, yeyakho leya, that brown calf . . . *[Pointing]* . . . when your first child comes into this world, that cow will be big. You must slaughter it to celebrate.

MLANGENI: Yima kwedini. *[Exits and returns with a stick]* Ziph' ezakho, ziph' ezakho. *[NOVUSUMZI enters]* Here's my wife ! *[Holding her]* We were standing like this kwedini, in front of the priest.

SIZWE: *[In a playful mood]* Do you take this woman to be your wife in sickness . . .

MLANGENI: I do, I do, *[Trying to shake his hand]* Yity' apha . . .

NOVUSUMZI: No, my turn, ndiyafuna nam.

SIZWE: Do you take this man to be your husband in sickness and in health, for richer or poorer, till death do you fall apart.

NOVUSUMZI: Yes, I do.

MLANGENI: My favourite part! *[Trying to kiss NOVUSUMZI]*

SIZWE: Not now, not now . . .

MLANGENI: You are jealous, you are jealous maani sizwe! *[Laughs and moves around the house]*

SIZWE: *[Seriously]* I'm leaving the village next week ntang' am. I will be working Embuthweni in one of the big companies there.

MLANGENI: Hamba ntang' am, kodwa uzubhale. *[SIZWE exits]* Ungawalibal' amanz' olwandle.

> BAWO uKHOVU and SIZWE take and lift black cloths, at the same time making sounds to symbolise the end of the scene. They then use white ones to symbolise the start of a new scene – this action is carried out throughout the play. NOVUSUMZI gives MLANGENI a bucket and ikhuba; NOVUSUMZI shakes the keys, MLANGENI smiles on the other side of the "door". As he moves, there's lot of joy. Suddenly he stops next to SIZWE who is sitting down. SIZWE beats the bucket with a small stick and MLANGENI continues with the journey to the garden.

MLANGENI: Molo Tata.

> The OLD MAN he is addressing does not respond, just looks down shamefully; he makes a sound every time MLANGENI wields his spade. A song accompanies the scene. NOVUSUMZI shakes the keys again and throws them down on the ground. SIZWE takes a small plate, eats from it once; NOVUSUMZI makes a sound. The action becomes faster and NOVUSUMZI takes a small tin with corn and pours it on top of her head. Then she runs to the river to wash herself. Having done that, she goes to MLANGENI in the garden. She looks him straight in the eyes and whispers in his ear. NOVUSUMZI turns to go back home; MLANGENI watches her with smile on his face.

MLANGENI: *[Turns to BAWO uKHOVU]* Ndizakuba nomntwana. *[Decides to follow his wife. To NOVUSUMZI]* Wait . . . what do you have in the kitchen?

NOVUSUMZI: As I told you – spinach with mashed potato.

MLANGENI: Bring everything to the table. Let's celebrate my wife! *[Putting down his garden tools]* Igama lakhe nguNtsika yekhaya.

NOVUSUMZI: Ukuba yintombi.

MLANGENI: *[In a happy mood]* Uzakubayinkwenkwe. *[He feels her stomach]* Awu Nkungw' Enamandla, I dreamt about a boy, my first born son of Thuli alinyathelwa, Ozandla zimanzi kodwa zibambene. He was running around in this house. Then he decided to go to the river. I followed him and watched him swimming. I was on my toes in case he drowned but he was a brave boy and nothing bad happened.

NOVUSUMZI: That was really your dream?

MLANGENI: Of course! And now we need to pay for all those toys in the shop . . . the child will soon come to life. Awu ndizakuhamba naye. *[Taking a chair]* Ndithi tiki, tiki, wen' ufana nobani, wen' ufana nobani.

NOVUSUMZI: *[Laughs]* You mustn't take him gambling!

She prepares uMqombothi for MLANGENI; he carries on smiling, looking away. Once she serves him, he drinks then stands up full of energy.

MLANGENI: *[Tickling her]* Awwwu! Lentwana mayifund' ukwenz' imali.

NOVUSUMZI: *[Teasing him]* Then he will miss everything, and gamble every day. My child is not going there. *[Long pause]* Ngcayimili ndiyakuthanda.

MLANGENI: Your beer is sweet, lovely . . . Ndiyakuthanda nam, you make a good strong beer. Tomorrow we will slaughter a sheep

NOVUSUMZI: Why?

MLANGENI: For my mother. But also tell your mother, your sister and your father to be here tomorrow – a proper family dinner, we will make known the news that you are pregnant.

MLANGENI takes a nip of brandy and pours it outside the house; while doing so he mumbles some words and his clan name. NOVUSUMZI is looking at him. MLANGENI sits ebuhlanti until he falls asleep.

At this point, BAWO uKHOVU and SIZWE take and lift black cloths and make sounds to symbolise the end of the scene; they then use white ones to symbolise the start of a new scene.

NOVUSUMZI wakes MLANGENI ebuhlanti and goes to prepare breakfast; MLANGENI enters the house.

NOVUSUMZI: Don't tell me you slept there the whole night.

MLANGENI: I've mentioned my son's name to my father several times. Ntsika, the name will stand. I think he likes the name.

NOVUSUMZI: Nkung' enamandla, don't tell your friends in the garden that I'm pregnant – they can bewitch our child before he is born.

MLANGENI: I will try . . .

NOVUSUMZI: Ungawalibali amanzi. *[Giving him water]*

MLANGENI: uNtsika must stay warm inside the house.

NOVUSUMZI: Don't stay until late in the garden.

MLANGENI: Feed my dog at least by 6 o' clock.

MLANGENI exits, NOVUSUMZI shakes the key; MLANGENI walks to the garden. SIZWE beat the bucket with the stick while MLANGENI continues the journey to the garden. SIZWE starts singing. MLANGENI reaches the garden; BAWO uKHOVU enters.

MLANGENI: Molo tata.

BAWO uKHOVU: Indlu yakho iyatsha Mlangeni.

MLANGENI stares at the OLD MAN in disbelief then takes his things and runs to his house.

MLANGENI: *[Entering his house]* What's happening Novusumzi?

Looking around, he sees her sitting in a corner, afraid.

NOVUSUMZI: There were people who wanted to see you, they were very angry . . .

MLANGENI: Why . . . who was here?

NOVUSUMZI: uNqaba noThembekile, they are saying, they are saying . . . their dogs are dying in their households but yours is still alive.

MLANGENI: *[Staring with disbelief]* Iph' inja, iph' inja Novusumzi?

He runs out to look for the dog. SIZWE becomes the dog and looking away, turns to MLANGENI. Then he lifts his leg, moving it around as if it is the dog's tail. MLANGENI enters the house.

Moving fast, he picks up his spear and is about to go out

NOVUSUMZI: Uyaphi Mlangeni?

MLANGENI: I'm going to Nqaba's house.

NOVUSUMZI: Not with that attitude . . .

MLANGENI: Novusumzi. . .

39

NOVUSUMZI: That spear can turn and stab you, Nkung' enamandla . . .

MLANGENI: You are not married to a dog, Novusumzi, ooNqaba abazovela bangene apha benze unothanda xa ndingekho, yindlu yendoda le.

NOVUSUMZI shakes the key in the door and quickly turns to MLANGENI.

NOVUSUMZI: Our son uNtsika will need you. *[Coming close]* You can teach him so many things Nkung' enamandla, ukuboph' ikhuba – how to shove the spade in the garden, to gamble only once the season comes.

BAWO uKHOVU and SIZWE act out their routine signifying the ending and beginning of scenes.

MLANGENI: Tomorrow its Saturday, you will take a rest. Don't forget to lock the door.

MLANGENI takes the bucket and Ikhuba and proceeds to the garden.
SIZWE beats the bucket with a small stick.
NOVUSUMZI throws away the key as SIZWE starts eating.
She is now heavily pregnant; her stomach is a big round ball.
Every time SIZWE eats, NOVUSUMZI feels a pain in her stomach.
All the while, MLANGENI is working in the garden.
Enter the OLD MAN and stares at MLANGENI.

BAWO UKHOVU: Nkung' Enamandla, you will never have kids. Take your coat, and go rest at home. Your wife is pregnant with someone else's child.

MLANGENI stares at the OLD MAN in disbelief. Then he runs home quickly. When he enters the house, NOVUSUMZI is sitting afraid in a corner; but she suddenly jumps up and hugs him.

NOVUSUMZI: I'm afraid! I thought those people might come again and kill me. *[Moving away]* Do you want tea?

MLANGENI: No.

NOVUSUMZI: Food?

MLANGENI shakes his head, takes his bottle of brandy and drinks; then he walks out to SIZWE'S house.

MLANGENI: *[Drunkenly, with a crying voice]* Khawuvule Sizwe!

SIZWE: *[From inside]* Ndisemanzini Mlangeni.

MLANGENI: My house is falling, Sizwe! An old man told me something today. He said I will never have kids but my wife is pregnant! Sizwe, she is pregnant, and who can be the child's father?

SIZWE: I'm sorry Mlangeni.

MLANGENI: Kuzakulunga Nyana KaNyuluba, Indlu yam izakuphinda ime kwakhona. *[Walking away]* Can you do a favour for me, my old friend? Go to my healer uVumazonke, tell him all what is happening in my house. He will instruct you what to do.

SIZWE: I'm going today, Mlangeni.

SIZWE prepares to leave on his journey – to take the bus;
MLANGENI talks again with the old man.

MLANGENI: Tell me the truth, who is the father of that child?

BAWO uKHOVU: Tell me your dream, your last dream.

MLANGENI: *[Angrily]* There was a boy inside my house, a small boy, he fled to the river. I followed him. I watched him swimming. I was standing on my toes in case he drowned, but he was a brave boy. My son was a brave boy.

BAWO uKHOVU: Your ancestors are standing far away from you.

MLANGENI: What must I do?

BAWO uKHOVU: There is a tall tree standing by your window. *[Slight pause]* Cut that tree down and slaughter a goat. Then tell your ancestors to come home.

In preparation of slaughtering a goat [played by the same actor who was the old man], MLANGENI and SIZWE walk around the animal, talking, until MLANGENI takes a spear and kills it. They take out the intestines; as they do this, the actor playing the goat becomes an ancestor with a white face.

MLANGENI: Nkungw' Enamandla, Zandla zimanzi kodwa zibambene, ukwenjenje kukuzam' ukucim' umlilo.

ANCESTOR: Zandla zimanzi kodwa zibambene, Nkungw' Enamandla. Indlu kababin' izel' amadangaty' omlilo.

SIZWE smears blood all over MLANGENI who cries out loud and kneels in front of him; SIZWE hugs him. NOVUSUMZI puts a blanket on top of MLANGENI.

The ancestor plays with a bracelet on the ground. SIZWE is also playing with a bracelet and they both raise a black cloth and a white cloth.

MLANGENI wakes up wearing clothes though he has not washed off the blood.

NOVUSUMZI puts down the bucket and Ikhuba in front of him.

MLANGENI walks out to the garden, staring straight at the old man.

MLANGENI: Xhego lam I've done everything. I slept in the kraal. I've made a ritual. I've slept everywhere in my house but my dreams are not coming true. What must I do to hear the whispers of the dead?

SIZWE: *[Entering]* Your healer uVumazonke told me to give you this. He said you are lucky to be alive. Drink this twice a day and burn this herb all around your house – you will see everything in your dreams.

MLANGENI: Ndiyabulela Sizwe, ngendiyintoni ngaphandle kwakho
SIZWE exits.

BAWO UKHOVU: Your wife is pregnant with Sizwe's child.
OLD MAN takes the herbs to the river; MLANGENI arrives at home and stands at the door staring straight at NOVUSUMZI.

MLANGENI: Novusumzi, who is the father of your child? *[She ignores the question]* I'm talking to you Novusumzi!

NOVUSUMZI: You, Nkung' Enamandla.

MLANGENI: Why? After all I've done for you! I gamble with my last cent to make you my wife. I went in the market to make sure that we become better people. But all of you . . . you killed me. Novusumzi, you of all people, you!
He places clothes in front of her.

MLANGENI: Goduka Novusumzi yiya kokwenu, umnchazel' uyihlo ukuba uwachithil' amazimba Othuli alinyathelwa.

NOVUSUMZI: I'm sorry. *[Trying to hold him but MLANGENI avoids her]*
She cries while MLANGENI takes a brandy, going next to the kraal.

MLANGENI: Nina bendlw' emnyama kababini, Nkungw' enamandla, ndicel' uxolo ngokuniphathel' ihulekazi elizenomngqakhwe emzini kabawo. Ndiyathebisa ndizakulihlamb' inyala.
He goes back to the house and finds NOVUSUMZI still sitting in the chair with labour pains.

MLANGENI: Undivile Novusumzi.

NOVUSUMZI: He raped me, I wanted to tell you . . .

MLANGENI: Save that for your father – maybe he is hungry enough to eat your lies.

NOVUSUMZI: Andiyindawo Mlangeni, ngumzi wam loo, I was chosen by your father to marry you . . .

MLANGENI: Then go to him, he is sleeping there in the grave. Tell him you are living in this house and you will never come back again.

NOVUSUMZI: I wanted to save our marriage! You were always busy in the garden – you know that you can't have kids.

MLANGENI: *[Long pause]* Bendicel' undikhwelele kwam Thabisa.

The dog barks; MLANGENI stares at NOVUSUMZI – she stands up.

MLANGENI: Hlala phantsi.

MLANGENI and NOVUSUMZI both sit, waiting. Suddenly there is the sound of a key turning. SIZWE enters; he is amazed to see MLANGENI. NOVUSUMZI meanwhile feels more and pains. They become so bad that SIZWE calls for help. Enter NONZWAKAZI, woman of the village. SIZWE and NONZWAKAZI take NOVUSUMZI out. SIZWE re-enters.

SIZWE: I'm sorry Nkungu Enamandla.

MLANGENI: Why? *[SIZWE puts the key down in the table]* Your cow has grown now. Take it out of that kraal. Slaughter it – to celebrate your first born child.

SIZWE exits.

Lights fade.

END

The Good Candidate

One man's bid to take on the powers that be

By Hans Pienaar   Directed by André Stolz

Zethu
Dlomo

Mpho Osei Tutu   Welile Nzuza   Motlatji Ditodi   Thulani Mswepi   Siphiwe Mabunagane

Fumani
Shilubana

Jan 30: 8pm
Feb 2: 1.30pm
Drama/Kyknet
Theatre
DF Malan St
Foreshore

Artscape

Somewhere in Africa, Raphael Tondoni has made peace with his future as a carpenter producing beautiful coffins for the families of the dead in his city township. So when he is asked to stand for parliament because his community trusts him, he is reluctant to agree. But the actions of the local police commander force him to change his mind and he sets off on a journey the end of which nobody could have foreseen.

Hans Pienaar's new play draws on his experiences in covering elections across Africa, but it is also a romance; Julia knows that when you fall for a good man, life is not necessarily a piece of cake. And it shows how scam artists and the poor alike yearn for that one opportunity to break free from their circumstances.

CHARACTERS

RAPHAEL TONDONI: Carpenter who specialises in colourful coffins, also chair of the local burial society. He is a good man, not interested in making money, has compassion for his clients and their problems. His hubris, however, is a tendency towards purity, to the extent that he judges people accordingly.

YESTERDAY: Raphael's friend. Honest township dweller who just wants to survive, and has a flair for organisation.

JULIA: Good-time girl with brains, who did what a girl has to do to see the world and rise up in society. Her first love was Raphael, and she tries to get back to him half-heartedly. She wants to form him to her desires.

MAGNA: Fake witchdoctor, or magic man, who conjures remedies for all sorts of ills, but is really a man of the people, not interested in exploiting them, more to act as a kind of slum psychologist.

KONI: Cowardly petty thief, who sees a chance to get some power by joining the Brown Bombers. But he has enough brains in the end to see whom he should throw his weight behind.

THE LIEUTENANT: Power-hungry, locally based policeman who has just got promotion. He ruthlessly stamps his authority over the township which he believes he rules.

MP: Scheming politician who will do anything to keep power. He is touched by Raphael's honesty though, and understands enough of democracy to fear his potential – prompting him to scheme even more.

BRA ZONDI, MA MIRIAM: Members of the burial society, but forgetful of details in their old age.

CROWD MEMBERS; Seven in total

BROWN BOMBERS; Members of a youth militia.

SCENE 1

A small square-like space in a jumble of shacks. Front right are the paraphernalia of a carpentry business: a coffin on which the carpenter is planing away. Behind him, upright are more coffins in the shape of a bird, a fish, a US dollar bill etc. In the centre leads one road around a corner, front left the rest of it goes off-stage. Singing can be heard in the background, a lament at somebody's funeral. Suddenly a youth comes running, bewildered – a dead, roasted chicken in his hand.

KONI: *[Skids to a halt, looking for hiding place, dashes into a shack, gets chased out again]* Ai, ai, they're going to catch me.

YESTERDAY: Get out of here, you scum. Go take your loot elsewhere. This is an honest man's place.

> *KONI dashes into a coffin, but lets the chicken fall. Just then the funeral procession enters the square. Four bearers are followed by a group of dancers who gyrate wildly, beating their chests, slapping the coffin with pangas.*

MOURNER 1: How happy we are!

Amina will be our messenger

To our forefathers.

MOURNER 2: They will listen to us now.

Maybe she'll even speak to the gods.

How we are suffering!

MOURNER 3: Oh, joyful day!

> *RAPHAEL sits on a chair behind his coffin, preparing to continue with his work. MOURNERS break away.*

MOURNER 4: We've done enough now.

MOURNER 1: Can we get our money now?

RAPHAEL: I am not paying you anything. I didn't hire you.

MOURNER 3: *[Protesting, gesticulating]*: But you said, "Show some respect to the dead."

MOURNER 2: That is what we are doing.

MOURNER 4: She has so much respect now she can go to parliament.

RAPHAEL: She'll fit right in. There nobody does anything – like dead people.

MOURNER 1: We moaned, and groaned, we took considerable time off from our daily work.

RAPHAEL: Daily work? What daily work?

MOURNER 1: We have things to do, important things.

MOURNER 3: We keep a watch. And that place we were watching, has gone unobserverd for several hours.

MOURNER 4: What evils are now going to breed out there?

RAPHAEL: I didn't promise you anything.

MOURNER 4: But you . . . you are the chairman of the burial society. You have to pay us.

RAPHAEL: OK. Take a coffin.

MOURNER 2: Ow, chief, you know we can't do that! Then people will think we are planning to die.

One spots the chicken lying there, holds it up behind RAPHAEL's back; they tiptoe off with it.

RAPHAEL: Everybody is dying. It's the fashion these days.

MOURNER 3: We can't die. They'll take our things.

RAPHAEL: That would be the best plan you had in a long time.

LIEUTENANT and MESCHAK burst on the scene, hitting left, right and centre with quirts.

Coffin gets dumped right there; everybody flees.

LIEUTENANT marches up to RAPHAEL, who keeps on planing.

LIEUTENANT: You.

RAPHAEL stops planing, gets up, reaches for a hammer then gets whipped on the wrist so he has to drop it again. He turns around, faces LIEUTENANT, who eyeballs him.

LIEUTENANT: You. You do you know who I am.

RAPHAEL: No.

LIEUTENANT: I am a Lieutenant. Look at my epaulettes. *[He lifts them up with his quirt]*

RAPHAEL: Be careful, they might fall off.

LIEUTENANT: *[Steps back in alarm, pats himself on shoulder while checking]* Don't make fun of me. I am the law. Who are you?

RAPHAEL: My name is Raphael Tondoni.

LIEUTENANT: Well, Raphael Tondoni, you are harbouring a thief.

RAPHAEL: Here in these shacks? It's possible.

LIEUTENANT: Possible, you say. Hey, Meshack, this man admits he's hiding thieves.

RAPHAEL: People are hungry and many steal – to stay alive.

MESHACK: Stealing is against the law. *[Storms at RAPHAEL; LIEUTENANT stops him]*

LIEUTENANT: Who are you to speak on their behalf?

RAPHAEL: I am the coffin maker here. I speak on my own behalf.

LIEUTENANT: You are hiding thieves in your coffins.

RAPHAEL: It's true. Go on, have a look. That is the most popular thing people steal around here. Death.

LIEUTENANT: You are making fun of me. Do you know I got promotion? Yes! Yesterday.

RAPHAEL: So what are you now?

LIEUTENANT: Lieutenant. It means I am an officer. It means I am the boss here. I can have this whole place searched by just snapping my fingers.

RAPHAEL: So go ahead. Start with the coffins. Let's see what comes out of them.

LIEUTENANT: *[Glares at him, as MESHACK starts opening first coffin]* Don't tell me what to do. *[He stops MESHACK from opening the coffin in which KONI is hiding]* You have spirits in there. I know you, you want to ambush us.

RAPHAEL: I am not a military man, I don't know anything about an ambush or any other bush.

LIEUTENANT: So you're saying I come from the bush?

RAPHAEL: No, Lieutenant, you are coming straight from an office.

LIEUTENANT: *[Impressed with himself, straightens up]* You can see that?

RAPHAEL: I can smell it.

LIEUTENANT: How? We have aircon in the office.

RAPHAEL: Well, it makes you smell like nothing.

LIEUTENANT: *[Looks for a moment as if he will attack him, then relaxes, sniffing the air around him]* It's true. I don't smell like any of these rubbish people here.

> LIEUTENANT and MESHACK march off again. YESTERDAY appears from shack.
>
> RAPHAEL continues to work.

YESTERDAY: What are you doing brother? You can't talk to that man like that.

RAPHAEL: That buffoon? He's too stupid to talk to any other way.

YESTERDAY: Telling him he smells like . . . nothing.

RAPHAEL: He does. He smells like a ghost. With his guns and his arrogance he won't live long.

Coffin lid jumps open, KONI gets out, giving others a fright.

YESTERDAY: See, the ghosts are also getting nervous.

KONI grabs RAPHAEL's hands, goes on his knees.

KONI: Thank you, my brother, thank you. You saved my life.

RAPHAEL: No, I didn't. I am not going to become your protector.

YESTERDAY: You scum, you pimple on a grandmother whore's bum! You scab on a donkey's testicle! Go back to your village.

KONI: What was I supposed to do? The chicken jumped into my arms.

YESTERDAY: It was a dead chicken. It was fried.

KONI: Everything has a second life near this coffin maker.

RAPHAEL: Look, brother, you were lucky, and we were lucky the Lieutenant didn't find you . . . Now beat it and don't come back.

KONI scampers off, with some more 'thank you's'.

YESTERDAY: What were you thinking?

RAPHAEL: What if they killed him? Then the army would have come in and they would be all over us.

YESTERDAY: You must go . . . and hide . . . stay out of trouble . . . like me.

RAPHAEL: Run away? Me? I am a poor man. You are a poor man. I'll be making coffins for the rest of my life. I'm staying here. At least I can pretend that this is a good, normal life.

YESTERDAY: Our lives will never be normal. Not like in the old days.

RAPHAEL: You read too many foreign magazines. From last year. That's why you have such a good name. Yesterday. You have no future because today you're always ducking and diving.

YESTERDAY: Tomorrow will be even worse. That's the only time today will be better.

RAPHAEL: Relax, Yesterday. Everything turned out OK. The Lieutenant thinks I gave him a compliment.

JULIA sashays in, dark glasses on; RAPHAEL continues as if nothing has happened, so that she practically has to go and sit on his lap, under his raised hammer.

JULIA: Ooh, I knew that.

RAPHAEL: Know what?

JULIA: That Raphael, the good man of the village, is just like the rest. He likes to knock up poor, unsuspecting women.

RAPHAEL: *[Laughing]* You're very beautiful, Julia, but you won't seduce me into . . .

JULIA: If you don't want to beat me with your hammer, you can always put your . . . screwdriver into me.

RAPHAEL: You came all the way to tell me what I know already: you'll put any tool in your pouch.

JULIA: *[Put off]* I missed you.

RAPHAEL: What did you miss about me? I don't have any money.

JULIA: You don't have any money, but . . .

RAPHAEL: So what do you want from me?

JULIA: *[Goes up to him and strokes his crotch]* What I want from you is to take you in my hand and stroke you until you rise up like a mountain and shoot off inside me like the stars across the sky. I'll make you the biggest man this world has ever seen . . .

RAPHAEL: *[Breaks away from her embrace]* You know those days are past for us. There are other men who can help you better.

JULIA: *[Defeated, pouting]* Why are you like this? What have I done? Have you no pity?

RAPHAEL: Why do I have to pity you? You know how to get around.

JULIA: Because my father died.

RAPHAEL: Your father, Zimi?

JULIA: No, my other father, Mosa. My real father.

RAPHAEL: Your real father is Zimi. Who was this Mosa?

JULIA: Mosa made my mother pregnant in the village, and then he came to the city, came here. Then my mother followed him, but he never wanted to know her, or about me. Now his family came to see us.

RAPHAEL: And they want you to pay for the funeral.

JULIA: They say we brought shame on them but that we can rid ourselves of this shame if we pay.

RAPHAEL: And you believe this?

JULIA: They only want us to make a contribution.

RAPHAEL: But they know you don't have any money. Why don't you just refuse?

JULIA: They brought a witchdoctor to come and see us.

RAPHAEL: Ahhh . . . you know better than that, Julia. You just promise the witchdoctor a chicken and he'll tell you anything you want to hear.

JULIA: But my mother . . .

RAPHAEL: You're not your mother. You're a city girl. You don't even know what a witchdoctor is.

JULIA: But what if it's true? He said my father's spirit will become an ngodzi. He'll come to make us pregnant with monsters at night.

RAPHAEL: It's all rubbish, Julia. The only men who lie more than witchdoctors are pastors in the church.

JULIA: I have a plan.

RAPHAEL: Only one plan will work: forget the father who forgot you.

JULIA: They want us to buy T-shirts for the whole family.

RAPHAEL: T-shirts!

JULIA: With my father Mosa's face on them.

RAPHAEL: That will cost hundreds of dollars!

JULIA: My plan is to sell them to the family.

RAPHAEL: The only thing you know how to sell is your pussy.

JULIA: *[Hurt, swings around]* I learnt a lot of things by selling myself.

RAPHAEL: It won't work. They will all promise to pay for the T-shirts, and then, after the funeral, you won't see them again.

JULIA: What is the burial society for?

RAPHAEL: What do you mean?

JULIA: Doesn't the burial society have a lot of money in the bank?

RAPHAEL: No, no, no. That money is for proper burials. To buy a space in the graveyard. To get the body from the mortuary. To bribe the police. Not for T-shirts.

JULIA: I will give it back to you with interest.

RAPHAEL: Julia, it's not even my money. It belongs to the members of the burial society.

JULIA: They will never know. They will only see their money has grown.

RAPHAEL: Julia, no.

JULIA: I see. It's just my luck. Why did I fall in love with a good man? Fall for a good man and all you will do for the rest of your life is suffer.

Song of the Good Man

Fall for a bad man
Life is like a piece of cake
Fall for a good man
All you get is heartbreak

Cakes are best for eating
Until only crumbs are left
Then all a bad girl does
Is find another chef

Good men make you angry
It's your life they will delay
Good will leave you hungry
Drive your dreams away

Fall for a bad man
Life is like a piece of cake
Fall for a good man
All you get is heartbreak

RAPHAEL: Julia, you don't love me.

JULIA: Raphael, I loved you once, and loved you again. I will always fall in love with you. You are my dove, and I am yours.

RAPHAEL: I, too, loved you once. But then you left me. Now I don't love you anymore.

JULIA: You only love your coffins. And your burial society. All those old women . . . It's because you're not a man anymore. *[Stomps off, RAPHAEL continues working on his coffin]*
   Lights fade out.

SCENE 2

Scene: As before. YESTERDAY comes out of the shack, tries out his cellphone; there is no signal. MAGNA the witchdoctor enters with a string of chickens in both hands.

YESTERDAY: Hey, Magna, you're a witchdoctor, help me with this thing.

MAGNA: No, brother, that's white man's magic.

YESTERDAY: It's like your magic, sometimes it works, sometimes it doesn't.

MAGNA: How now, brother, it works all the time. Where do you think all these dead chickens came from?

YESTERDAY: You didn't use magic to kill them. You used the eternal stupidity of your clients.

MAGNA: Don't say that. You'll jinx my business.

YESTERDAY: How come business is so good? I haven't seen you with so much loot before.

MAGNA: It's the elections, man. I'm working as hard as a real doctor. I've even started with bookkeeping.

YESTERDAY: But you can't read or write.

MAGNA: Nobody else can either. I make up my own figures. Numbers have their own magic.

YESTERDAY: How come the elections are making you so rich?

MAGNA: Well, you know, they changed the rules this year. Anybody can now become a candidate.

YESTERDAY: You want to go to parliament!

MAGNA: No, no, it's not me. It's all these businessmen who think because they are clever enough to cheat people, they are clever enough for parliament. So they come to me to find out what their chances are.

YESTERDAY: And they must pay with a chicken.

MAGNA: No, that's not what happens. I take the chicken and shake it, like this. *[Vigourously shakes a chicken]*

Song of the Shaken Chicken

I am just a chicken
Hunting worms all day
But when they need prediction
I will have the final say
The Shaken Chicken
The Shaken Chicken

I feel it in my wishbone
When I get so shaken
Then my legs are prone
For any old direction

The Shaken Chicken
The Shaken Chicken

But keep it all together
That's my life's big aim
Or else the bad weather
Means the pot of blame
The Shaken Chicken
The Shaken Chicken

I'll cross many rivers
A bird that's free and bold
I'll only get the shivers
When I catch a cold
The Shaken Chicken
The Shaken Chicken

YESTERDAY: I see – if the chicken dies, the man goes to parliament.

MAGNA: It's the other way round. If the chicken lives, THEN he'll go to parliament. There are eight hundred candidates for this city alone but only forty seats. So most will not make it.

YESTERDAY: Oh, I see, and if the chicken lives, you won't be able to eat it.

MAGNA: You see, if the chicken lives, they take it with them and put it in a big cage by the front door so all the people passing by can see the ancestors are on their side.

YESTERDAY: You're a smart one, Magna, YOU should go to parliament.

MAGNA: No, I'm happy to just be a psychologist.

YESTERDAY: What is a psy-cho-lo-gist?

MAGNA: That's what the white journalist said I am. He interviewed me. A psychologist is somebody who shrinks your head.

YESTERDAY: And why do you want to shrink people's heads?

MAGNA: There are too many big men with big heads.

YESTERDAY: Well, start with your own then. Just because a white man came to interview you, you think you are now a pygmy king with skulls round your neck?

MAGNA: Well, he is going to write about me and the chicken test. More white people will come to visit me, you'll see.

YESTERDAY: And you are going to shrink their heads?

MAGNA: Only if they ask.

YESTERDAY: As long as you don't kill chickens for them. They don't like that.

MAGNA: Hey, that journalist paid me well, man. Twenty American dollars.

YESTERDAY: Twenty dollars! You're not only famous, you're rich. What are you going to do with so much money?

LIEUTENANT: *[Off stage]* All people must go to the coffin maker's house!

MAGNA: What do you think? Maybe I must buy a cellphone.

YESTERDAY: To talk to the spirits?

LIEUTENANT: *[Off stage]* Lift your feet.

MAGNA: I don't need a cellphone for that. I want to talk to my wife in the village.

> *Sounds of troops marching off-stage followed by the LIEUTENANT's voice on a loudspeaker.*

LIEUTENANT: *[Off-stage]* All people must come to the coffin maker's house!

> *BROWN BOMBERS march in with an elaborate, ostentatious drill. MAGNA and YESTERDAY get up; doors slam, people stand glumly among the shacks. Two soldiers carry in boxes of food parcels.*

LIEUTENANT: Come on, you scumbags! Drag your filthy bodies here. The government wants to speak to you.

YESTERDAY: All the government wants is our money. We don't have any!

LIEUTENANT: Shut your trap, before I shove my boot into it.

> *More grumbles from the gathering CROWD; militias lift their rifle butts, people draw back.*

LIEUTENANT: I have been sent here under protest. I told the commander you are just a lot of good-for-nothings who deserve to be sent back to the bush, rubbish that just lies in the streets.

CROWD 2: Get on with it, officer.

LIEUTENANT: However, orders are orders. The government is a caring, generous . . . *[Looks at paper in his hand]* . . . in-sti-tu-tion. And so they have sent three boxes of food for you lazy bastards.

YESTERDAY: It's not the government. It's the Italians. It's written on the bag.

LIEUTENANT: Is that so? Then there must be a mistake. I'll just have to take it back. *[Gestures to soldier, who carries one box off-stage]*

> *Crowd members now turn on YESTERDAY, who takes a defensive stance.*

CROWD 2: Look what you have done now. Just shut up, or we'll lose all the food!

CROWD 5: Go and fight with the Lieutenant in another place.

LIEUTENANT: And another thing. I told the government they should punish you, rather than give you food. Because you won't vote for the government in the election.

CROWD 5: I voted for the government.

CROWD 2: I voted for the government! *[Points at another CROWD member]* It's him, he didn't! Not me. Give us the box.

There is a rush for the box and the soldiers have to shove the people away.

LIEUTENANT: OK, some of you voted for the government but there are some people who didn't vote for the government. We'll have to split up the food then.

MESHACK moves the second box off-stage to loud protestation.

The LIEUTENANT gestures to the crowd to help themselves to what remains; this leads to a frantic scramble during which most gets lost. BROWN BOMBERS march off.

RAPHAEL, who has been standing and watching, decides to say something.

RAPHAEL: People! Listen to me. Listen to me.

They look up, pay attention, since all the packets have been gathered by now.

RAPHAEL: Give me the packet. Give me back that packet!

There is remonstration but YESTERDAY gives him a packet.

RAPHAEL: Look at this. You really want to fight over this? A nut bar. A can of sausages. Cigarettes. A condom. You can't live from this. This is not going to kill your hunger.

CROWD 5: At least it is something.

RAPHAEL: But you are selling your souls!

CROWD 1: We don't have souls to sell. They've been bought up already.

RAPHAEL: Exactly. Isn't it time to say: We are dead people already. We are ghosts. We don't have anything left that they can take.

CROWD 6: We have our votes.

RAPHAEL: But a vote is useless if you just spend it on anything. Don't let the Lieutenant fool you. Your vote is your property that you own when you go and vote, and stays your property forever.

CROWD 6: They can see who voted for who.

RAPHAEL: How? Your name is not on that voting paper. It's just your cross.

CROWD 1: They have magic. They use computers.

CROWD 2: Here's the magic man. Let him tell us: is it magic?

RAPHAEL: Tell them, is it magic?

MAGNA: *[Caught off guard, improvises]* OK, OK, try this: How many letters does the alphabet have?

CROWD 6: Three dozen.

CROWD 4: Twenty-eight! Eleven!

MAGNA: You don't know. But you still believe the alphabet is magic.

CROWD 2: Because all powerful people know the alphabet. Like pilots.

CROWD 3: Like police officers, doctors.

CROWD 4: Like Jesus.

MAGNA: But one letter can cancel out all that magic. The one you use for voting.

CROWD: How do we know it is a letter if we don't know the alphabet?

MAGNA: *[At a loss, picks up a stick]* OK, try this, then. Everybody has a stick. No matter how poor, you'll find a stick somewhere. So you put that on the ground. *[Puts stick down with great showmanship]*

MAGNA: But this stick now, it's on its own and you don't know what it can do: become a snake, or a gun. *[Makes appropriate gestures of snake hissing, gun firing; the CROWD recoils]* You have to stop that magic. *[Runs over to get another stick, puts it across the other]* See? That is why your vote is a cross.

RAPHAEL: There you have it – if the magic man says it's not magic, it can't be magic.

> At first the CROWD seem to fall for his trickery, but then gather their wits.

CROWD 1: What rubbish.

CROWD 5: You think we're stupid? Those crosses get counted.

CROWD 2: But it is magic. Every time there is an election, the Lieutenant brings us food.

RAPHAEL: But he only gives you a little. He keeps the rest.

CROWD 7: We must go and get it. It is our food.

RAPHAEL: No, that is just what he wants. You go to the police station to take back the food parcels and he'll just beat you up. We must be clever. We must make him understand.

CROWD 6: Understand what?

RAPHAEL: That we won't be bought off with food, that we need food because we are hungry, not because we have a vote to sell.

CROWD 5: Why don't you go and talk to him then?

CROWD 2: Yes, Raphael, you go and tell him.

RAPHAEL: No, no. I'm not your leader. I am just the chairman of the burial society.

YESTERDAY: But everybody trusts you.

RAPHAEL: Forget it.

CROWD 5: Raphael, you always say that, you're just a wimp.

CROWD 2: You're like Magna's shaken chickens.

CROWD 5: We don't need you. We just need some sticks.

CROWD 7: And not to make crosses.

CROWD 1: No, to use it properly

CROWD 5: We'll tell that Lieutenant what's what.

But some in the crowd are getting cold feet.

CROWD 6: I must go and sell my tomatoes.

CROWD 7: I must go see my sick aunt.

The rest exit marching off, waving sticks. Lights fade.

SCENE 3

Scene: Same as before. YESTERDAY sits on a coffin with a huge bandage around his head. JULIA is nursing him, RAPHAEL sits on coffin.

JULIA: Ai, you men remain stupid creatures.

YESTERDAY: Ouch, you're hurting me.

JULIA: Don't cry like a baby now. You should have known this would happen.

YESTERDAY: You're right. The Lieutenant just said, "boo", and they all turned on their tails. Sticks flying.

JULIA: What did you think would happen anyway? That Lieutenant gave the food to his own people long ago.

YESTERDAY: I couldn't just let them get beaten up. It's . . . solidarity.

JULIA: Solidarity doesn't fill your stomach.

RAPHAEL: I'm tired, Julia. I must do . . . I don't know, something. Yesterday could have been in that coffin. Sunday is God's day of rest. But that is when my work week starts. By lunch time, I have sold my first coffin. By Sunday evening, the stench of death is all over this place.

JULIA: Men have to fight. But they also have to know when they will lose the fight.

RAPHAEL: How is it going with your father's funeral?

JULIA: I still don't have the money. Now they're saying his name would have been good had I not appeared.

RAPHAEL: It seems that when people die, all dignity disappears.

JULIA: But what about you two? Now the Lieutenant knows who the leaders are. Next time, he'll come for you first. ·

YESTERDAY: If we could only get these people to plan better.

RAPHAEL: They are too poor. When you're hungry, you can't think properly. You can't even organise yourself.

YESTERDAY: They can organise funerals, though. If somebody dies, you have mourners, band members, coffin bearers, preachers, relatives, all over the place.

RAPHAEL: That's democracy! Only when we're dead are we all equal.

YESTERDAY: That magic man was right. About the sticks.

RAPHAEL: Magic Man is a clown, Yesterday.

YESTERDAY: But he's a psychologist too.

JULIA: *[Sniggers]* Psychologist. You only get them in magazines.

YESTERDAY: No, take him seriously, just for once. That cross, that X, really cancels out the whole alphabet. The alphabet that produces all that talk, all that rubbish the ministers speak on the radio. Enough for twenty alphabets.

RAPHAEL: Masters of the alphabet.

YESTERDAY: Maybe we mustn't give up on this election thing.

RAPHAEL: I'll go and vote, don't you worry.

YESTERDAY: No, we must go further. You know that preacher Godson, he, too is a candidate.

RAPHAEL: And now God's son is visiting the Magic Man.

YESTERDAY: Raphael, stop making silly jokes. We need a candidate to state our case.

RAPHAEL: Yes, but who?

> *YESTERDAY just gazes intently at RAPHAEL. Eventually it dawns on RAPHAEL, who gets up and walks away in denial.*

RAPHAEL: Me! Forget it! I am not a politician.

YESTERDAY: Everybody trusts you. People here will put their lives in your hands.

RAPHAEL: People put their deaths into my hands.

YESTERDAY: Life, death, it's all the same for these people. If the spirits of all the people you have buried would be able to choose one man as their candidate, who do you think it would be?

RAPHAEL: I don't believe in spirits.

YESTERDAY: But the spirits believe in you. Why do people leave you their savings when they're dead?

RAPHAEL: Because they want a good funeral. They don't want to bankrupt their families.

YESTERDAY: But what do they care? They're dead. No, it's because they have hope, hope that their money, their hard work, could be used for something more than surviving every day.

RAPHAEL: *[Sees his point, but doesn't want to concede]* I'm not an angel, Yesterday. I make a living out of other people's misery.

YESTERDAY: Come on, Raphael, who are you kidding? Everybody knows you give them a discount on their coffins.

RAPHAEL: They're not supposed to tell.

YESTERDAY: But they do. That's the point. People talk about you. You, Raphael Tondoni, are the only honest man in this township.

RAPHAEL: The only fool too.

YESTERDAY: Only if you don't make something out of it. Take the trust people have put in your hands and make something out of it. Something that is not a coffin, to be buried in the ground or burnt up in smoke.

RAPHAEL: To be a candidate you need money. Which I don't have because of . . . *[Laughs]* . . . my discounts?

YESTERDAY: So it's only money? Then you'll think about it? Yes?

RAPHAEL: I didn't say that.

YESTERDAY: But you didn't say no. Now you've got me excited. Every candidate needs an elections agent. That'll be me! *[Scampers off in excitement, babbling away]*

JULIA: So what do you say?

RAPHAEL: All I want to be is a carpenter making coffins.

JULIA: *[Begins to give him the makeover, feels him up in his crotch]* I know you, Raphael, you're thinking about it. You said you wanted to do something. You're excited.

RAPHAEL: *[Breaks away from her, but she follows him]* Yes, it is an exciting idea. But not for me.

JULIA: Just who are you fooling. You're not made for this miserable life. Just one level above a grave digger. *[RAPHAEL listens, lets her come from behind and caress him]* Go to the barber and look at yourself. What a strong man you are. A big chest with a full heart in it. You can inspire people. You can make them follow you. *[RAPHAEL, against his better judgement, lets her continue]* And I'll be by your side. I know something about the world out there. All the sharks and wolves. How to tame them.

RAPHAEL: You want to change me into one of them.

JULIA: There is nobody like you, Raphael. All those other men with their cars and cigars, and their big fat pockets . . .

RAPHAEL: Are you trying to seduce me?

JULIA: *[Circles him running her finger over his face and head]* I just think you should take it seriously, this chance you have.

RAPHAEL: That is what I don't want to be – a serious man in a black suit.

JULIA: Then you'll have to sleep with me.

RAPHAEL: And how do you get that?

JULIA: Because that's the only way you can prove you're not a serious man.

RAPHAEL: And if I don't sleep with you?

JULIA: Then you'll have to go to parliament.

RAPHAEL: And what do you care?

JULIA: I just care about you. I love you. Can't you see?

RAPHAEL: You betrayed me, Julia. You said you loved me before . . . and then you went with other men.

JULIA: I've come back to you because I know you can forgive me. Because you're that kind of man.

RAPHAEL: So if I stay out of parliament, I will be able to forgive you.

JULIA: That's why I love you. You understand me.

RAPHAEL: Come here.

> He makes a grab for her, and for a moment it looks like he'll hit her, but then he kisses her, caresses her. She drags him into the shack. RAPHAEL looks dazed. Lights fade, noises of township; this, too, fades.
>
> Silence for a minute, then lights up as YESTERDAY returns with MA MIRIAM. He knocks on RAPHAEL's door.

YESTERDAY: Raphael! Come out! Bra Zondi and Ma Miriam are here. We have news for you. Great news.

> RAPHAEL appears, putting on a shirt.

YESTERDAY: He will only be a minute. Raphael, Raphael!

RAPHAEL: Greetings, Ma Miriam.

ZONDI: We heard you want to stand for parliament!

RAPHAEL: *[Throws hands up]* What have you told them?

YESTERDAY: Everybody is excited about it. Everybody.

MIRIAM: And we are going to help you.

RAPHAEL: Ma Miriam . . .

MIRIAM: No, no, there won't be any problem.

ZONDI: We already spoke to the other members.

RAPHAEL: But there is nothing to tell them. I . . .

MIRIAM: We will lend you the money.

RAPHAEL: What money?

YESTERDAY: *[Uncomfortable]* I told them you . . . the only thing that's keeping you . . . that you asked for money.

RAPHAEL: I asked for money? But you know that's not true!

YESTERDAY: Well, sometimes, you know, one has to tell a little lie.

RAPHAEL: Except this one is a big lie. Ma Miriam, I did not ask for any money. The money belongs to the burial society, and the burial society alone.

MIRIAM: We can talk to Miguel, and Misha and Indisuna, and they will all agree: let's use the money for something other than a funeral . . .

YESTERDAY: . . . for a change, is what I told them.

RAPHAEL: OK, just stop right there. Stop! I am not going to run for parliament. I am sorry Ma Miriam, Bra Zondi, but Yesterday misrepresented me.

ZONDI: But . . . the people want you.

RAPHAEL: The people don't always know what's good for them. Now, excuse me . . .

ZONDI: There comes a time when every man is tested, Raphael. This is your test. You should not fail it now. Otherwise there is really no hope left.

YESTERDAY: Leave him for a while, Ma. I'll work on him tomorrow.

They exit. Lights fade

SCENE 4

Scene: As before. The MP in front of a crowd, the LIEUTENANT by his side.

MP: We are all gathered here, people, for a very significant day. It is not often that a member of parliament visits you, but today . . . I am here. I fly to many places to talk about important things because I have to do my bit to help save the world from the mess it is in. But today I am here – for you.

CROWD MEMBER 3: Jesus saved us too. Where is he now?

MP: Without people like me, global warming, started by Western capitalists, will consume the world. Without people like me, development won't come to our country. Without people like me, there will be no conferences to talk about development.

CROWD 5: We want food not conferences.

MP: We get the food for you from donors. These donor people, because they are the oppressor, and because they force their cultures on us, will only deal with people who know how to do conferences.

CROWD 6: You're a beggar in a suit.

MP: Am I wearing a suit?

CROWD 3: So we're not important enough for you to wear a suit?

MP: That is not true. You are the most important people on election day. Without people like you, elections can't happen. And then I put my suit away to show that I'm like you.

CROWD 2: Then take off all your clothes, because we have nothing.

MP: I have heard that's what people like you do, walk naked in front of the police. But that will not get us anywhere. Our donors will think we are barbarians.

CROWD 5: We are barbarians.

CROWD 3: We are cannibals! We'll eat you up.

MP: Listen to me, people. Listen! I will share a secret with you. I need you, and you need me. We can enter into a contract today. Vote for me and I'll make sure that you get the benefit.

CROWD 3: What benefits? Give us suits?

MP: I will make sure that our donors, when they come to the country, will visit this constituency. Then they will put up their clinics here. And their schools. And distribute their food here. Not in Tulakwana next door.

CROWD 6: And they'll buy a big ambulance for you. That looks like a Mercedes-Benz.

MP: You are the best township precisely because you are the poorest and look the worst. That is something we can use. That is the contract I propose. You bring out all your sick, all your hungry children, and I bring the donors.

CROWD 2: You feed on the hungry! *[But this time the others quieten him down]*

CROWD 4: Shut up, let the man talk.

MP: You see, previously the government would hide the beggars and the cripples but now we show them to the world. It's called "good governance", or "transparency". That way, we come on the world agenda, and people take notice of us.

CROWD 4: How will the money come to us?

MP: Through television. I bring the TV cameras here, because I have connections at the TV station. They see all this filth, that you cannot read and write. And then the donors will come here because they too have to be on TV. That's how it works.

CROWD 1: My child has a skew leg. Give me five bucks for her.

MP: We will find ways to work together. But first you have to vote for me so I can stay in parliament.

Crowd gets worked up. RAPHAEL has had too much, and now steps forward; grabs the megaphone from the MP.

RAPHAEL: Don't listen to this man. He is a crook and a thief!

MP: Who you are?

CROWD 3: It's Raphael Tondoni, the chairman of the burial society.

MP: Oh, the local gravedigger.

RAPHAEL: This man is not a real MP. Real members of parliament represent their people, their constituencies. This man represents only himself.

LIEUTENANT: You are a troublemaker. You want to undermine the state.

RAPHAEL: People like him sit around all day long scheming how to get more money. People like him only come here during elections.

MP: Don't listen to him. He doesn't know how things work.

RAPHAEL: This man did not come to save you. He is a vulture. People like him want you to stay poor and miserable, because that's how he gets his money.

MP: Only people like me can make things change.

RAPHAEL: What change? You get a new model 4 x 4 so you can bring more foreigners to stare at us? Get the Lieutenant a new uniform, made in China?

LIEUTENANT goes up to RAPHAEL; RAPHAEL moves away, points to shacks.

RAPHAEL: Look at these shacks. Do you even know what this place is called?

MP: I have it on Google map. I travel a lot.

RAPHAEL: Because you have to tell the same story to every township, don't you? You promise them all you will bring TV cameras to them.

LIEUTENANT: They will only come to places where there are no troublemakers.

RAPHAEL: So that's your democracy! No trouble, no backchat, no danger — only rows of starved people, crippled people.

CROWD 6: *[Gets worked up]* This man is a swindler!

CROWD 4: He has no plan for us.

CROWD 2: Let's throw him out.!

LIEUTENANT orders policemen with him to load their guns; they stand in front of the frightened MP who backs off. CROWD gets shoved to one side.

CROWD 2: *[As crowd members leave]* Now he is going to come back for us.

CROWD 6: We'd better make ourselves scarce!

RAPHAEL halts the dispersing crowd members in their tracks.

RAPHAEL: People, listen, before you go. *[He remains silent for a while, pensive]* Look, some of you asked me to stand for parliament.

CROWD 3: Now you too want to join them.

CROWD 4: And become like them.

RAPHAEL: Listen, listen! I don't want to become like them. At first I said no – because I don't want to be a politician. But I cannot close my eyes to what is going on here.

CROWD 1: Bad things are happening here.

RAPHAEL: This government is not one for the people. We need to change that. And the only way is to vote in elections. Everybody!

CROWD 5: For the right man.

RAPHAEL: And so, if you don't want me as candidate, I'll go, and continue to make coffins. If you say yes, then I'll put myself in your hands. Then I am your man on election day.

CROWD silent. Then they suddenly erupt. They get excited and try to hoist RAPHAEL on their shoulders. He lands up standing on a coffin.

CROWD 2: Yes. We want you Raphael.

CROWD 5: We need someone we can trust.

CROWD 6: You are one of us.

CROWD 1: Raphael for parliament!

RAPHAEL: And as my elections agent I propose Yesterday.

CROWD 1: On one condition.

RAPHAEL: What's that.

CROWD 1: That we change his name to Tomorrow.

RAPHAEL: We'll change Yesterday's name to Tomorrow, today!

> ### *Song of Tomorrow*
>
> *In the land of tomorrow*
> *You don't have to worry*
> *You just beg and borrow*
> *And never say you're sorry*
>
> *Yesterday belongs to the past*
> *And not much will ever come back*
>
> *In the land of tomorrow*
> *You don't pay your bets*
> *You just tell everybody*
> *To forgive your debts*
>
> *Things will stay the same today*
> *You will live your life in despair*
> *In the land of the future*
> *Hope will have no end*
>
> *Hope will last forever and ever*

CROWD 2: Yes, let's go with Yesterday so we can start on your campaign.

CROWD 6: Our time has come!

CROWD 5: Today belongs to us.

CROWD 3: Let's get to work!

> *They hoist YESTERDAY on their shoulders, carrying him off.*
>
> *JULIA peeks from the shack, gestures to her kanga, RAPHAEL passes it to her.*

JULIA: Hey, they really like you. They really want you.

RAPHAEL: Like Zondi said, every man will be tested – once in his life.

JULIA: Oh, I can just picture you. When you rise to speak in parliament, everybody else will fall silent. You'll knock them down in your charcoal suit.

RAPHAEL: Juliaaa . . . didn't you hear what they said? About suits?

JULIA: What happens here and what happens in parliament, are two different things.

RAPHAEL: That is precisely what I want to change.

JULIA: And I'll be your advisor. I'll teach you everything you need to know.

RAPHAEL: I am not going to start wearing a suit now. I'll dress like the people dress.

JULIA: That's fine, Raphael, but there are other things.

RAPHAEL: Like what?

JULIA: Have you ever eaten in a restaurant?

RAPHAEL: No.

JULIA: If you go to parliament, you'll have to do a lot of eating in restaurants.

RAPHAEL: That's why they're all so fat.

JULIA: You have to learn how to use a knife and fork. How to fold a napkin. How to drink wine in a glass.

RAPHAEL: Only if I can share my food and wine with someone from here.

JULIA: That's called socialism. Which doesn't work.

RAPHAEL: I am not going to change into one of them. Otherwise, what's the point of representing the people.

JULIA: All I'm saying is that if you want to be effective, you should not give people a stick to beat you with.

RAPHAEL: You sound like our MP.

JULIA: I know that world. I know how vicious they are. You have to play them at their own game.

RAPHAEL: The people see me, Raphael, and that is who they want. They don't choose me to go play goalkeeper in somebody else's team.

JULIA: But you'll win, Raphael, and that will change things.

RAPHAEL gets up, walks to one side, struggling with what he has to say.
JULIA looks on, gradually the horror and hurt grow on her face.

RAPHAEL: Julia, I've been thinking about a lot of things. About the elections, about you and me.

JULIA: I'll be by your side. Together we can start a whole new life.

RAPHAEL: No, Julia, it is not going to work.

JULIA: I'll never betray you again. I'm your's now.

RAPHAEL: You said earlier that I'm not a serious man. Well, now I am. This is my fate, to act for the people.

JULIA: You're telling me this now, after you had your way with me.

RAPHAEL: I'm sorry. I should not have slept with you. I didn't have the clear mind that I have now.

JULIA: You are betraying me!

RAPHAEL: I didn't promise you anything. It is precisely because there is promise in the air now that I have to break with you. Because I can't promise you something I can't deliver.

JULIA: But I'll take my chances.

RAPHAEL: No, Julia. In a quest like this, one has to remain pure.

JULIA: So that's what this is about. You still see me as a whore.

RAPHAEL: You know that's not what I am saying.

JULIA: *[Dives into the shack to get her belongings]* Well, just you remember. Jesus Christ did not care who he was saving – prostitutes, cripples, soldiers, coffin makers . . .

RAPHAEL: If I am to succeed, I cannot allow myself to be contaminated.

JULIA: Contaminated? You know what, you are already contaminated. By your fucking purity. First parliament was not pure enough for you. Now I'm not pure enough for you. Who is? Where around you do you see any purity? Purity is baby food!

RAPHAEL: You have too many charms. You will distract me.

JULIA: Don't try to soften up what you said.

RAPHAEL: When the elections are over . . .

JULIA: Forget it, Raphael. I made a mistake coming here. I don't like people like you, after all. Go and wash your corpses, that's the only time people are pure.

She stomps off; RAPHAEL looks in her direction, makes as if to go after her then turns around, troubled. Lights fade.

SCENE 5

Scene change: Stage Right is a police station, old colonial building, very delapidated. Has verandah and window on which POLICE is clumsily painted. In the centre is an awful looking cage with barely enough space for two people to stand in. To left is an alley, to which RAPHAEL will be forced to move his campaign table. At the start of the scene, at centre stage, he has an easel and blackboard on which is written in large letters: RAPHAEL TONDONI – THE GOOD CANDIDATE. He and YESTERDAY spell these out to passers-by. There is also a chair and a small table.

RAPHAEL is standing in front of the blackboard, elaborately spelling out his name to an illiterate passer-by, who exits when the LIEUTENANT appears.

LIEUTENANT: Move your table.

RAPHAEL: What for?

LIEUTENANT: It's in the way.

RAPHAEL: I am a candidate in the elections. I can put up my table where I want to.

LIEUTENANT: You're obstructing the traffic.

RAPHAEL: What traffic? Nobody has cars around here.

YESTERDAY: Not even donkey carts.

LIEUTENANT: You have to be further than ten yards from the police station.

RAPHAEL: OK, I'll move.

Takes table and blackboard, moves it to end of stage. YESTERDAY comes to help him.

YESTERDAY: But what about that poster, hey? Right next to your door.

LIEUTENANT: That belongs to the government.

RAPHAEL: Really? The one saying vote for the MP.

LIEUTENANT: It shows people who their MP is.

RAPHAEL: Well, I want to lay a complaint. For transgressing the election rules.

LIEUTENANT: Sorry, I can't allow that. The police has to stay impartial, we can't interfere.

YESTERDAY: And you know very well we can't afford to travel all the way to the Electoral Commission, you scoundrel.

He attacks the LIEUTENANT; RAPHAEL has to drag him back.

RAPHAEL: Calm down, YESTERDAY! Don't waste your time on fools like him!

They busy themselves preparing their little stand. YESTERDAY looks uncomfortably at RAPHAEL, plucking up courage to speak.

YESTERDAY: People won't notice us in this spot. But maybe it's just as well.

RAPHAEL: That's not what an elections agent should say.

YESTERDAY: I don't know if you really want me as your agent anymore.

RAPHAEL: You're the best man for the job.

YESTERDAY: Not after what I have to tell you.

RAPHAEL: *[Alarmed]* What happened?

YESTERDAY: It's the money.

RAPHAEL: The burial society's money?

YESTERDAY: It has disappeared.

RAPHAEL: How do you mean, *disappeared?*

YESTERDAY: It's not in my shack anymore.

RAPHAEL: Then where is it now?

YESTERDAY: I don't know. That's what I'm trying to tell you.

RAPHAEL: But you had it this morning.

YESTERDAY: I thought I had. I thought it was still under my mattress.

RAPHAEL: Is all the money gone?

YESTERDAY: All of it.

RAPHAEL: Somebody must have stolen it.

YESTERDAY: That's the only explanation.

RAPHAEL: But who would do such a thing?

YESTERDAY: Everybody knew we had the burial society's money.

RAPHAEL: Which means it can be anybody.

YESTERDAY: It has to be that scoundrel whose life you saved.

RAPHAEL: The boy who stole the fried chicken?

YESTERDAY: Who else?

RAPHAEL: Come on, Yesterday, you can't just accuse him.

YESTERDAY: He must have thought you would protect him again if he got caught.

RAPHAEL: Don't tell the burial society yet. Let's try to find him first. And ask him.

YESTERDAY: We have to go and tell the Lieutenant.

RAPHAEL: What is that going to help?

YESTERDAY: At least then we followed the right procedure.

RAPHAEL: *Right procedure?* How often am I going to hear those words?

YESTERDAY: We also have rights to use the police.

RAPHAEL: At least we can try.

They walk over to the police station, knock on the door.

Eventually the LIEUTENANT opens, stretching his arms after his nap.

RAPHAEL: I'm sorry, for disturbing you from your . . . meditation.

LIEUTENANT: What do you want?

YESTERDAY: We want to report a theft.

LIEUTENANT: My typewriter doesn't have a ribbon.

YESTERDAY: Use your pen, then.

LIEUTENANT: It ran out of ink.

YESTERDAY: So you're not going to help us?

LIEUTENANT: Don't ask me to waste my time on petty matters.

YESTERDAY: But you chased that good-for-nothing, Koni, right into my shack. You remember? Was that a petty matter?

LIEUTENANT: We were not after him, we were after the chicken. My men were hungry.

RAPHAEL: You admit it, just like that.

LIEUTENANT: I don't have anything to hide. Besides, he gave himself up in the end.

YESTERDAY: And you didn't tell us?

LIEUTENANT: Why should I? We sorted him out. Capture, trial, punishment all in one. Great procedure.

RAPHAEL: You killed him.

LIEUTENANT: Mister Tondoni, what do you think of us? We did no such thing. That Koni is alive and better than he has ever been.

YESTERDAY: Yes, There he is.

Sounds of marching. The first of four BROWN BOMBERS appears; they enter, marching in elaborate, almost comical fashion.

LIEUTENANT: Troop 1, 2 Halt!

RAPHAEL: You turned him into a Brown Bomber!

LIEUTENANT: These young men are members of the Youth Alliance for Protection of our Independence.

YESTERDAY goes for KONI, who falters, but recovers when YESTERDAY is pulled away by RAPHAEL and the LIEUTENANT. They come to a halt in a comical mess.

LIEUTENANT: Koni Tafadudzi, step forward.

KONI: *[Points at himself]* Who me? *[Then steps forward awkwardly in a move they had obviously not practiced]*

LIEUTENANT: Yes. Turn right! Did you commit any crime?

KONI: *[Shows enough consternation on his face for us to know he had, indeed, stolen the money]:* No, I did not.

LIEUTENANT: There you have it, whatever you want to accuse him of, he didn't do it.

YESTERDAY: But you can see he did! He looks as guilty as a hyena in a graveyard.

LIEUTENANT: Watch what you're saying. He is a servant of the state. Show some respect.

YESTERDAY: Respect! This lot? These scumbags who beat up old women and children!

LIEUTENANT produces a notebook and pencil, which he licks before writing.

YESTERDAY: Oh, now suddenly you have a pencil, now you can write! Just spell my name right. And it's not Tuesday!

RAPHAEL: Come on, Yesterday. You've made your point.

LIEUTENANT: We'll be watching you.

RAPHAEL and YESTERDAY retire to their corner, licking their wounds.

RAPHAEL: What am I going to tell the burial society?

YESTERDAY: We need that money. We have to make posters, print flyers and hire transport.

RAPHAEL: It's a lost cause. We might as well give up.

YESTERDAY: No, that is the one thing we cannot do.

RAPHAEL: We should move from here. Get away from that scoundrel.

YESTERDAY: No, that's what he wants. We are going nowhere.

RAPHAEL: You're right. We are staying just here.

They continue to write and shout to people to register and vote for RAPHAEL. Lights fade.

SCENE 6

Scene: Same as before.

MIRIAM: *[Approaches RAPHAEL's table, excitedly]* Raphael, Raphael! I must tell you something.

RAPHAEL: *[Turns around, ready to confess about the money]* Look, Ma Miriam. I am so sorry.

MIRIAM: It's a dream. I had this dream! *[MIRIAM turns RAPHAEL around to face her]*

RAPHAEL: You often have dreams, Ma.

MIRIAM: But this one! This time! I was dreaming of a man on the clouds. There was a light shining from him, a bright light like the clipping of the sun.

RAPHAEL: Eclipse.

MIRIAM: Yes, the clipping. Then that man started to walk, and he came down, to us, here in our township

Song of the Man on the Cloud

You come down from your cloud
And your clothes are so shiny
You can make us feel proud
And no longer so tiny

Everything you touch will glow
All of us looking up will know
This will be their special day

You will say we are chosen
And will rise up to heaven
Where we won't stop with eating
Between every meeting

I am longing to touch you
Even if you make a demand
That we show a giving hand

RAPHAEL: Sounds like Jesus Christ.

MIRIAM: It's obvious. That man in my dream – it's you! You are going to save us.

RAPHAEL: *[Tries not to show his alarm. Meanwhile Bra ZONDI approaches too]* Look at me, Ma Miriam. I am not that man in your dream. I don't walk on clouds, I put people in the ground.

MIRIAM: But you are going to parliament. You can do a lot for us.

ZONDI: Raphael, you must promise us.

RAPHAEL: Bra Zondi, I already have . . . and I have been trying to tell Ma Miriam that . . .

YESTERDAY: *[Drags Koni in by the ear, pushes him into Raphael's arms]* You cowardly dog! You squeaking mouse! You're nothing without your gun, hey? Tell them what you told me.

KONI: Bra Raphael, I'm sorry, I'm sorry!

RAPHAEL: What did he do now?

YESTERDAY: He confessed. Come on, tell them.

KONI: *[Goes on his knees before RAPHAEL]* Forgive me, Bra Raphael.

RAPHAEL: You have to ask the burial society for forgiveness.

MIRIAM: What did he do?

KONI: I won't do it again.

MIRIAM: What did you do?

KONI: *[Lies whimpering, pitying himself]* I didn't want to do it.

YESTERDAY: He stole our money. Your money.

MIRIAM: *[Shocked, wants to attack KONI]* Why did you do that? *[Confused]* But . . . but . . . isn't it with Raphael?

KONI: They made me do it.

YESTERDAY: *[Pulls KONI to his feet again]* Who made you do it?

KONI: Don't hurt me . . .

YESTERDAY: *[Shoves KONI about]* Where is the money!

KONI: It was the Lieutenant! He has it.

RAPHAEL, MIRIAM, ZONDI, YESTERDAY: You gave it to the Lieutenant?

KONI: He told me to take it.

YESTERDAY: How did he know about it?

KONI: I told him. I saw you putting it under your mattress.

YESTERDAY: You betrayed us after we saved your sorry ass.

KONI: Hey, brother, please, I didn't want to go to jail.

YESTERDAY: But did you have to become a Brown Bomber?

MIRIAM: Where is that Lieutenant? We must go and see him.

RAPHAEL: No, Ma Miriam, that won't help.

ZONDI: But we must do something.

RAPHAEL: We can't do anything. *[Everybody asks or gestures, Why?]* The MP backs him. He's probably behind it all.

MIRIAM: *[Shattered]* But he took our money! It was such a lot of money.

All sit or stand around, disconsolate.

YESTERDAY: It's do or die. We simply have to get Raphael in parliament.

ZONDI: Then he can expose all this stuff going on.

MIRIAM: Is it true you will earn a lot of money?

RAPHAEL: Probably. But I'm not going to parliament for the money, Ma.

YESTERDAY: What Ma Miriam is saying, you can then pay back the society then.

RAPHAEL: Of course, Ma Miriam. You'll get your money back. Even if I don't go to parliament.

YESTERDAY: See? We must now all work harder to get Raphael in parliament. Even if it becomes mission impossible.

ZONDI: And this scoundrel?

YESTERDAY: Let him go. Let's not give them a stick to beat us with.

KONI: *[Stumbles away and off right, turning around to shout and gesture at them]* I'll get you back for this! You're lucky the Lieutenant wasn't here. You shouldn't mess with the Yapis!

ZONDI: I'll go and talk to the wrestlers.

MIRIAM: Maybe the washerwomen is a good place to start.

> *Exit MIRIAM, ZONDI, YESTERDAY.*
>
> *Sounds of car stopping, doors slamming, electronic key tweetering, enter the MP and JULIA. She has a T-shirt on with the face of her father.*

MP: Raphael Tondoni, I want to talk to you

RAPHAEL: About what.

MP: I have a preposition *[sic]* for you

RAPHAEL: *[To JULIA]* I see you have buried your father.

JULIA: Our MP was so kind as to . . . find me the money.

RAPHAEL: Which he got where? Stealing from poor people?

MP: Careful what you say. Stay with the facts.

JULIA: An MP gets a very good salary.

RAPHAEL: And you would know exactly how much. *[He glares at her; she glares back]*

MP: Look, people make contributions to my campaign because I am so popular. The Brown Bombers, too, bring me money, from their own pockets. Very reliable, very idealistic, these youngsters. They give one hope for the future.

RAPHAEL: Spare me the speech.

JULIA: Just listen to what he has to say.

MP: I've come to make you an offer.

RAPHAEL: I'm not for sale, forget it.

MP: I'm not trying to bribe you. I'm offering you something.

RAPHAEL: What can you offer me? A soiled woman?

MP: I want you to join us.

RAPHAEL: Join you two!

MP: Not us, the new party we're forming.

RAPHAEL: What new party?

MP: The idea is to only form it after the election. Otherwise, if we announce it now, the president will just smash us up. Set his goons on us, intimidate the workers, or get us killed.

RAPHAEL: But that's . . . fraud! People think they're voting for you on one ticket and then you turn around.

JULIA: It's called politics.

MP: I've been watching you. You are a real talent, a real find. You can go far. But then you must play the game.

RAPHAEL: I will create my own game and play by my own rules – the rules of the people.

MP: Oh, an idealist! I was like that too. But how will this new game work, with only one player?

RAPHAEL: There are many who think like me.

MP: Too many, Raphael, too many. That's the problem. There are too many poor people. Look at all this, this hopeless mess. How are you ever going to fix it?

RAPHAEL: *[Uncomfortable]* As long as we make a start.

MP: The only way to get out of this mess is to get out of it. These people cannot be saved. But you can save yourself.

RAPHAEL: And then? After I've saved myself?

MP: Think ahead. One day when you have children, you will want to give them a proper education. Overseas. Which costs money. But at least we can save our children. Our names will live on through them.

RAPHAEL: The people have put their trust in me. My name depends on the people.

MP: The people can keep on trusting you. Just not in this constituency.

JULIA: All we are suggesting is that you put yourself up as candidate somewhere else.

RAPHAEL: But I have already registered here.

MP: The official process can be adapted.

RAPHAEL: *[Gets up, walks up to MP until their faces are centimetres apart]* I know I must not get angry with you. But what I would like to do now is punch you . . . right here! *[Points to MP's nose]*

MP: *[Glaring back at RAPHAEL]* You are a stubborn man. And stubborn men always end up paying for it.

RAPHAEL: You can't touch me. You'll feel the wrath of the people when you lose on election day.

MP stomps off, telling JULIA also to come but she breaks away from his grip, rushes back to RAPHAEL.

MPs car key:[Off stage] Bleep bleep . . . bleep bleep . . . bleep bleep . . .

JULIA: Raphael, be sensible! First get to parliament, and then you can save the people.

MPs car door closes, car revs.

RAPHAEL: And when you're done with him? Are you going to ditch him too?

JULIA: Like how you ditched me for your politics. I do what I have to do. I had to save the name of my father.

RAPHAEL: You've made your choice – and I've made mine.

MP hoots car hooter: [Off stage] Hoot, hoot! Hoot, hoot!

JULIA: I'm going to vote for you, Raphael, no matter what you think of me.

RAPHAEL: Then I'll spoil my own vote. To cancel out yours.

JULIA: I'll vote for you because you'll see the light Raphael, you'll come around.

MP hoots car hooter: [Off stage] Hoot hoot hoot hoot . . .

Enter MAGNA, goes to sit with RAPHAEL.

MAGNA: Hey, Raphael, I heard about that money, man. I'm sorry.

RAPHAEL: Yes, I don't know what to do.

MAGNA: You know what I can do. I can make people forget.

RAPHAEL: Come on, I lost their money. They will not forget.

MAGNA: I make people forget the plans they had with their money.

RAPHAEL: I will not forget that the society trusted me.

MAGNA: If people forget they don't become greedy.

RAPHAEL: The society members are not greedy people.

MAGNA: No, Raphael, but I am.

RAPHAEL: Explain.

MAGNA: You know, since all these candidates came to me with their chickens, I have made plans for my money. Now I can't sleep. All I can think of is what I am going to buy.

RAPHAEL: It's your good luck. Just use the money.

MAGNA: And after the election? What will I do then? Then I'm used to my new cellphone, my new camera, my new radio. Then I would want a new bicycle, new shoes. I would even want to buy underpants.

RAPHAEL: You can do with a new hat.

MAGNA: Raphael, I want to forget about all this money, and you must help me.

RAPHAEL: How?

MAGNA: You must take the money. For the election.

RAPHAEL: Me, take money from you? I don't believe in your magic.

MAGNA: I don't care. All this money is going to kill me. And my magic.

RAPHAEL: But even if I get money, I should give it back to the society.

MAGNA: Raphael, listen to me. The people want you in parliament. I want you in parliament. I have seen the other candidates. *[Shakes his head in contempt]*

RAPHAEL: You just have a bad conscience and now you want to purify your money.

MAGNA: You can call it what you like. I want my money to work. Do some real magic.

RAPHAEL: *[Ponders the offer]* Okay, I'll accept. But then you must help me with something.

MAGNA: Just bring me a chicken.

RAPHAEL: No seriously, you must. When I get to to parliament, you must help me to remember what I'm doing there.

MAGNA: I will make that rooster crow every morning at your window.

RAPHAEL: It's a deal.

They exchange high-fives, very pleased with themselves.

MAGNA: Raphael, let me teach you another trick.

RAPHAEL: Don't overdo it.

MAGNA: You must reward the people who want to vote for you.

RAPHAEL: Isn't that called . . . bribery?

MAGNA: You just give them something to drink. Something they cannot afford. Like Coca-La-Cola.

RAPHAEL: *[Laughs]* That's the way of the MP and the government. I am not like them.

MAGNA: It's simply to lure people here to come and listen to you.

RAPHAEL: Magna, you go back to your magic, and leave me to my campaign.

They exit, laughing and teasing each other. Lights fade.

SCENE 7

Scene: Same as before. RAPHAEL stands with leaflets in his hand. In the middle of the set stands a stack of Coke bottles, most of them empty. He now has a fair-sized but poorly made poster of himself. Pedestrians come past, get ambushed by the Coke offer, or stand and listen and/or read what RAPHAEL has to say.

RAPHAEL: Coca-Cola, a free Coke for everybody!

YESTERDAY: Vote for Raphael Tondoni. Here, this is his face and his name.

CROWD 6: But I can't get to a voting station.

RAPHAEL: Don't worry, just tell us where you live and we'll go fetch you.

CROWD 6: How? My leg is lame.

RAPHAEL: We have a wheelbarrow.

YESTERDAY: We're running out of Coke.

RAPHAEL: We're running out of money too. We have to keep some for election day.

YESTERDAY: Raphael, we just got to stick it out.

Song of Sticking It Out

You say left
I say right
You say deaf
I say bright

We stick it out
We stick it out

I say slow
You say fast
I say throw
You say last

We stick it out
We stick it out

You say up
I say down
You say stop
I say don't

We stick it out
We stick it out

They say run
We say stand
They say sun
We say sand

We stick it out
We stick it out

They say bread
We say fire
They say dead
We say liar

We stick it out
We stick it out

Ma MIRIAM enters.

MIRIAM: I'm so glad you got our money back. It was like magic!

RAPHAEL: Listen up, people. Most of you cannot read or write. You don't understand how things work. There are liars and cheats who want to take the little you have. All this has to come before parliament.

CROWD 6: Take us back to the bush.

RAPHAEL: In the bush you can be yourself. You don't have to worry. You can live like your forefathers lived. But times have changed. We have to move on.

CROWD 6: Yes, move on to nowhere!

MIRIAM: Will you be quiet! The man has important things to say.

CROWD 6: But what does it help if he can only buy us a Coke? We need casava and some meat.

Exits stage right. The LIEUTENANT appears.

LIEUTENANT: *[Cocksure, full of schadenfreude]* Hey move! Hey, get off that bucket!

YESTERDAY: I'm not moving from that bucket.

RAPHAEL: We moved already for here to there and now we are back here.

LIEUTENANT: OK, It's better that you stay here, I can see you directly from my office.

YESTERDAY: Why?

LIEUTENANT: Because I'm investigating you.

YESTERDAY: What for? This time we have money for a lawyer. In a suit.

LIEUTENANT: Aha, money, you say. That you got from where?

MIRIAM: We gave it to him. Us, the burial society. We can do with it what we want.

LIEUTENANT: Are you sure it's your money, Ma?

MIRIAM: Of course I'm sure. *[Turns to RAPHAEL, suddenly unsure]* Hey, Raphael? He's confusing me. How else could he buy all these Cokes?

LIEUTENANT: How else, indeed.

YESTERDAY: You're just bluffing. And bullying us. It's not going to help, Lieutenant, we already have hundreds of supporters. Thousands!

LIEUTENANT: We'll have to see about that when I present my evidence.

RAPHAEL: Evidence of what? We kept book of everything.

LIEUTENANT: Did you? Shall I tell these people how much money you really have?

RAPHAEL: I have nothing to hide.

The MP appears, starts handing out DVDs.

MP: People of the city! I have come to bring you gifts.

CROWD 6: Look, a DVD. It shines.

CROWD 4: Give me one too.

MP: Vote for me, and there will be more on election day.

CROWD 3: What must we do with this? We don't have a TV.

CROWD 4: We can look at the DVD like we look at the radio!

MP: When you choose on election day, you must ask yourself: What can your MP do for you? Does he have the . . . *[He raises his arm and fist from his elbow in gesture of triumph]* . . . to do what it takes to do things for you?

YESTERDAY: What are you trying to you prove? That you can fart harder than other people?

MP: People, we need to make ourselves strong. Our nation must rise and throw off the shackles of oppression! We have the right to take our place among the other nations on the globe.

CROWD 5: Yes, give us globes and electricity.

MP: I have made a start with that. This DVD shows Michael Jackson, my friend. The proof is on this DVD, of us shaking hands.

CROWD 6: Michael Jackson?

CROWD 5: I want one too. I want to hear Michael Jackson.

CROWD 3: I want to — we want to see Michael Jackson. But we don't have a TV.

MP: Oh, so you don't have a TV? *[Snaps his fingers. KONI staggers in with a TV set. Excited crowd members help him to hook it up]* One day, people, one day, this TV will show how our ministers visit New York! It will show our president at the United Nations! It will show how one of you goes to the moon!

CROWD 5: I can't see, turn it this way! No, he made it face this way! This way!
Crowd turns it around one way, then another, pulling it to and fro.

MP: Now, now, remember this belongs to everybody! So let's put it in front of the police station. Then the police can watch it for us.
Crowd members pick up the TV set and put it on the verandah where the LIEUTENANT strokes it possessively.

CROWD MEMBERS: But the Lieutenant will take it for himself.

MP: No, the Lieutenant won't do that! He is a servant of the people. Aren't you Lieutenant?

LIEUTENANT: *[Awkward, clearly eyeing it for himself, gestures dismissively at the crowd]* Yes, sure. You can take turns. You can queue here.

RAPHAEL: I can't stand this anymore! *[Pushes MP away. LIEUTENANT wants to intervene but MP blocks him]* How can you fall for this? Isn't it obvious what he's doing?

CROWD 5: The question is: What can you do for us? Do you know Michael Jackson?

RAPHAEL: I can also bring you gifts – once I am an MP. But I would rather bring you common sense.

CROWD 4: Common sense like in Coca-Cola?

CROWD 6: You can't even organise enough to drink.

RAPHAEL: Look, I made a mistake. *[He takes the last Coke from its crate and pours it on the ground]* This man promises you everything. I promise you nothing. No, I promise you worse than nothing. Because your vote is a cross, it crosses out even the nothing you have.
CROWD falls silent as he speaks. MP tries to intervene.

RAPHAEL: Voting is an act of purification. In the polling booth: Just you and your conscience remain. And your conscience is not looking for a new dress, or a new cellphone, and it doesn't want to go to the moon.

MP: These are the words of a preacher. But behind his back it's all about money.

CROWD 3: Look who's talking.

MP: Raphael is not interested in money? He's lying. He's a liar.

CROWD 3: You're the liar. We all know he is an honest man.

CROWD 5: Yes. Even if he gets power.

MP: He's a liar when he says he's not interested in money.

CROWD 4: Proof! Prove it!

CROWD 6: Show us the evidence before we wring your neck!

MP: I have all the proof I need. Just give me a chance *[Raises his hands for silence, not perturbed at all, which lets the crowd calm down]*

MP: To prove it, the Lieutenant needed some time. But now . . . *[Stands aside, LIEUTENANT steps up to RAPHAEL, grabs his wrist, and snaps a pair of handcuffs around it].*

LIEUTENANT: *[Quickly reads from a piece of paper]* Raphael Tondoni, with the powers vested in me as officer of the peace, I arrest you for the crime of thievery and concealment of crime and property.

> CROWD *sighs collectively, steps back in surprise.* YESTERDAY *tries to stop* LIEUTENANT, *gets a blow to the head from a soldier who cuffs him, drags him to the cage, semi-conscious.*

CROWD 4: What did he do?

LIEUTENANT: Tell them, you miserable . . . amateur.

RAPHAEL: Tell them what? This is all a plot.

LIEUTENANT: There is no plot. We have all the evidence. Here . . . *[Produces a file, thick with paper work].*

RAPHAEL: If you're talking about the burial society money . . .

MP: Aha, how did you know? See everybody, it's a confession. That always makes things easier.

RAPHAEL: I have nothing to confess. That money was stolen, but the only one who can tell you about it is Koni.

MP: Koni? The secretary of the Yapis in this area?

RAPHAEL: *[Shakes his head]* Now he's your secretary!

MP: Why should he not be? Such an upright young man.

> KONI *arrives, haughty, yet uncomfortable enough to show he's acting out his part of the plot.*

LIEUTENANT: Ah, here he is. Koni, this man is accusing you of theft.

> KONI *steps forward, hits* RAPHAEL *in the stomach, puts his hand in his pocket, and throws a wad of money at* RAPHAEL.

KONI: Again! Take this back, you piece of scum. I would rather work than take anything from you.

MP: Koni, tell all the good people here what happened.

KONI: On that day, Mister Tondoni here, while I was selling a chicken in his street . . . he said I must give it to him.

MP: *[Impatient]* Come on, not the chicken, the money.

KONI: He told me the burial society had a lot of money, enough to make

him and me rich. He said he would get them to give him the money, and
that I should then steal it from his house. He would then pretend he lost it
and we would share it.

MIRIAM: But we gave him the money because we wanted to . . .

MP: Did you really want to? Or did he talk you into it?

MIRIAM: *[Growing confused]* He would only become a candidate if we gave
him . . .

LIEUTENANT: You see! He twisted your arm.

MIRIAM: My memory is not so clear anymore.

MP: You see, these poor old people, so forgetful, so easy to cheat.

MAGNA: *[Pushes through crowd, points to RAPHAEL's stand and poster]*
Now wait here. I gave him the money. He bought all this stuff with all my
money.

MP: Another one who fell for his trickery.

MAGNA: Everybody here knows I don't fall for anybody else's trickery.
Raphael did not ask for that money, just to get it stolen by somebody else.
Ridiculous.

MP: And how are you going to prove that? Shake a chicken?

MAGNA: Let the people judge me on my reputation: Would I give money to
a thief?

LIEUTENANT: Maybe it was because you were in on it too.

KONI: Because the money you gave was a lot less than the society's.

MAGNA: How do you know so much about my money affairs? *[Confronts
KONI, who backs off in fright, LIEUTENANT has to intervene]*

LIEUTENANT: Come now, don't bully the youth.

MAGNA: Everybody knows he's a good-for-nothing.

LIEUTENANT: He signed the statement. He made his cross . . . in the right place.

MAGNA: You should arrest him. It's blasphemy!

LIEUTENANT: No, I'll arrest you. That way we'll get some order here and we
can interrogate you to find the truth. *[Puts MAGNA in cuffs too]*

MP: Well, I rest my case. How can you trust a candidate anyway, who
takes money from a Magic Man. We live in the modern world where
superstition has no place. Especially not in parliament.

MAGNA: Tell that to all the MPs who visit me in secret.

MP: Slander will get you nowhere.

LIEUTENANT: OK, people. The show is over. We can all go home now.

Sullen CROWD turns away, disperses quietly, RAPHAEL and MAGNA are led away to the cage on right, where they are locked up. MP and LIEUTENANT remain behind, MP walks to RAPHAEL's stand. He takes a sheaf of leaflets, slowly tears them up.

SCENE 8

Scene: Same as before. MAGNA, YESTERDAY and RAPHAEL hang from a chain on a pole.

RAPHAEL: I should never have come to the city, the bush is better.

YESTERDAY: You don't belong in the bush, Raphael. You're a leader.

RAPHAEL: It's only in the bush that you can be a proper leader.

YESTERDAY: If you go to the bush, you'll become a rebel.

RAPHAEL: If that's my destiny . . .

YESTERDAY: First we have to get out of here.

MAGNA: Someone will come to help us.

RAPHAEL: Who? Everybody will be scared now. They'll think I've failed, that they've failed, that it's a lost cause.

YESTERDAY: You're right. It will be no use trying to convince them we're innocent.

RAPHAEL: Whether we like it or not, the bush is the answer for now.

YESTERDAY: This whole system isn't working.

MAGNA: It's the people who can read and write who are in control. They write down your name and you are guilty.

YESTERDAY: In the bush at least you don't have this problem of reading and writing.

MAGNA: Or of money.

RAPHAEL: You can be yourself. You can live like your forefathers lived. In the bush I can be pure again. If you learn to write, it is for writing, not to win power. If you have money, it's to buy things, not to cheat people with.

MAGNA: In the bush I don't have to shake chickens.

YESTERDAY: Maybe you two are right. If we get out of here, and go back to the bush, we can start over.

MAGNA: I have a plan. Here comes Koni. Pretend to sleep.

He gestures to the others that they should pretend to sleep; they "fall asleep" standing up in each other's arms in a contorted position.

KONI arrives, carelessly carrying a rifle, looking at pictures in a magazine. At first he doesn't realise MAGNA is awake, gets a fright when he speaks.

MAGNA: So you made a cross on that piece of paper.

KONI: *[Proudly]* It's my signature.

MAGNA: How do you know it's yours?

KONI: The Lieutenant made it for me.

MAGNA: So what do you do when the Lieutenant is gone, like now? Can you even make a cross?

KONI: I don't have to prove anything. I am in charge here now.

MAGNA: Making crosses is magic, you know.

KONI: Magic? The Lieutenant signed that statement . . . it's the truth now!

MAGNA: You know if you do magic when you are not a magic man, the forefathers will be angry.

KONI: I did not touch that pencil!

MAGNA: Still, it's your cross. *[HE makes a 'cross sign' across his throat]*

KONI: *[His attempted resolve falters, but he regains it]* Ha, now I can see what you want to do. You want to trick me.

MAGNA: You can keep me here, and Yesterday. But Raphael does not belong here. You should free him.

KONI: And then? I'll get caught. It's either me or him.

MAGNA: You know he won't turn you in. He already let you go once.

KONI: He was stupid.

MAGNA: Think Koni, think about Raphael. He will even act for scoundrels like you.

KONI: The MP will look after me.

MAGNA: That MP does not care about you. If he cares, it's like the hungry cat that cares for the fat mouse.

KONI: What's in it for me if Raphael goes free?

MAGNA: He will vanish back to the bush. There he can be a real leader. Get some people with guns.

KONI: That will be treason.

MAGNA: And what you're doing is not treason against the forefathers? Making bad magic with your bad crosses?

KONI: Can you talk to the forefathers? Tell them I didn't make that cross?

MAGNA: Have you got a cellphone?

KONI reaches for a phone in his pocket. MAGNA busily presses a few keys on the phone, speaks as if in a whisper behind his hand.

MAGNA: They say they can't help you.

KONI: Why not?

MAGNA: You've run out of airtime.

KONI: But you must do something!

MAGNA: How can I help you chained up like this.

Noise of a funeral procession, similar to that in Scene 1. KONI suddenly hears it; begins to panic.

MAGNA: It's too late anyway. That's the forefathers. They're on their way already.

KONI: On their way? Here?

MAGNA: They are very jealous of people who want to be like them.

KONI: So what am I going to do now?

MAGNA: Maybe you should run away.

KONI looks at him, hesitates, then tries to bolt, but is turned back by a configuration that looks like a coffin (which JULIA is carrying and hiding behind).

KONI: Take these spirits away! They'll kill me!

MAGNA: Release us!

The coffin cuts off KONI's escape route. Eventually it corners him against the police station.

RAPHAEL, YESTERDAY: Come on, unlock these chains! Be a brave man now!

MAGNA: There is only one thing to do, Koni. Face up to it!

KONI: I didn't mean to! The Lieutenant made me do it! I didn't make the cross.

Shaking, terrified, KONI holds out the keys. MAGNA and YESTERDAY escape. The coffin mask gets put down, and JULIA is revealed as the carrier.

RAPHAEL: Julia!

JULIA: *[Unlocks MAGNA's chain]* Yes, it's me. You must run now.

RAPHAEL: What are you doing?

JULIA: *[Forgets about YESTERDAY, speaks to RAPHAEL who is still chained to the pole]* I don't like my life anymore, Raphael. Once you fall for a good man, you've had it.

RAPHAEL: I can't give you what you want, Julia.

JULIA: What I want is not to be the slave of men, I'm tired of it. All of them want to use me, except you. I can see that now.

RAPHAEL: It took you a while, Julia.

JULIA: I know that. But you betrayed me too. You chose your purity over me.

RAPHAEL: I had to do it. I didn't mean to hurt you.

JULIA: You have, Raphael, you have. But, you see, I have forgiven you.

[RAPHAEL and JULIA reach out for each other]

YESTERDAY: Guys, this is not the time to be romantic.

JULIA and RAPHAEL pull back from each other, JULIA turns to unlock YESTERDAY.

He takes the gun from KONI; she turns back to RAPHAEL but does not yet unlock him.

JULIA: Doesn't my forgiveness mean I can be like you too?

RAPHAEL: I am not a good man anymore. I am now a renegade, a bandit.

JULIA: Well, make me one then to.

RAPHAEL: You will only suffer.

JULIA: Fall for a good man, and what you get is heartbreak.

RAPHAEL: No, Julia, I can't do this to you.

JULIA: Then I'll chain myself to this pole with you. Either we stay together in chains, or we do it in freedom. *[She embraces him]*

YESTERDAY runs back in; he has a gun. He sees what is happening; beckons to RAPHAEL.

YESTERDAY: Don't be stubborn, Raphael, let the woman come.

RAPHAEL: Unchain me.

JULIA unlocks the chain; they flee, hand in hand. KONI is left behind whimpering.

After a few moments, glancing fearfully in all directions, he follows them.

KONI: *[Shouting]* Raphael, Julia, wait for me! I'm coming with you!

Lights fade; come back on again. MP enters; spotlight trains on him as he inspects everything, making a weak attempt at bringing order.

MP: And so the candidacy of Raphael Tondoni has come to an end. Like so many other promising careers, it degenerated into fraud and thievery. Is there no hope for us in our darkness?

Song of Hope and Darkness

We are creatures of the darkness
The light of day is overrated
It burns and blinds and marks us
Unless our eyes are shaded

It's in the deepest shadows
That we find out who we are
If we're headed for the gallows
Or towards a lucky star

It's when things get blacker
That hope shines like a jewel
And hides that it is an actor
In the place of what is real

Lights fade.

END

THE MARKET THEATRE PRESENTS:

SHOES&COUPS

A DEPARTMENT OF ARTS CULTURE INCUBATION PRODUCTION

WRITTEN AND DIRECTED BY PALESA MAZAMISA   MENTOR DIRECTOR MARALIN VANRENEN

SIPHO ZAKWE   MICHELLE MOSALAKAE   ZIZI PETENI   SIHLE NDABA

16 NOVEMBER - 2 DECEMBER 2018

'The intellectual was rejected and persecuted at the precise moment when the facts became incontrovertible, when it was forbidden to say that the emperor had no clothes.'

- Michel Foucault

INTRODUCTION

In the tradition of satire, *Shoes & Coups – A Paradox of the Absurd,* uses humour, irony, exaggeration and ridicule to illustrate the politics of idealism and power as demonstrated through the relations between government, citizens, and big business.

The current global political climate has seen the voices of citizens increasingly usurped by the demands and excesses of narrow political and conglomerate business interests, for whom, it appears, undermining basic democratic, constitutional and human rights principles is par for the course. Tragically, these actions generate adverse social, financial and economic repercussions that affect especially the poor, working, and middle classes as well as weakening the ethical, moral and philosophical principles that seek to uphold the integrity of a nation. Citizens suffer when gross, and shameless, misconduct by political and business interests becomes a fait accompli. When those who are entrusted to lead a nation disregard and mock the privilege of leadership, they risk breaking the social contract with the people and to the constitution they have sworn to uphold. Such misconduct destroys the ability of a nation to reconstruct itself as it sinks deeper into a quagmire of corruption, despondency and, often times, sheer absurdity.

In as much as *Shoes & Coups* is entertainment and parody, it is also a plea to reflect on this erosion of democratic, constitutional and human rights principles, and hopes that audiences will reflect on the processes employed by political and business interests to subvert dignity and common decency in their pursuit of inexhaustible financial gain and satisfaction of a relentless lust for power.

Humour serves not as a substitute for critical engagement but rather as an alternative lens through which to view the issues that matter and are important to society. Ultimately, it seeks to add to the debate that ensues when citizens ask, often in exasperation: how did we get here?

CHARACTERS

THE GREAT SUCCESSOR | 30-years old, self-involved Lascivia, daughter of the Supreme Leader of the Ultimate State of Lascivia; she aspires to be a top designer, but her dreams are shattered when she is forced to take over the country when her father dies suddenly in a car accident.

MS. TRACINDA PURCHASE | Deputy CEO of one of the world's most powerful and influential businesses, The Corporation; she is hungry for the CEO position which she can attain only if the Successor signs over powers to her to run the Ultimate State of Lascivia.

NIMROD | the son of the Supreme Successor's favourite butler, the Successor's advisor and much mistreated friend who seems to be more capable of running the country; he's in a predicament as he tries to save the country from both The Successor and Ms. Purchase.

THE PRAISE SINGER [iMbongi] | a praise singer and unofficial voice of the people who also informs The Successor of the state of mind of the citizens of the Ultimate State of Lascivia.

THE VOICE | the nagging intercom that keeps hounding Ms. Purchase.

Shoes & Coups premiered at the Market Theatre, Johannesburg on 21 November 2018 with the following cast:

THE GREAT SUCCESSOR	Michelle Mosalakae
NIMROD	Zizi Peteni
TRACINDA PURCHASE	Sihle Ndaba
IMBONGI / THE VOICE	Sipho Zakwe

GUARDIANS OF TIME [1]

There is a melody of change in the distant wind
The final trumpet was blown to mark the ending of a wicked era
Anarchy is the colour of these clouds
The coming rain will be a reign of true spiritual freedom
Every spirit is beginning its blossoming with the arrival of the new sun
Every righteous bone shakes restlessly in the bodies aligned
With nature's ferocious cries
Her teardrops are drumbeats that awaken the hibernating giants
Who have slept through centuries of conditioning
While you slumbered, the materialistic greed
Has developed a gluttonous appetite
The whispers of revolution echo in the minds of the young
A new breed of warriors have risen
Who no longer desire to be chained by the laws of amoral men
The once meek and humble are inflamed with frustration
The indigo youth starve for truth and are rebelling for change
A thick veil was placed over the spiritual eyes of the young
The most high speaks to you through the wind
The instructions are crystal clear to the listening souls.
Oh, guardian of the benevolent light
Oh, warriors of change
Inhale your conditioned fears
Victory is yours
Your enemies are mere mortals
They are children of MEN

[1]*Guardians of Time, Copyright © 2018 Lemuel LaRoche, Tree of Life: The Human Ascension*

ACT 1

SCENE 1

Music. Lights rise. The office of **THE GREAT SUCCESSOR** *of the Ultimate State of Lascivia is a mismatch of official state objects and fashion design studio – mannequins, fabric and shoes. A sewing machine sits on her desk, and a large portrait painting of a young woman hangs on the wall.* **IMBONGI**, *the praise singer, enters the stage followed by* **THE GREAT SUCCESSOR** *and* **NIMROD**, *her personal assistant. They strut around the stage with gravitas. They stop in the centre of the stage and* **IMBONGI** *heralds her.*

IMBONGI: Hail thee, Great Successor of the Ultimate State of Lascivia. Hail thee Supreme Leader, Commander of the Highest Order, Chief Protector, First Empress, Conqueror of the Dominion, Her Excellency, the Highest of the High. Hail thee our leadership, the most honourable, most gracious, most beautiful leader of leaders. Hail thee, eminent ruler loved by all and destined to greatness and eternal recognition. Hail thee, servant of fairness and justice. Hail thee, oh brave one, fearless in the face of danger, guardian of your people, mother of the nation, spirit of our ancestors, champion of the unborn. Hail thee, hail thee!

> *THE GREAT SUCCESSOR steps forward. She is wearing a hideous designer outfit. She turns around, clearly fishing for compliments.*

NIMROD: Madam Successor, as always you look exquisite. Whose . . .

SUCCESSOR: *[Cutting him off]* Nimrod, you know very well that this is my own design.

NIMROD: But Madam Successor, your talent has no limits. Surely you can't blame me for mistaking it for an original Prada.

SUCCESSOR: *[Sitting down on the couch]* Don't patronise me Nimrod. You know I don't care for it. What's on our agenda for today?

NIMROD: *[Rushing to stand next to the couch]* Don't be angry Madam Successor. It's just that I'm overwhelmed by your style. It's so voguish and . . .

SUCCESSOR: *[Shouting]* WHAT IS ON OUR AGENDA TO-DAY, NIMROD.

NIMROD: Yes, yes, yes, Madam Successor. Today is an important day. Today we are signing Proclamation Gallus Gallus Domesticus.

SUCCESSOR: Why Nimrod?

NIMROD: *[Hesitant]* Wha . . . uhmm. What do you mean Madam Successor?

SUCCESSOR *[Sighing]* That ridiculous name Nimrod. Gallus Gallus Domesticus. Why not Proclamation Lascivia for example?

NIMROD: *[Excited]* Oh, but Madam Successor, it's the scientific term for a chicken.

SUCCESSOR: *[Sighing]* A chicken?

NIMROD: *[Excited]* Yes. A chicken.

SUCCESSOR: *[Annoyed]* Why Nimrod? Why?

NIMROD: Why? But of course in honour of your father, The Supreme Leader who died *[Sobs]* who died . . .

SUCCESSOR: Nimrod. Pull yourself together.

NIMROD: *[Regaining his composure]* It was because of a chicken that your father died so tragically. It was only proper to name the proclamation after it, you know, so that we may never forget. *[Pauses]* M`adam Successor, Proclamation Gallus Gallus Domesticus puts into effect the hand-over of the management of the Ultimate State of Lascivia to The Corporation.

SUCCESSOR: *[Closely and lovingly inspecting her shoes]* Whatever. Details Nimrod. I want details.

NIMROD: Ms. Tracinda Purchase, the Deputy CEO of The Corporation is due to arrive in the next hour. She will bring the original documents for both you and her to sign.

SUCCESSOR: *[Still admiring her shoes]* And . . .

NIMROD: And, well if you remember, it's a 20-year agreement. It gives power to Ms. Purchase to officiate as de facto leader of the Ultimate State of Lascivia. It will be a seamless transfer of power. The citizens won't know the difference.

SUCCESSOR: Is that so Nimrod.

NIMROD: Yes Madam. We have arranged it so that the nerve centre of the operation will be housed within The Corporation and will be overseen by the very capable Ms. Purchase. Of course you will be kept abreast of all decisions to be taken well in advance. No decisions will be acted upon without your final approval and . . .

SUCCESSOR: *[Waving him to slow down]* Nimrod . . . *[Sighs]* Exactly how does this agreement benefit me?

NIMROD: Madam Successor the benefits are aplenty.

SUCCESSOR: Really?

NIMROD: *[Excited]* Oh, Madam Successor, surely an increase in productivity and efficiency in the management of our fine nation is nothing to frown upon! Not to mention the benefits to our economic growth, job creation, infrastructural development and . . . need I go on? Might I remind you Madam Successor that the citizens expect a better quality of life now that you are in power. You are young and they are looking to you to reinvigorate this nation with your youthful spirit. Also, in your inauguration speech you made a commitment to the people. So this is exactly what we need to ensure that you keep your promises.

SUCCESSOR: I'll ask again. Exactly how does this agreement benefit me, Nimrod. And don't tell me about promises to the citizenry for heaven's sake. I could have said anything that day. It was very busy.

NIMROD: But Madam, I have provided you with a detailed summary of the agreement on no less than twelve occasions, outlining each of the clauses, the issues you should take note of such as the conditionalities, as well as the financial implications of the deal over the 20-year period of management. Have you even read through the document?

SUCCESSOR: *[Looks up from shoes]* Is that a tone?

NIMROD: No, of course not, Madam Successor. I was just gently inquiring about . . .

SUCCESSOR: *[Cutting him off]* Gently inquiring?

NIMROD: Ye-yes Madam?

SUCCESSOR: Nimrod.

NIMROD: Yes Madam.

SUCCESSOR: Do I need to remind you of my schedule? Why is it that all I'm doing is reminding you how busy I am?

NIMROD: I am aware you're busy Madam.

SUCCESSOR: Really?

NIMROD: My devotion is solely to serving you, which is why I have done all to make this an expeditious affair.

SUCCESSOR: So how did it escape you that I have more pressing concerns that do not afford me the time to peruse some papers you have concocted?

NIMROD: These are no concoctions Madam Successor. I can assure you. These documents are . . .

SUCCESSOR: Oh stuff it, Nimrod! Do you know that I have had to design original works for the Paris Fashion Week, Milan Fashion Week and

Johannesburg, Nairobi and Lagos are coming up? Do you think it's child's play? Do you even understand the pressure I'm under? I'm a top designer AND I have to run a country at the same time. Hmmm?

NIMROD: I meant nothing by it Madam Successor. Of course I appreciate the complexities of your genius, not to mention the time and commitment that come with creating the works of art as you do so resplendently Madam Successor, while running this country.

SUCCESSOR: Do you now Nimrod?

NIMROD: *[Ignoring her sarcasm]* As I was saying, in summary, Ms. Purchase, through The Corporation, will take over the complete management of the State, including all its resources, which will allow you much needed time to dedicate your life to your passion and true talent – one the world should not be deprived off.

SUCCESSOR: That's it?

NIMROD: For now Madam Successor.

SUCCESSOR: *[Changing her mood]* Brilliant Nimrod! You're good for something after all.

NIMROD: Thank you Madam Successor. Of course you will be generously compensated with a substantial fee on all transactions, on top of the royalties from the country's resources and a monthly allowance of no less than $100-million.

SUCCESSOR: *[Laughs uncontrollably, then gets angry]* $100-million? You think that is generous Nimrod? Do you know what this country is worth? A miserable $100-million does not even begin to account for the wealth bequeathed to me in this soil. The soil I allow you and your wretched citizens to step on with your dirty feet. $100-million!

NIMROD: But it's money for jam Madam Successor.

SUCCESSOR: Money for jam? MONEY FOR JAM? Are you joking? *[She clasps her chest dramatically]* Are the stakes so low Nimrod? Are they? You think that giving away my nation's wealth in return for $100-million is money-for-jam? Enlighten me. Whose money is it to begin with Nimrod?

NIMROD: Yo-yours?

SUCCESSOR: Oh, I wouldn't have thought you were aware of that the way you are busy negotiating such fraudulence . Clearly you are out to deceive me.

NIMROD: But Madam, you explicitly asked me to come up with a way to keep the country running smoothly while you focus on your design career.

SUCCESSOR: Aha! And so I did. But I do not recall requesting you to arrange anything to do with money and jam.

NIMROD: But Madam Successor . . .

SUCCESSOR: I'm not signing anything without the financials being re-done. I refuse to live on $100-million a month when I'm worth trillions . . . gazillions.

NIMROD: *[Mumbles]* Huh, as if . . .

SUCCESSOR: What was that?

NIMROD: I said it might be too late for that.

SUCCESSOR: *[Looking at him with suspicion]* Too late for what?

NIMROD: Changes to the agreement.

SUCCESSOR: *[Laughs uncontrollably again]* Oh, Nimrod. Full of jokes today. For a moment it sounded like you're trying to turn me into a commoner who takes instructions. *[Pause]* Oh . . . you're serious?

NIMROD: Uhm. I think so . . . ?

SUCCESSOR: You think so? You think that as the ultimate ruler of this land, what I do is subject to interpretation and discussion? You think that I, Lascivia, the Great Successor of the Ultimate State of Lascivia, have to seek approval over my land from anyone?

NIMROD keeps quiet as he frantically searches on his tablet.

NIMROD: *[Showing her the tablet]* But Madam it states in here that ...

SUCCESSOR: *[Screaming]* NIMROD, you may never take a decision that puts me in a position like this. I DON'T BEG FOR ANYTHING WITHIN THE BOUNDARIES OF MY OWN NATION. MY NATION NIMROD. Got that?

NIMROD: Got it. Got it.

SUCCESSOR: *[Even angrier]* And for that matter, I don't even like jam. So NO MONEY FOR JAM, you hear. I don't want to hear anything about jam. Not home-made, not apricot, not strawberry, organic and don't even mention marmalade. Don't you ever tell me about jam again! In fact as of now, I'm banning jam. It's outlawed. Issue an executive order at once.

NIMROD makes notes on his tablet. THE SUCCESSOR paces up and down murmuring about jam.

NIMROD: It's been taken care off. Parliament is rushing it through the processes, and they have allocated thirty-two minutes to discuss the bill.

SUCCESSOR: A whole thirty-two minutes?!

NIMROD: You have a legion of dedicated cadres Madam Successor . . . The Bill will then be published in the Government Gazette for input from our citizens. They will have a full twelve minutes.

SUCCESSOR: Twelve minutes! Who needs that much time in the age of instant messaging? Does nobody in parliament use social networks? Why did we buy them all the expensive gadgets if they're not prepared to use them?

NIMROD: Madam, democracy is a consultative process. It says so in the instruction manual provided gratis when we bought the Democracy programme from The Corporation. There are entire chapters on it.

SUCCESSOR: In English Nimrod.

NIMROD: *[Takes out tablet]* The manual states that parliamentarians will need to consult a representative group of a minimum of fifty citizens to ensure maximum participation or at least giving the impression thereof.

SUCCESSOR: That's your excuse? Please inform those numbskulls that modern technology reaches even beyond our borders. If they need representatives, they can just go online and buy them. They should learn to be more innovative in this day and age.

NIMROD: May I suggest this for the next piece of legislation Madam? *[Madam Successor scowls at him; he ignores her]* It should be rubber stamped into an Act by eleven this morning after which it shall be announced on national radio.

SUCCESSOR: Not good Nimrod. Not good.

NIMROD: We're doing our best given the circumstances Madam Successor.

SUCCESSOR: You're making me work over-time Nimrod. Bloody jam. And sort out this agreement at once. Or must I do that too?

NIMROD: That's why I sent you the document so many times Madam Successor.

SUCCESSOR: You just don't get it, do you? How can I make you understand the pressure I'm under?

NIMROD: No need Madam Successor. I am feeling your strain as much as you do.

> THE SUCCESSOR starts giggling. Her mood has changed suddenly and she looks at NIMROD expectantly.

NIMROD: *[Annoyed but playing along]* What?

SUCCESSOR: *[Giggles]* Oh nothing . . . *[Looks to NIMROD expectantly]*

NIMROD: *[Sighs]* What's making you so cheerful suddenly Madam Successor?

SUCCESSOR: *[Pretending to be pressured to respond]* Ok, ok. Nimrod. Since you're forcing me . . . I'm launching a new label.

NIMROD: What might that be Madam?

SUCCESSOR: *[Laughing in an exaggerated manner]* Shoes Nimrod, shoes!

NIMROD: Just what the world needs Madam Successor. More shoes.

SUCCESSOR: *[Ignoring him and pointing to the shoes]* You see these? Hmm. Original Lascivianas. Do you know how I begged and humiliated myself to get the world's top designer to create these for MY label? This is the only pair you will find anywhere in this world. Custom made for me by the great Fifou. FOR ME. *[Laughs]*

NIMROD: I'm starting to see the significance.

SUCCESSOR: Oh. Do you really understand the significance of this? Do you know what I've been put through in that industry? I've been mocked and laughed at, taunted, ridiculed as the talentless spoiled brat daughter of some erstwhile dictator. Do you know what the deal with Fifou means to me? My reputation? My influence?

NIMROD: Everything?

SUCCESSOR: YES, Nimrod. E-V-E-R-Y-T-H-I-N-G. Do you think Fifou would do this for just any one?

NIMROD: *[Dramatically]* Never.

SUCCESSOR: But you thought I am worthy of a lousy $100-million a month? Conditionalities? What's that Nimrod? Can you even spell it? *[Circling him]* Who am I Nimrod? Who am I?

NIMROD: *[Stands to attention]* You are the Great Successor of the Ultimate State of Lascivia, only child of the Supreme Leader who died tragically choking on a chicken bone when his limousine crashed into a tree as his driver swerved to avoid hitting a wandering free-range chicken.

SUCCESSOR: You had better remember that Nimrod! Do you think you can manage that? My father bought this country for $1.6-billion. The first billionaire on this continent. That was thirty-one years ago. Ok. If it weren't for his financial savvy, saving this country from total bankruptcy and economic disaster, you would not be standing here, the second most powerful person in this nation. Remember that Nimrod.

NIMROD: I couldn't forget it if I tried.

SUCCESSOR: Or start looking for a new friend who is a world leader at thirty.

NIMROD: I would never Madam.

SUCCESSOR: Your attitude suggests otherwise.

NIMROD: No, no madam. You're my only friend. My best friend. And no one deserves all this more than you.

SUCCESSOR: *[Calms down]* Ok. Good. We understand each other. *[Suddenly syrupy]* Remember, you are the son of my father's favourite manservant. We mustn't argue like this darling. We've known each other all our lives. We're practically brother and sister. Daddy would have hated seeing us fight like this.

NIMROD: I'm not fighting Lasci . . . Madam Successor.

SUCCESSOR: *[Admiring her shoes again]* It's good to get these things off my chest you know. Anger just clogs my arteries and kills my creativity. So what's this about the purchase?

NIMROD: No, it's Ms. Tracinda Purchase. Purchase is her surname.

SUCCESSOR: Tracinda Purchase?

NIMROD: Yes, madam. Tracinda Purchase.

SUCCESSOR: What kind of a name is that? Are you mocking me Nimrod?

NIMROD: Surely Madam Successor, you're not expecting me to account for other people's sense of the absurd when it comes to naming their children.

SUCCESSOR: *[Looking him over]* Go on.

NIMROD: Tracinda Purchase. Highly ambitious. Already sold us several of their programmes including Democracy, which included a free template for human rights. Touted as the next CEO of The Corporation. Wants this deal badly. Without it, she has no chance at becoming its CEO – and she knows it. You have the upper hand. She needs you more than you need her. It's a zero sum game. Make her sweat a bit.

SUCCESSOR: Nimrod, listen carefully. I am a leader. It is beneath me to make people sweat. Honestly Nimrod.

NIMROD: I meant just for your own amusement Madam Successor.

SUCCESSOR: Oh well, in that case, impressive, Nimrod. So my father's money sending you to study that useless course of philanthropy at Sorbonne has paid off after all.

NIMROD: Philosophy, Madam Successor.

SUCCESSOR: What?

NIMROD: Never mind.

SUCCESSOR: *[Casting him a nasty look]* I never don't not mind Nimrod. That's what I pay you for. To mind all those trivial things you commoners concern yourselves with.

NIMROD: *[Phone rings; he checks it]* Madam Successor she's here!

SUCCESSOR: Who?

NIMROD: The Purchase.

    Music.

SCENE 2

Music. THE GREAT SUCCESSOR stands staring into nothingness. MS. TRACINDA PURCHASE enters the room. She strides confidently to THE SUCCESSOR who moves to the other side as soon as MS. PURCHASE nears her. MS. PURCHASE is surprised and confused. THE SUCCESSOR continues. NIMROD and IMBONGI's faces turn to horror. Finally she stops the childish game and turns to face her.

MS. PURCHASE: *[Stretching out her hand in greeting]* Great Successor, at last . . .

SUCCESSOR: *[Turning around]* Oh, no need for formalities Tracinda. You may call me Lasci . . .

    As THE SUCCESSOR turns, her eyes fall on TRACINDA PURCHASE's shoes – they are the exact same pair as she is wearing. NIMROD and IMBONGI turn away, fearing the worst.

SUCCESSOR: *[Takes a few moments to compose herself]* Madam Successor would be just fine.

MS. PURCHASE: *[Surprised by the sudden change in attitude]* Ok. Well then, Ms. Purchase will do for me, thank you.

    THE SUCCESSOR tries hard not to focus on MS. PURCHASE's shoes but she can't help herself.
    MS. PURCHASE also becomes more reticent. NIMROD jumps in.

NIMROD: *[Laughing nervously]* Ms. Purchase, please do have a seat.

    MS. PURCHASE takes a seat while THE SUCCESSOR remains standing looking the other way, clearly trying to keep her cool.

NIMROD: I trust that you travelled well, Ms. Purchase.

MS. PURCHASE: *[Sniggers]* As well as one does in a private jet.

SUCCESSOR: *[Turns when she hears 'private jet']* Oh. Gulfstream?

MS. PURCHASE: G650.

SUCCESSOR: *[Smiling slyly as she flips her hair]* Oh, that little thing. Mine's a 747-8 V-I-P.

MS. PURCHASE: *[Offended]* Oh.

IMBONGI: *[Sniggers]* Phhh.

NIMROD: Ahum, shall we get to the business then? Madam Successor? Ms. Purchase?

MS. PURCHASE: I should think so. Time is money, I should hope even for you people.

SUCCESSOR: *[Raising eyebrows]* You people?

MS. PURCHASE: Yes.

SUCCESSOR: Do you care to elaborate Ms. Purchase?

MS. PURCHASE: No.

NIMROD: All Ms. Purchase means is that she is looking forward to signing the deal as soon as possible.

SUCCESSOR: *[Flashing a fake smile]* I see.

MS. PURCHASE: It's been a long time coming, and oh, my condolences.

SUCCESSOR: Extraordinary. How very casual about a leader as great as my father, whose misfortune is the sole reason for your presence here today and your ascent up the corporate ladder.

NIMROD: Shall we get started ladies?

BOTH: *[Turning to Nimrod]* LADIES?

NIMROD: My apologies, Madam Successor and Ms. Purchase shall we get started with the proceedings.

SUCCESSOR: *[Looks at the shoes and suddenly changes her mind]* It would be inhospitable for me not to offer Ms. Purchase an opportunity to freshen up.

MS. PURCHASE: Oh no, no need. I was hoping for a quick 'in and out'. I'm expected back tomorrow morning.

SUCCESSOR: Is that right? You have it all worked out I see.

MS. PURCHASE: As I do.

THE SUCCESSOR turns to NIMROD, ignoring MS. PURCHASE.

SUCCESSOR: Nimrod, please see to it that Ms. Purchase freshens up. And Nimrod please inform her that I insist.

MS. PURCHASE: But . . .

NIMROD rushes MS. PURCHASE out of the room. Lights fade.

SCENE 3

MS.PURCHASE is in the reception room on the phone. The reception room has a couch and a coffee table.

MS. PURCHASE: Sonia, it is the strangest thing. I fly half way around the world to get here only to be received like social leper. *[Shouting]* A leper Sonia, a LEPER. You're a hypochondriac, you of all people should have memorised the catalogue of extinct and current diseases. *[Pause]* I don't care about the weather. I'm not here to enjoy the stupid weather. It's almost 10:00. I told them it would be an in and out. *[Pause]* I should leave here no later than six this evening. *[Pause]* Yes, my time. *[Pause]* What board meeting? Who called the meeting? And why does George call for a meeting on the one day in the year I'm not at the office? *[Pause]* He is a low-level manager, what business does he have calling for such a high level meeting? *[Pause]* I knew it. He's been coveting my job for years. Well, he won't get it. You better make sure that meeting doesn't happen until I'm back. *[Shouting]* I don't give a damn what you do Sonia. I pay you a lot of money to make my life easy. Make sure THE MEETING DOES NOT HAPPEN.
    She is furious, throws the phone away, which breaks, then takes a cigarette from her bag. As soon as she lights up, a loud voice is heard.
THE VOICE: Smoking is strictly prohibited at Palace Lascivia.
MS. PURCHASE: *[Looking up and around]* You shut up!
THE VOICE: Insolence is not appreciated at Palace Lascivia.
    MS. PURCHASE hurls an object in the direction of THE VOICE.
THE VOICE: The use of violence is not encouraged at Palace Lascivia.
    MS. PURCHASE lets out a scream. Lights fade.

SCENE 4

NIMROD rushes back into THE GREAT SUCCESSOR's office; he's out of breath. THE GREAT SUCCESSOR is crying in front of the mirror.

SUCCESSOR: *[Softly at first]* Those are my shoes.
NIMROD: *[Confused]* What? Lascivia? What's wrong?
SUCCESSOR: *[Frantic]* Those are MY shoes. What is she doing wearing them? MY original design. Fifou made them for me only.

NIMROD: *[Consoling her]* Lascivia . . . I know you've worked hard to get that designer and that they mean a lot to you but, Lascivia, they ARE just shoes.

SUCCESSOR: *[Quiet at first, then becomes angry]* Just shoes? Just shoes? Is that what you think? You think my life's passion is just about shoes?

NIMROD: *[Forceful]* YES . . . *[Then changing]* Madam.

SUCCESSOR: These are more than just shoes you pitiful idiot.

NIMROD: *[Sternly]* Lascivia I don't care for the insults. These are just shoes. You can't put the shoes before the interest of this nation. What would your father think?

SUCCESSOR: My father? Don't you use his name!

NIMROD: I'm sorry I just meant that . . .

SUCCESSOR: My father would be impressed that his daughter has such foresight. I'm starting a shoe label. I'm adding value to the economy. I'm creating factories, employment, improving the standard of living for my people.

NIMROD: Of course.

SUCCESSOR: *[Falling apart crying]* How did this happen Nimrod? No one else is supposed to have them except ME. I've been lied to. He's a liar that Fifou. They are all liars. Frauds. Who do they think they are to deceive me like this? What else are they lying to me about?

NIMROD: Lascivia . . .

SUCCESSOR: *[Shouting hysterically]* It's Madam Successor to you.

NIMROD: *[Ignoring her]* Calm down Lascivia. Stop this nonsense.

   THE GREAT SUCCESSOR *wails, walking from one side to the other, frantic and exasperated.*

SUCCESSOR: *[Angry]* I want that swindler ruined. Call the head of intelligence. I want this sorted out now!

NIMROD: We can't do that Madam Successor.

SUCCESSOR: Why not?

NIMROD: We no longer operate like that.

SUCCESSOR: Since when?

NIMROD: Since your father died.

SUCCESSOR: And who made that decision? I want names, dates of meetings, people involved, machinists. I want to know everything about this.

NIMROD: Madam Successor, I'm not in a position to do so.

SUCCESSOR: NIMROD, you are turning this into a debate. The intelligence service is devoted to gathering information for purposes of my personal security and defence.

NIMROD: Actually, no. According to The Corporation's section on Intelligence Services, the objects, powers and functions must be pursued in compliance with the law.

SUCCESSOR: *[Looking confused]* Exactly Nimrod. I AM the law NIMROD. What do you think they are referring to by 'the law'? . . . *[Tearful again]* My shoes . . .

NIMROD: You will have your meeting and worry about the shoes afterwards. I need you to focus Lascivia. Can you do that? *[THE SUCCESSOR shakes her head still in tears]* We're going ahead. There's a lot more at stake than you realise in this deal. You will pull yourself together and let's negotiate you a new one. You hear me? A new deal. Now go freshen up. I will call Ms. Purchase.

SUCCESSOR: *[Disconcerted]* Ok.

NIMROD: Lascivia . . . *[THE SUCCESSOR turns around]* You are not your shoes. *[THE SUCCESSOR nods with appreciation and presses her hand to her heart]* Thank you Madam Successor.

   Light fades.

SCENE 5

Music. IMBONGI prepares to praise THE GREAT SUCCESSOR.

IMBONGI: Hail thee, daughter of the soil, purer than light, the most reliable, we are not worthy of your presence! Hail thee, emblem of all between the earth and moon, greater than the sun! Hail thee, flower of the moist earth, origin of air, more wholesome than water! Hail thee, most radiant, luminous glow of the people, incandescent being and representative of the humble people of the Ultimate State of Lascivia! Hail thee, oh glorious one. Hail thee!

   NIMROD and MS PURCHASE enter as IMBONGI prepares to continue with his praise. But, horrified to see them walk in, he stops and motions them to leave the room. They leave. Music starts again. IMBONGI prepares to praise THE GREAT SUCCESSOR.

IMBONGI: Hail thee, daughter of the soil, purer than light, the most reliable, we are not worthy of your presence. Hail thee, emblem of all between the earth and moon, greater than the sun. Hail thee, flower of the moist earth, origin of air, more wholesome than water. Hail thee, most radiant, luminous glow of the people, incandescent being and representative of the humble people of the Ultimate State of Lascivia. Hail thee, oh glorious one. Hail thee.

> THE GREAT SUCCESSOR enters, taking in the praise singing; NIMROD and MS. PURCHASE follow after her.

> MS. PURCHASE cringes in amazement and shock.

NIMROD: Madam Successor, you've outdone yourself on this occasion. If only more people would acquire your discerning taste for fashion, the world would be a better and safer place indeed. I'm sure Ms. Purchase agrees with me.

SUCCESSOR: *[Slyly]* It would be in her best interest to do so. After all, she is here to see me for a purpose. Am I right?

NIMROD: As always you are Madam Successor.

> THE SUCCESSOR walks over to the desk and sits down. NIMROD follows her. MS. PURCHASE is left standing by herself.

SUCCESSOR: Nimrod, do you think that where Ms. Purchase comes from, it is customary to stand during meetings?

> MS. PURCHASE walks over to the couch and sits down. As soon as she sits down, THE GREAT SUCCESOR gets up.

SUCCESSOR: So Ms. Purchase, what is the nature of your visit to the Ultimate State of Lascivia?

MS. PURCHASE: *[Looking at Nimrod]* The nature of my visit? Your advisor didn't inform you? Norman?

NIMROD: Actually it's Nimrod.

MS. PURCHASE: What is?

NIMROD: No, never mind.

SUCCESSOR: I know what he thinks you are here for. But what do you think you are here for?

MS. PURCHASE: Let us get to the business at hand, please. *[Taking out documents from her case]* As proposed, these contain the terms of agreement between you, on behalf of the Ultimate State of Lascivia, and myself, on behalf of The Corporation.

SUCCESSOR: I see. And who came up with the terms of agreement?

MS. PURCHASE: We did.

SUCCESSOR: We did?

MS. PURCHASE: *[Ignoring her]* Please refer to sections A to D for detailed explanations on how the transfer will take place. Then refer to T to Z for the financial agreements. These stipulate the terms of agreement including costs to company . . .

SUCCESSOR: Costs to company?

MS. PURCHASE: We are taking a big risk.

SUCCESSOR: Risk?

MS. PURCHASE: Yes risk. You're lucky The Corporation is even offering this service to you. But it's nothing to worry your pretty little head about.

SUCCESSOR: Pretty little head?

MS. PURCHASE: *[Irritated]* Do you have anything useful to say Madam Successor?

SUCCESSOR: Something useful to say?

THE GREAT SUCCESSOR turns to her desk and gets ready to operate her sewing machine. She runs the machine as an agitated MS. PURCHASE tries to convey the business to her.

MS. PURCHASE: Listen. My turnaround strategy for this country will over the next five years reposition you as one of the top three economically viable countries in the world. Under my visionary leadership, this country will be a model of financial stability, the hub of innovation in the region, and a risk-free, safe and stable destination for investment.

SUCCESSOR: And exactly how will you achieve this?

MS. PURCHASE: Refer to sections E to K.

THE SUCCESSOR walks around to the back of the couch. She stands behind MS. PURCHASE. She is quiet for a while and then lowers her head to her ear.

SUCCESSOR: I DON'T THINK SO, MS. PURCHASE. IF . . . that's your real name.

MS. PURCHASE: *[Stands up and turns around]* Excuse me? You're questioning my name?

SUCCESSOR: Nimrod, please arrange something to eat for Ms. Purchase as we go through the documents.

MS. PURCHASE: Oh no. No need Ronald. I've eaten.

NIMROD: It's Nimrod actually.

MS. PURCHASE: What is?

NIMROD: Never mind.

MS. PURCHASE: *[Turning to THE SUCCESSOR]* You can't do this. We've already agreed in principle.

SUCCESSOR: Principle? You expect me to sell my country, my people, just because of some lousy principle?

MS. PURCHASE: Rules are rules Madam Successor.

SUCCESSOR: Ha! You're trying to throw the rule book at ME? In case you'd forgotten, I MAKE THE RULES IN THIS TERRITORY.

MS. PURCHASE: That may be the case, but there is an international code of conduct by which we are guided. YOUR RULES, Madam Successor, are NOT, exempt from this.

SUCCESSOR: You think so?

MS. PURCHASE: I know so, little Miss.

SUCCESSOR: Are you trying to patronise me?

MS. PURCHASE: You are a thirty year old, hopeless designer if rumours are to be believed.

SUCCESSOR: Rumours? NIMROD, you're making me deal with this surly individual who not only listens to rumours, but will repeat them in public? *[Slaps him]* What's wrong with you Nimrod?

NIMROD: Huh . . . but . . .

SUCCESSOR & MS. PURCHASE: Shut up!

SUCCESSOR: Well, this thirty year old is no neophyte Ms. Purchase.

MS. PURCHASE: Ha ha ha . . . *[Tries to speak but continues laughing]*

SUCCESSOR: I wonder how amused you'll be when I lay a charge with the International Criminal Court.

MS. PURCHASE: *[Trying to stop laughing]* For what?

SUCCESSOR: Attempted bribery, treason, wrongful and illegal extraction of resources from my country to stack your war chest and human trafficking. Ha!

MS. PURCHASE: War chest? Human trafficking?

SUCCESSOR: You seem to think me and my people are for sale. The next thing you'll have my people working at slave wages for your profits while you completely deplete my resources and destroy the environment of my country. And then you will bankrupt my economy. Can I allow that?

[To NIMROD] i don't think so, NIMROD.

NIMROD: *[Escorting MS. PURCHASE out]* Ms. Purchase, I'm sure you would like a bite to eat. Let me show you out.

> *While exiting, he shoots looks of anger at THE GREAT SUCCESSOR, who is busy inspecting her shoes. After a few moments, he returns.*

NIMROD: What is this about?

SUCCESSOR: The deal is off.

NIMROD: Off?

SUCCESSOR: Off.

NIMROD: Why? And when did you develop a conscience?

SUCCESSOR: A conscience? Nimrod, she should not have undermined me like that.

NIMROD: What are you talking about?

SUCCESSOR: She's probably on the phone right now, laughing and sniggering away with those traitors.

NIMROD: What?

SUCCESSOR: Those frauds, neo-convicts, pseudo-beings parading as homo-sapiens who sold her my designs.

NIMROD: Designs?

SUCCESSOR: My shoes Nimrod. My shoes!

NIMROD: Oh no. Not the shoes. No . . .

SUCCESSOR: Oh yes. The deal is off Nimrod. Nobody gets away with this kind of theft. She can forget about becoming CEO of that stupid corporation. Who does she think she is, rocking up in here with my shoes?

NIMROD: What will we tell the nation? They are expecting the announcement today.

SUCCESSOR: What do they know?

NIMROD: They were told there will be an injection of foreign investment to boost the economy.

SUCCESSOR: Well, it's settled then. No one knows that The Corporation was to run the country. We will tell them that they came to rob us. They are frauds whose intentions were to enslave our people to eternal corporate servitude, and that The Great Successor won't have it. *[Standing clenching her fist]* My people, my land, my resources are not for sale!

> *The national anthem comes on as THE GREAT SUCCESSOR professes her dedication to the nation. Lights fade.*

SCENE 6

MS. PURCHASE is in the visitor's lounge. She takes another new phone out of her bag. She makes a call.

MS. PURCHASE: What's the status Sonia? *[Pause]* I'm still fine. As fine as I was an hour ago when we spoke. *[Pause]* Update Sonia. What's going on with that meeting? Have you rescheduled? *[Pause]* What do you mean it's not possible? I'm the Deputy CEO of The Corporation, how can there be an executive management meeting without me? *[Pause]* You get on this and prove to me that you're worth the money I'm spending on you. *[Throws the phone away; it breaks like the first one]*

THE VOICE: We value our goods at Palace Lascivia.

MS. PURCHASE: *[Pointing aimlessly in the air]* You! You stay out of my business.

THE VOICE: While a resident at Palace Lascivia, your business is my business.

MS. PURCHASE: *[Sitting down]* I can't believe this. They're trying to unseat me at the corporation I built to greatness, and I'm being harassed by an intercom which I sold to these useless individuals.

THE VOICE: Harassment: aggressive pressure or intimidation. We subscribe to principles of non-violence at Palace Lascivia.

MS. PURCHASE: Non-violence? You're talking about non-violence when you have that little monster running amok . . .

THE VOICE: Speaking ill of The Successor will not gain you favour at Palace Lascivia.

MS. PURCHASE: I'm not here to gain favour. I'm here to honour a deal. A deal we agreed on.

THE VOICE: Agreements come and go at Palace Lascivia.

MS. PURCHASE: I noticed. No honour. You people have NO honour what so ever.

THE VOICE: We only take on what we are able to manage at Palace Lascivia.

MS. PURCHASE: What's that supposed to mean you lifeless piece of. . .

THE VOICE: We encourage reflection of all actions taken at Palace Lascivia.

MS. PURCHASE: Who installed you? You can't possibly be a product of The Corporation? Or else the technocrats didn't follow the instructions properly. I will report you.

THE VOICE: *[Laughs]* To whom?

MS. PURCHASE: To whom? To whom? *[Pause]* Uhmm . . .

THE VOICE: *[Interrupts with stern voice]* In future, ensure you are prepared for anything Ms. Purchase. Life is full of surprises at Palace Lascivia.

MS. PURCHASE: *[Defeated]* You're just not going to stop are you?

THE VOICE: Defeat is neither policy nor practice at Palace Lascivia.

MS. PURCHASE: Oh, just shut it. And before you say it, I know rudeness is not encouraged at Palace Lascivia.

THE VOICE: *[Laughing]* Good girl. We might teach you some manners yet at . . . Palace Lascivia.

Lights fade as laughter sounds out.

SCENE 7

Music. A voice sounds over the intercom.

ANNOUNCER: This is a live broadcast on Radio Lascivia-FM, the preferred station of the citizens of the Ultimate State of Lascivia. Citizens, as of this hour, jam has officially been outlawed under the new national regulation, THE ELIMINATION OF ALL FORMS OF JAMS ACT, 2016 (ACT NO. 232 OF 2016), which decrees that: [A] Jam, meaning a preserve, conserve, jelly, marmalade, fruit spread, compote, or fruit butter, shall not be consumed in any form; [B] Jam, in noun or verb form, shall not be used to construct sentences, nor used in thoughts, dreams or as an artistic expression; the only exception is made for the song 'We're jamming' by the great Bob Marley; [C] Jam, as an expression of monetary value, such as MONEY FOR JAM, shall be punishable by the highest offence afforded in the Ultimate State of Lascivia. In this regard, large-scale manufacturers of jam will have exactly 14 days to dismantle their operations. Should manufacturers require more time for such dismantling, a legal application must be submitted to the Department of Liquidations. Those who refuse, or in any other manner avoid arrest, risk being shot under Regulation 1305.02, 'Shoot to Kill'. Please note that in the Act, all words or expressions to which meaning has been assigned has the meaning so assigned unless the context indicates otherwise. Where the context indicates otherwise, use your discretion at your own risk of contravening the meanings so assigned. Thank you and please remember your many viable new 'jam-free' options courtesy of the Great Successor: [A] cheese and scones; [B] money for nothing; and [C] traffic congestions.

SCENE 8

Sounds of protest heard in the background. Lights go on and THE GREAT SUCCESSOR is seen pacing up and down in the office before NIMROD rushes in.

SUCCESSOR: *[Looking outside]* What's going on Nimrod?

NIMROD: They are protesting Madam Successor.

SUCCESSOR: I can see that. Why? *[NIMROD keeps quiet]* Why Nimrod? Is it the jam?

NIMROD: No Madam Successor. As it turns out, not many citizens liked jam nor expected money for jam to begin with. The jam legislation has been well received. Haven't you seen the news coverage?

SUCCESSOR: Nimrod, I have a country to run, a new label to launch. Do you think I have time to wade through the arbitrary opinions of the media? Now tell me – why are my children protesting?

NIMROD: The people are hungry, Madam Successor.

SUCCESSOR: Hungry? For what?

NIMROD: It's not a figure of speech Madam Successor.

SUCCESSOR: In English Nimrod.

NIMROD: *[Sighs]* Unemployment is high. People are not working Madam Successor. Food prices are rising, the cost of living is unmanageable. Between bread cartels and banks, people are struggling to make ends meet. They can't continue living like this.

SUCCESSOR: Well, why don't they just pull themselves up by the bootstraps?

NIMROD: *[Offended]* I beg your pardon.

SUCCESSOR: Pull themselves up by the bootstraps.

NIMROD: Are you serious?

SUCCESSOR: No, are YOU serious? Honestly Nimrod! How many pairs of boots have they been given?

NIMROD: You can't blame them for conditions created by your father and his cronies.

SUCCESSOR: *[Takes a deep breath]* How dare you speak of my father like that? After all he's done for them. Clearly they don't want to work. Look at me. I'm launching my own label. Why can't they be innovative and take some initiative?

NIMROD: Madam Successor you are in a position to launch whatever it is you wish. It's not the same for them.

SUCCESSOR: Whose fault is that, hmm? Mine? I've just assumed power and I'm being blamed for all this? And, if they're so unhappy, why don't they do something about it?

NIMROD: Well, that's what they are doing now. *[Pointing outside]* That's why they are out there on the streets.

SUCCESSOR: But what for Nimrod?

NIMROD: They know why Ms. Purchase is here.

SUCCESSOR: How Nimrod? How did that happen?

NIMROD: Not sure.

SUCCESSOR: Not sure? Nimrod? Why are you in my service if you can't be bothered to find out what these indigents, these peasants, are on about? We wouldn't be in this predicament had you not stopped me from exercising my right to employ the services of my intelligence agency to . . .

NIMROD: They see Ms. Purchase's visit as your attempt to trade and sell our nation's resources while you keep the wealth, and leave them in total destitution.

SUCCESSOR: Oh, what rubbish! I'm doing them a favour. I'm saving them from modern-day slavery. You know the terms of that agreement will only serve The Corporation.

NIMROD: You haven't read the documents.

SUCCESSOR: Well, whatever . . . you know what I mean.

NIMROD: No, I don't know what you mean. You've changed your mind because of some petty . . .

SUCCESSOR: Petty? You think corporate espionage is petty?

NIMROD: It's espionage now?

SUCCESSOR: Do you think someone who has no qualms about stealing an original design can be trusted to run an entire country? What else will she steal from us? Our identity? Our culture? Our language?

NIMROD: No more than what you've already done.

SUCCESSOR: What?

NIMROD: Nothing.

SUCCESSOR: Issue a statement saying that The Corporation came here to deceive us and that, like my father, I have saved this nation from total collapse.

NIMROD: Madam Successor, contrary to what you people in the higher echelons of our society believe, not all citizens are simpletons. They won't accept it just because you're making an official statement.

SUCCESSOR: Since when? You mean to tell me that the common sense and obedience of this nation has been eroded in just one day? They were model citizens yesterday and now today they have their own will?

NIMROD: Things have a way of changing without explanation and at their own time.

SUCCESSOR: I'm not interested in your theories Nimrod. This is not a lecture on Philanthropy. Who's behind this? Is it that fraudster Fifou? I won't have foreign interests meddling in my affairs. Get the intelligence men to look into this.

NIMROD: Respectfully, I doubt Fifou could find this country on a map.

SUCCESSOR: I see, too clever by half. I want the names of people involved in this and see to it that they are sentenced before the highest court of the land within three hours.

NIMROD: There are processes Madam Successor.

SUCCESSOR: Processes for what?

NIMROD: You can't convict people without trying them first before the court.

SUCCESSOR: Oh, no Nimrod darling, sweetheart. You are being misled. Where did you get this dodgy information from?

NIMROD: *[Takes out his tablet]* Well, it says here that democracy is founded on the primacy of the law, provided such law falls within the provisions stipulated by The Corporation.

SUCCESSOR: I'm starting to think that this Democracy programme is designed to set us up for failure. Ignore that stupid manual and track down those traitors.

NIMROD: We will need to find another way to deal with this situation.

SUCCESSOR: Nimrod. Are you the traitor? Are you behind all this?

NIMROD: LASCIVIA!

SUCCESSOR: Ok, ok. But I won't be mocked like this in my own country. I need this resolved as a matter of urgency. GO!

As NIMROD walks out, MS. PURCHASE rushes in.

MS. PURCHASE: What's going on?

SUCCESSOR: Democracy is going on Ms. Purchase. Have you heard of it?

MS. PURCHASE: Have I heard of it? Lest you forget, I invented, exported and implemented it in no less than seventy-two percent of the world's nations.

SUCCESSOR: Aha! That explains its spectacular failure.

MS. PURCHASE: Your father's technocrats were incompetent and had little knowledge of applied democratic systems. What we export is tried and tested and has yet to fail where applied accordingly.

SUCCESSOR: Oh, is that what it is! We're too incompetent to execute your failed system.

MS. PURCHASE: My failed system? I don't think so. We keep telling you people that Democracy is foolproof provided you use our 12-step programme.

SUCCESSOR: If your system were foolproof it wouldn't matter how many steps we skipped.

MS. PURCHASE: Oh, what do you know anyway! *[Pointing outside]* What are they complaining about now?

SUCCESSOR: As per your Democracy manual, the people are exercising their right to express their unhappiness with your attempt to usurp this honourable nation.

MS. PURCHASE: Usurp? If there's any usurping Madam Successor, you are party to it.

SUCCESSOR: No. You deceived me.

MS. PURCHASE: How?

SUCCESSOR: You came here under the pretence of helping this nation, but all you're trying to do is climb the corporate ladder through corporate espionage.

MS. PURCHASE: Corporate espionage? That's quite an accusation Madam Successor. So you renege on the deal and now you're trying to make me out to be an enemy of your citizens. Very clever. That's never been done before.

SUCCESSOR: You can be sarcastic but you're leaving here tonight with nothing. Go and explain that to your bosses . . . on your way out of your job.

MS. PURCHASE: *[In total shock]* What! What do you know? What have you heard?

SUCCESSOR: You don't understand, do you? I'm a head of state. I get to know what I want, when I want, and about whom I want.

MS. PURCHASE: What have you been told? And by whom?

SUCCESSOR: Calm down.

MS. PURCHASE: Calm down? Are you involved in this plot to unseat me?

SUCCESSOR: Now that's quite an accusation Ms. Purchase.

MS. PURCHASE: Well, are you?

SUCCESSOR: *[Laughing]* You think that someone of my stature has time to plot the downfall of an overly-ambitious worker? *[Even more raucous laughter]* No wonder you're on your way out – paranoid old bag!

MS. PURCHASE: You talentless little tart. I'll . . .

NIMROD walks in before THE GREAT SUCCESSOR can respond.

SUCCESSOR: Yes?

NIMROD: Not good.

SUCCESSOR: What do you mean 'not good'?

NIMROD: They're marching on the palace.

SUCCESSOR: So? Just shoot them. *[Nimrod is horrified]* As a warning.

NIMROD: The police refuse.

SUCCESSOR: What do you mean they refuse?

NIMROD: They are part of the protesters.

SUCCESSOR: What? Well, get the army in, you dunderhead.

NIMROD: Uhm. They too are part of the protesters.

THE GREAT SUCCESSOR screams.

MS. PURCHASE: Will I be able to get out of this place?

SUCCESSOR: I have a major crisis unfolding and all you can think about is your own escape?

MS. PURCHASE: There's a meeting I can't afford to miss.

SUCCESSOR: *[Walks around to MS. PURCHASE]* Are you serious?

MS. PURCHASE: I need to be out of here no later than six this evening. *[Sternly]* I demand to be out of here by 18.00 hours.

NIMROD: Sorry Ms. Purchase. But they've taken your jet hostage.

THE GREAT SUCCESSOR bursts out laughing.

MS. PURCHASE: Taken what hostage?

NIMROD: Your private jet Ms. Purchase.

MS. PURCHASE: Who takes a plane hostage? What kind of place is this? They had better not be eating my caviar.

NIMROD: I tried to tell them that it's your plane. They don't believe me.

MS. PURCHASE: It's Russian. The finest.

THE GREAT SUCCESSOR is still laughing.

NIMROD: For all they care your caviar could be Cambodian Ms. Purchase. As far as the people are concerned the plane is grounded.

MS. PURCHASE: *[Turns to THE GREAT SUCCESSOR]* I don't know why you're laughing, because if I'm not leaving, you're definitely not going anywhere either.

THE GREAT SUCCESSOR stops laughing abruptly.

SUCCESSOR: Nimrod!

NIMROD: I need both of you to stay calm.

MS. PURCHASE: This is a joke. Are you staging this for my entertainment? If so, I'm not interested.

NIMROD: Both you of you have offended the people.

MS. PURCHASE: I don't even know them. I don't want to know them. I made an agreement with her. The lies you decide to tell your people are YOUR problem.

NIMROD: It's your problem now too. They know you're here and they distrust you as much as they do The Great Successor. They are saying that the Democracy programme you sold us was outdated.

SUCCESSOR: After all I've done for them, they have a nerve to distrust ME?

NIMROD: Madam . . .

SUCCESSOR: Don't madam me! Go find out what is going on. I need details, Nimrod. Details!

NIMROD exits, leaving THE GREAT SUCCESSOR and MS. PURCHASE in the office.

SCENE 9

The protests continue. THE GREAT SUCCESSOR and MS. PURCHASE try not to look scared. But it is evident that they are worried about the situation. They hear iMbongi approaching, followed by NIMROD.

IMBONGI: Fear thee, queen of sorrows, troubled by the ire of the people! Fear thee, lady of torment who incurred the wrath of her citizens! Fear thee, ruler of disgrace who tramples on the soul of the nation! Fear thee, lady of darkness whose enmity infuses the spirit of the nation! Fear thee, fear thee!

SUCCESSOR: Get this louse out of here. *[Turning to NIMROD]* What's the status?

NIMROD: Not good.

MS. PURCHASE: Not good?

SUCCESSOR: Not good?

NIMROD: They've started to reverse toyi-toyi.

SUCCESSOR: Reverse toyi-toyi?! No!

NIMROD: I tried to stop them.

SUCCESSOR: Do something Nimrod. I can't have such imprudence. They can do it on my grave. Not while I'm alive.

NIMROD: I will do my best.

SUCCESSOR: Not good enough Nimrod. Reverse toyi-toying ends NOW!

MS. PURCHASE: What's a 'reverse toyi-toyi'?

NIMROD: [As the iMbongi demonstrates] An indigenous form of protest through dance. But in reverse it's the rudest of all. It's simply not done.

SUCCESSOR: Absolutely uncouth for a nation reared by my father whose manners were impeccable. But where do they get this from? Who is influencing them?

MS. PURCHASE: Oh, this is ridiculous! And for that matter, nowhere in our programme is there provision for merging indigenous systems with Democracy.

NIMROD: Ridiculous to you, Ms. Purchase, but people have a right to express themselves as they chose.

SUCCESSOR: No, no, no! They may not under any circumstances reverse toyi-toyi against me. You heard her – there is no provision for that in any of The Corporation's programmes,.

MS. PURCHASE: I DON'T CARE. I need to go home! Do something.

SUCCESSOR: [Falls down into a chair] They're reverse toyi-toying against me?

NIMROD: If you would listen to their demands and act upon them, maybe we can save this situation.

SUCCESSOR: What demands? What more do they expect in addition to what my father has already given them. They have wardrobes full of superior clothing.

NIMROD: Your interpretation of what a need is may differ from theirs. That's why they're protesting.

SUCCESSOR: But I'm The Great Successor Lascivia, leader of all leaders. How can they reverse toyi-toyi against me?

IMBONGI: Well at least it's not the side-step toyi-toyi. That's real trouble!

SUCCESSOR: OUT!!!

MS. PURCHASE: Reverse toyi-toyi, side-step toyi-toyi . . . you're ruining the reputation of The Corporation! I will renounce this agreement if things continue like this.

SUCCESSOR: You renounce when you may not have a job when you get back?

NIMROD: That's if you get out.

BOTH: Shut up!

The sound of protest increases; then a loud bang.

MS. PURCHASE: *[Terrified]* This . . . it's the sound of my death knell.

SUCCESSOR: Oh, get over yourself. We need to solve this. This is not the time for drama. I thought you were some high-powered professional. And to think I nearly handed over management to you.

MS. PURCHASE: My whole life I've worked so hard to get this far. The obstacles, the wars I've fought.

SUCCESSOR: Aha! So you did come here to fill your war chest! You thought you'd get away with it.

MS. PURCHASE: I need to go home. They will get rid of me if I'm not at this meeting.

SUCCESSOR: Nimrod, draft a memorandum and get it out NOW. And let it be known that all those who abide by the order to stop protesting will receive a pair of original Lascivianas in three different colours for their entire family.

NIMROD rushes out. Light fades with the increasing sound of protest.

ACT 2

SCENE 1

MS.PURCHASE is in the reception room pacing as she speaks on the phone.

MS. PURCHASE: Update Sonia. *[Shouting]* For heavens sake, why did I employ you? Or are you part of them? *[Pause]* Who? You're asking me who? The traitors, that's who! *[Pause]* Sonia, I want the truth. Did you know about this? *[Pause]* Then how is it that the meeting is scheduled conveniently when I'm out of the country? Hmm? *[Pause]* Ah . . . *[Pause]* Oh. *[Pause]* Ohhhh no . . . No?! . . . I see. And when exactly did you think

I was born Ms. Smith! *[Pause. Yelling]* I don't care if your surname is not Smith. I have bigger things to worry about than the name you inherited from your father. *[Pause]* I must calm down? After you're colluding with that rogue George?! Well I don't believe you Ms. Taylor. *[Pause]* What? Oh please. SMITH, TAYLOR, WHAT'S THE DIFFERENCE. *[Pause]* You have given me no reason to believe you, you scheming, ungrateful, disloyal, deceitful . . . Don't you dare drop the phone on me!

> *She throws the phone away, which yet again breaks, then throws herself on the chair and holds her chest in pain.*

THE VOICE: A heart attack is not convenient during these troubled times at Palace Lascivia.

MS. PURCHASE: *[Looking up and around]* I'm dying and you're telling me it's not the right time for you?

THE VOICE: We're having a crisis. Besides, narcissism is not tolerated at Palace Lascivia.

MS. PURCHASE: Narcissism?

THE VOICE: Yours is an attack of conscience, which has manifested as an anxiety attack.

MS. PURCHASE: Narcissism not tolerated? You're rather delusional for an intercom. Your leader is the epitome of narcissism.

THE VOICE: Now-now. Envy will only aggravate your anxiety attack.

MS. PURCHASE: *[Takes a new phone out of the bag]* Oh, what will I do now? I've insulted my PA, falsely accused her, now how will I find out what's going on at the office?

THE VOICE: *[Laughs]* Worry first about your life.

MS. PURCHASE: *[Looking up and around]* What? Are they going to kill us? Will my life end at the hands of some side-stepping toyi-toyi-ers?

THE VOICE: *[Laughs]* Perhaps.

MS. PURCHASE: I refuse to be bullied by some reverse and side-stepping agent-provocateurs. I refuse, I say!

> *THE VOICE laughs. Lights fade.*

SCENE 2

THE GREAT SUCCESSOR stands at the balcony with NIMROD and IMBONGI on either side. She is about to give a speech to the nation.

NIMROD: Citizens of the Ultimate State of Lascivia. In an act of pure selflessness and love, the leader of this great nation wishes to address you. *[PROTESTERS boo]* Citizens! Citizens please allow our honourable leader an opportunity to share with you her new plans for this wonderful nation bestowed unto her after the death of her father who, if I may remind you, died, oh, so tragically, choking on a chicken bone . . . were it not for that chicken! That chicken!

SUCCESSOR: My people. I stand before you today, the remaining survivor and only daughter of the Supreme Leader of the Ultimate State of Lascivia who died tragically choking on a chicken bone when his limousine crashed into a tree as his loyal driver swerved to avoid hitting a wandering free-range chicken. *[Wipes away a tear]* Esteemed people of Lascivia, allow me to remind you of the great legacy my father left you, a legacy that includes the purchase of Democracy, Human Rights, a Constitution like no other. Citizens, we are a wealthy nation, an educated nation, a peace-loving nation. We do not wilfully descend into our streets to protest in such objectionable ways – screaming, destroying, reverse-toyi-toying, and even side-step toyi-toying. NO. You have been given a lifestyle that most can only dream of. We provide you with a house, a luxury car . . .

PROTESTER 1: We can't afford petrol!

PROTESTER 2: Our cars are parked in our garages for months! We walk everywhere.

PROTESTER 3: The toll roads are breaking us. We can't afford them!

SUCCESSOR: *[Continues]* Yes, yes, yes . . . and wardrobe choices most people can only dream of. Yet, you are reverse toyi-toying with your government issued smart phones. You should be grateful instead of disparaging of my leadership. This is the only nation that satisfies all the material needs of its citizens. Where else do you get to eat fried chicken, croissants and blue cheese, burgers, champagne for breakfast?

PROTESTER 4: Our cholesterol is high, we suffer from diabetes, high blood pressure!

PROTESTER 5: We have no access to affordable health care and medication!

PROTESTER 6: The hospitals barely function!

SUCCESSOR: *[Somewhat unsettled but continues]* Yes, we have consistently remained on the top five list of best-dressed nations in the world. Let's not take this lightly. And so, my heart is filled with generosity and I feel it is only fitting that I give to you, all of the citizens of this nation, three pairs of my very own, newly designed Lascivianas in the colours of your choice. Yes, citizens, you too will walk in my shoes. But, we have learned from The Corporation that the Democracy programme makes no provision for indigenous forms of protest. And as a nation we must stay within the rules and regulations of the programmes we buy. Should you have any concerns or issues, please consult the online survey. It only has three hundred and forty questions. It should take no time to complete it. That is, if you are truly interested in Democracy. I am the mother of this nation. Yes, I am your mother. Respect yourself and respect this nation, respect me, your mother, and original Lascivianas shall be yours.

The PEOPLE protest loudly.
Light and sound fade out.

SCENE 3

Music. A voice sounds over the intercom.

ANNOUNCER: This is a live broadcast on Radio Lascivia-FM, the preferred station of the citizens of the Ultimate State of Lascivia. Lascivians, you are encouraged to fill out the online application forms to collect your three pairs of original Lascivianas. Please be advised that no two people in one family may collect the same colours. For the colour-blind, there are special forms to be filled out to avoid unsightly colour schemes and clashes. These are punishable by law if not reported within forty eight hours to the Fashion Marshalls. Please ensure you bring along proper identification, as well as items of clothing with which you will wear your Lascivianas. Any uncoordinated or offensive garments will be disposed of with immediate effect. The Great Successor is known for her refined and discerning taste. Please do not become an affront to the reputation of this nation, so carefully developed and branded over thirty years. You will be persecuted for any such transgressions. Thank you.

SCENE 4

The GREAT SUCCESSOR, NIMROD and MS. PURCHASE are in the office. The GREAT SUCCESSOR is feeling triumphant after announcing her solution for the nation. Soon the voice of IMBONGI is heard.

IMBONGI: Beseech thee, wicked woman of reprehensible morals! Beseech thee, for thou shall be alone and falter as the righteous overcome those who are against them! Fear thee, woman of little sense and no conscience! Fear thee, angel of destruction and turmoil!

SUCCESSOR: I thought I asked you to get rid of him. Why is he still here Nimrod?

NIMROD looks away, ignoring the question.

SUCCESSOR: Are you ignoring me? ME? Your mother! *[MS. PURCHASE sniggers]*

NIMROD: Madam Successor, you are a head of state, you are not my mother. We need to start thinking clearly about this situation. We need leadership.

SUCCESSOR: In English Nimrod.

NIMROD: What are we going to do Madam Successor? The people want answers.

SUCCESSOR: Answers, answers! They want answers. Answers to what? How is this for an answer – they can all go to jail.

NIMROD: You can't jail the entire nation.

MS. PURCHASE: *[Interrupts]* Oh, no, no, no! Who told you that? Of course you can jail an entire nation. Just look at America where we have secured a forty percent containment rate of the black male population. It's one of our most successfully executed strategies to date. *[Looks pleased with herself]* No wonder you have these barbarians roaming your streets.

SUCCESSOR: Are you referring to my citizens as barbarians?

MS. PURCHASE: *[Ignoring The SUCCESSOR]* As I was saying Rodney . . .

NIMROD: Nimrod.

MS. PURCHASE: What?

NIMROD: Never mind.

MS. PURCHASE: Please stop interjecting Norman. It's very disruptive. As I was saying, the Corporation has over the years perfected its citizen containment programme. In fact, our latest version is in such high demand precisely because of its success rate in securing consistent prison entry rates. And the business opportunities are tre-men-dous.

NIMROD: Why let an opportunity to make profit go to waste?

MS. PURCHASE: You're being sarcastic Rodwell. But our calculations have projected huge profits in construction, catering contracts, not to mention employing the inmates at a cost of uh . . . zero to manufacture products. It's genius. *[Laughs rather pleased with herself]*

NIMROD: So you're behind the rise of the prison industrial complex around the world.

MS. PURCHASE: We're very proud of it. All our clients across the world are highly satisfied with the programme.

SUCCESSOR: You think locking up all my citizens is the answer?

MS. PURCHASE: You suggested it.

SUCCESSOR: Nimrod, please. This odious woman. Do something NOW Nimrod. Now!

NIMROD: With all due respect Madam Successor, what will we tell our citizens?

SUCCESSOR: You may tell my citizens that soon they shall be wearing an original pair of Lascivianas, one of three different colours. What else could they possibly want?

NIMROD: The people can't eat your Lascivianas, it's not a solution at all.

SUCCESSOR: Are you suggesting that three pairs are not enough for this greedy lot? I refuse to give them more until they change their disgraceful behaviour.

MS. PURCHASE: You're even more witless than I thought you'd be. He's trying to tell you that your people want real change, they don't need those ghastly shoes of yours. But I have a comprehensive package of solutions that will . . .

SUCCESSOR: *[Laughs and then abruptly becomes serious]* This from the woman who has no qualms wearing my original designs in my country, my home, wasting my time? Now you have opinions about what my citizens need?

> *MS. PURCHASE looks down at her shoes and then at The GREAT SUCCESSOR's. She is visibly shocked to see that they are wearing the exact same pair.*

SUCCESSOR: Aha! *[Pointing at MS. PURCHASE]* Now what have you got to say? Huh? Huh? Nothing. Thief. Nimrod, arrest her at once.

MS. PURCHASE: You dare call me a thief?

SUCCESSOR: Arrest her Nimrod. Arrest her.

NIMROD: Lascivia I'm not arresting her. *[There is a stand-off]* STOP. BOTH OF YOU. Can't you hear them coming.

IMBONGI: *[Running into the room]* They're coming! This is it.

NIMROD: *[Pulls them aside]* Now both of you listen. Shoes are not of the essence right now. Do you hear me? *[Looking around]* We need to escape before they find us.

SUCCESSOR: I'm going nowhere. This is my country. I am Lascivia, The Great Successor, sole heir of The Supreme Leader who died tragi . . .

The door bursts open before The GREAT SUCCESSOR can finish her sentence. Lights go out. Screaming and shouting ensues.

SCENE 5

The GREAT SUCCESSOR and MS. PURCHASE are locked up in the office. Both look dishevelled and disoriented.

MS. PURCHASE: *[Walks to the door and tries to open it]* Oh, stop that! OPEN THIS DOOR NOW. *[Bangs on the door]* OPEN. OPEN I SAY. OPEN.

SUCCESSOR: They won't hear you, you idiot. Haven't you noticed the high level of security in this building?

MS. PURCHASE: Haven't I noticed? Huh?! We invented this security system.

SUCCESSOR: Well, thanks. You have insulated us so much we won't find an escape. The Corporation is to blame for this disastrous system. Ever since my father acquired it, things have gone horribly wrong in this country.

MS. PURCHASE: Ha! You want to implicate The Corporation in your father's poor, if not disastrous, management?

SUCCESSOR: You blame my father, my father, the Supreme Leader of the Ultimate State of Lascivia who died tragically choking on a chicken bone when his limousine crashed into a tree as his driver swerved to avoid hitting a wandering free-range chicken.

MS. PURCHASE: Enough of your father's death. We know how he died. I've seen the arrest of the chicken and its subsequent slaughtering repeatedly on the World News. You don't need to remind me over and over.

Rattling at the door; NIMROD enters.

SUCCESSOR: *[Getting up]* It's about time. Get us out of here at once.

NIMROD: *[Looks away and clears his throat]* Hmmm . . .

SUCCESSOR: Why are you standing there? Let's go.

NIMROD: I've come with a message from the people.

SUCCESSOR: A message from the people. Huh?

MS. PURCHASE: Let him speak.

NIMROD: Both you and Ms. Purchase are not to be let out of here. The people . . .

SUCCESSOR: The people, the people! What rubbish. Who are the people? I want names. Now.

NIMROD: Lascivia. *[MADAM SUCCESSOR starts to protest but keeps quiet]* I have warned you about this happening. The people have their demands and I've been asked to present them to you on their behalf.

NIMROD clears his throat. Suddenly THE GREAT SUCCESSOR and MS PURCHASE realise that NIMROD's behaviour has changed. They slowly become quieter as it dawns on them that NIMROD has something serious to say.

NIMROD: *[Looks away then starts to read from his tablet as messages come through]* We, the people of the Ultimate State of Lascivia, demand the following: 1. The immediate handover of the management of the nation to Nimrod, our brother, a loyal son of the nation, a commoner like ourselves; 2. The immediate installation of Free Will; 3. The deaths of The Great Successor Lascivia and Tracinda Purchase by hanging.

Both The GREAT SUCCESSOR and TRACINDA PURCHASE are utterly shocked.

SUCCESSOR: They are demanding that I be hanged? This beautiful body? Their mother? What kind of children are these?

MS. PURCHASE: I'm not even part of all this. I don't know you people and have never wanted to know you. All I do is sell Democracy and country management programmes. Why involve me in this chaos?

NIMROD: I've been pleading for them to let both of you go. At least leave and not return to the country. It was the least . . . and . . .

MS. PURCHASE: And what Rodriguez?

NIMROD: *[Angry]* Nimrod!

MS. PURCHASE: What?

NIMROD: I said my name is Nimrod. *[He walks away angrily and slams the door shut]*

Black out.

SCENE 6

The SUCCESSOR is sleeping. MS. PURCHASE takes out a new phone and moves to a corner to talk.

MS. PURCHASE: *[In a sweet voice]* Sonia . . . Sonia. . . . pick up the phone, Sonia!
> *MS. PURCHASE throws the phone against the wall as she screams.*
> *The SUCCESSOR wakes up confused. The first thing she does is check her shoes.*

SUCCESSOR: Do you mind? I'm trying to get some rest. I'm highly stressed.

MS. PURCHASE: No point being stressed when you're staring death in the face.

SUCCESSOR: I will die for no man or woman. I was born with a destiny and that is to lead this land. It is not in their power to dictate to or defy fate.

MS. PURCHASE: And you believe this.

SUCCESSOR: I know this.

MS. PURCHASE: Foolish girl.

SUCCESSOR: Hmmm, we shall see who is foolish when your lifeless body swings in the wind as the people watch your spirit evaporate into nothingness.

MS. PURCHASE: Oh. And you?

SUCCESSOR: They will have recognised their error and restore me as their rightful and only leader.

MS. PURCHASE: I hope for your sake that it will unfold as you believe it will. As for me, I expect you to make a plan to get me out of this . . . alive.

SUCCESSOR: I'm in no way obligated to do anything for you. My country was running smoothly until you decided that it needed to move into the new global era of systems and now look what it has come to?

MS. PURCHASE: Who advised your father to purchase the Free Will programme?

SUCCESSOR: I have no recollection of any acquisition of a Free Will programme. The citizens must have come up with it themselves.

MS. PURCHASE: Ha! That's laughable. You know that's not possible. In any case, I have done only what my job required of me.

SUCCESSOR: Aha, yes exactly – to sell us for a song and dance, to corrupt our systems, to exploit . . .
> *Laughter comes through the intercom system.*

THE VOICE: How many times have I listened to sorrowful musings of those held in these quarters. Ohhh . . . *[Yawns]* how very boring.

MS. PURCHASE: *[Laughs]* Exhibit A. *[Pointing to the ceiling]* This is what incompetence results in . . . an intercom system that is rude and speaks to you as though you are equals.

THE VOICE: Now, ladies, you ought to consider yourselves lucky I'm even speaking to you. No one else in this country wants to.

SUCCESSOR: What do you mean? I'm still the Great Successor of the Ultimate State of Lascivia.

THE VOICE: *[Laughs]* Not for much longer. *[Laughs again]* In fact, if rumours are to be believed, Nimrod will be inaugurated as leader within the next two hours.

MS. PURCHASE: Who is Nimrod?

THE VOICE: Who's Nimrod? You imbecile! I suggest you remember his name from here onwards.

SUCCESSOR: Nimrod? He has neither the gall nor sense to lead a country. He was born to serve me. He wouldn't take on the position even if they were to put a gun to his head.

THE VOICE: *[Laughs]* Do you believe so? *[Laughs again]* Good thing he put a gun to his own head. *[More laughter]*

   Lights fade.

SCENE 7

The door opens NIMROD enters. The GREAT SUCCESSOR and MS. PURCHASE stand up defiantly, ready to take him on.

SUCCESSOR: So I understand that you are trying to depose me from my rightful position. How long have you been plotting this Nimrod?

NIMROD: Lascivia, surely you don't believe that I had anything to do with all of this.

SUCCESSOR: And why wouldn't I believe so Nimrod?

NIMROD: I would never, ever . . .

SUCCESSOR: *[Holding up her hand to stop him from talking]* I'm not even interested in the story you're trying to fabricate. I have seen through you. Ever since my father died so tragically . . .

MS. PURCHASE: *[Interjecting]* Uh . . .

SUCCESSOR: Who died so tra . . .

MS. PURCHASE: *[Interjecting]* Ah, ah . . .

SUCCESSOR: Who died . . .

MS. PURCHASE: *[Interjecting]* No, no . . .

SUCCESSOR: *[Dramatically]* Ever since my father died you have done everything in your power to make this nation ungovernable.

NIMROD: Me? You are misreading the situation Lascivia.

SUCCESSOR: To think that I never realised how deep your resentment was towards me. Hmmm. Even as little children I remember the look of envy in your eyes every time my dear father who . . . *[MS. PURCHASE shoots her a warning look]* . . . my dear father who gave me everything I wanted, including you, my supposed loyal servant.

NIMROD: I never resented you. I repudiate these allegations with contempt and in the strongest terms.

SUCCESSOR: You may do so, but I am not as stupid as you make me out to be. I recognise betrayal.

NIMROD: Lascivia, you're speaking out of turn.

SUCCESSOR: I should have known as soon as this woman showed up wearing my shoes that this was part of a greater plot to unseat me.

MS. PURCHASE: I beg yours.

SUCCESSOR: Who advised my father to buy the Free Will programme so that I end up with an angry and confused nation?

NIMROD: I never acquired the Free Will programme, maybe it's a by-product of the updated democracy version your father bought before he died so tragically.

MS. PURCHASE: Uhh . . .

NIMROD: May I suggest that perhaps, just perhaps, the people acquired Free Will on their own? Maybe Free Will is available on the black market.

MS. PURCHASE: *[Laughs]* There is no Free Will. We didn't create it, and if The Corporation didn't create it, it doesn't exist. Please Ringo. Stop this.

NIMROD: *[Getting upset]* I came here to find a solution. But I can see that talking won't change anything. Have you considered Madam Successor that the people could be tired of how you and your father have been running this country?

SUCCESSOR: There's no such. No one ever tires of getting new things.

NIMROD: *[Exasperated]* It's not about new things. What about dignity, respect, self-worth?

> Both The SUCCESSOR and MS. PURCHASE fall over laughing hysterically. NIMROD gets angry.

MS. PURCHASE: Fine print, Rodney. Do you read the fine print ever? Dignity and those other things you mentioned are built into the democratic systems.

SUCCESSOR: You see, Daddy would never buy anything that didn't have dignity incorporated in it.

NIMROD: Dignity is not for sale.

MS. PURCHASE: Oh no, no. This is another example of greedy people. If they want more dignity, they will have to buy the upgraded versions and install them.

SUCCESSOR: *[Ignores her]* So what must I do Nimrod? They are holding me hostage and calling for my head despite all I've given them – including training in etiquette and elocution. Look at how well spoken they are. They can go anywhere in the world and they will be taken serious.

NIMROD: *[Shaking his head]* You need to start taking the will of the people more serious. *[To MS. PURCHASE]* You think your fancy systems can control people and prescribe what it is they need. *[Pointing to THE SUCCESSOR]* And you . . . you . . . I don't even know what to say . . .

SUCCESSOR: Well, don't waste your breath Nimrod. And rather listen to what I have to say.

NIMROD: No.

BOTH: What?

NIMROD: I said, NO.

SUCCESSOR: You're saying NO to what?

NIMROD: *[Walking away and turning at the door]* This stops here and now.
    THE SUCCESSOR and MS. PURCHASE are confused. NIMROD checks his tablet. A message comes in.

NIMROD: It's been decided. There will be a referendum.

SUCCESSOR: A referendum? You must be joking.

NIMROD: Well, The Corporation does allow for a Referendum.

MS. PURCHASE: You are deliberately misinterpreting the intent of the referendum. It's not meant to give citizens an opportunity to institute lawlessness.

SUCCESSOR: Nimrod, truly. I'm on my knees. Stop this while you still can.

NIMROD: Referendum Hamba 387 will happen and it will decide your fate, and . . . *[Pointing to MS. PURCHASE]* . . . and yours.
    Lights fade.

SCENE 8

NIMROD looks at both The SUCCESSOR and MS. PURCHASE with disgust.
There is a recognisable difference in his demeanour.

IMBONGI: Loathe thee, Successor of the Ultimate State of Lascivia,
dishonourable, disgraceful, deceitful chief of rogues! Loathe thee . . .

NIMROD: *[To IMBONGI]* You . . . out.

Turning to The SUCCESOR and MS. PURCHASE.

NIMROD: Both of you sit down. Be humble.

The SUCCESSOR and MS. PURCHASE sit down finally realising that
the dynamics have changed. There's the sound of the intercom going on.
NIMROD stands to order in anticipation of the announcement about to be
made. Music.

ANNOUNCER: This is a live broadcast on Radio Lascivia-FM, the preferred
station of the citizens of the Ultimate State Lascivia. The results of
Referendum Hamba 387 have been validated and certified. The citizens
have unanimously voted that the new leadership of the Ultimate State of
Lascivia will be assumed by Nimrod, a loyal servant of the people and in
whom the people believe and place their trust. It is so decreed that The
Great Successor Lascivia and Ms. Tracinda Purchase vacate the Ultimate
State of Lascivia by way of beheading.

MS. PURCHASE faints. IMBONGI sniggers when he sees MS. PURCHASE
passed out on the floor. The GREAT SUCCESSOR is in shock.

SUCCESSOR: Nimrod. You can't allow this.

MS. PURCHASE wakes up.

MS. PURCHASE: Wha . . . what's going on?

SUCCESSOR: Nimrod please. Don't let it happen. Not to me, your friend?
Your oldest friend.

MS. PURCHASE: *[To herself]* They want to behead me?

SUCCESSOR: Us. Both of us. I'm to go first.

MS. PURCHASE: But . . . but . . .

NIMROD walks out with IMBONGI. At the door he turns round to look
at The SUCCESSOR and MS.PURCHASE.

NIMROD: Bye Lascivia. I never did envy you. But you were not deserving of all this.

Lights fade.

ACT 3

SCENE 1

MS. PURCHASE is in a state of confusion. The GREAT SUCCESSOR is defiant.

SUCCESSOR: *[Screaming]* Nimrod. NIMROD! YOU TRAITOR! Come back here if you dare!

MS. PURCHASE: Stop it.

SUCCESSOR: Excuse me, but who do you think you are speaking to?

MS. PURCHASE: As you can see, we are both in this predicament. Taunting and insulting Rodwell is not the best option.

SUCCESSOR: *[Screaming]* Nimrod is his name!

> *The GREAT SUCCESSOR sits down on a chair looking away from MS.*
> *PURCHASE. They don't speak for a moment.*

SUCCESSOR: My shoes. How did you get them?

MS. PURCHASE: What?

SUCCESSOR: My shoes.

MS. PURCHASE: *[Annoyed]* Has it occurred to you that it is perfectly possible for two women to buy the same pair of shoes and wear them on the same occasion?

SUCCESSOR: WHERE DID YOU GET THEM?

MS. PURCHASE: *[Pauses before speaking]* Fifou.

SUCCESSOR: *[Screams]* I knew it! That bloody traitor of a man. How did you know about them?

MS. PURCHASE: The shoes? Do you mean to tell me that you value an ugly pair of shoes above the well-being of your nation?

SUCCESSOR: Ugly? Ugly? Are you even aware that these are my designs?

MS. PURCHASE: That explains it then.

SUCCESSOR: *[Starts to respond but restrains herself]* Did he call you?

MS. PURCHASE: Who?

SUCCESSOR: Fifou.

MS. PURCHASE: Yes.

SUCCESSOR: So he knew.

MS. PURCHASE: Knew what.

SUCCESSOR: Your trip. This deal.

MS. PURCHASE: And?

SUCCESSOR: Only Nimrod knew of this. Don't you think it's rather coincidental that as I'm being deposed of my position, your colleagues back at The Corporation are doing the same?

MS. PURCHASE: Oh no!

SUCCESSOR: He planned all of this.

MS. PURCHASE: The defective programmes I sold your father . . . he's been working with that double-crosser George all along.

SUCCESSOR: And the Free Will programme?

MS. PURCHASE: George. He must have designed it and traded it with Nimrod for a stake in the country after the revolt.

SUCCESSOR: We've been bamboozled.

The GREAT SUCCESSOR gathers measuring tapes.

MS. PURCHASE: I spent years refining those systems . . . years. Then someone comes up with Free Will and just like that . . . *[Snaps fingers]* . . . it wipes out the millions spent on my products, the time, the research, the dedication from my team.

The GREAT SUCCESSOR checks the strength of the measuring tapes.

MS. PURCHASE: *[Laughs]* Dignity.

SUCCESSOR: Didn't you sell it to us?

MS. PURCHASE: You never did install it.

SUCCESSOR: Maybe he did.

MS. PURCHASE: I would know. The Corporation created it.

SUCCESSOR: Maybe it had a defect.

Music. The GREAT SUCCESSOR gets up and hands a measuring tape to MS. PURCHASE. They fix tapes around their necks, preparing to hang themselves. The women hold hands. Light fades with the muffled sounds of the women drawing their last breaths.

SCENE 2

Music. The office formerly of THE GREAT SUCCESSOR has changed. A large framed picture of NIMROD hangs against the wall. NIMROD walks about proudly, enjoying the crowd. IMBONGI prepares to hail NIMROD.

IMBONGI: Hail thee, leader of all leaders, father of the nation, solely devoted to the upliftment of your people! Hail thee, leader of the common people, our protector, saviour, liberator and deliverer! Hail thee, purest of men, bearer of truth! Hail thee, revolutionary and fearless leader, indomitable servant of our people! Hail thee. Hail thee!

NIMROD prepares to deliver his speech.

NIMROD: My people of the Divine Nation of Nimrodus. I, father of this nation, thank you. Without your sustained support, this day would not have come to light. We have fought a good fight. We have persevered against the Coalition of the Callous and Undeserving. We have thwarted their endless and vicious attempts to undermine the will of the people. We are victorious. *[CROWD repeats: We are victorious!]* Victory is ours! *[CROWD repeats: Victory is ours!]* Our struggle for freedom is now complete. The true emancipation of this glorious nation is finally upon us. No longer shall we be at the behest of the fickle-minded or the greedy savage to whom we were nothing but plebeians to be abused and exploited to perpetuity. No longer! *[CROWD repeats: No longer!]* My people of the Divine Nation of Nimrodus, I, Nimrod, son of the loyal and favourite servant to Uncle Su, who died tragically choking on a chicken bone when his limousine crashed into a tree as his driver swerved to avoid hitting a wandering free-range chicken . . . *[Stops for a second]* . . . I stand before you in truth. I, Nimrod, promise to uphold the honour of this new nation. Our dignity is not in what we own and what we have. *[CROWD roars approval]* Our dignity is in who we are. *[Clapping and shouting]* And for this my people, FOR THIS I bestow upon you, yes all you noble citizens of the Divine Nation of Nimrodus, I bestow upon you the rank of nobility. *[Disbelief but loud approval from crowd]* Citizens of the Divine Nation of Nimrodus, we will now all be one in knighthood. You shall be knighted under the Orders of: 1] Nimrodus, 2] Nimrodia, 3] Nimroditi, and 4] Nimrodita. You my people are now all equal before the law. You are royalty. You are now worthy. Your dignity has been restored. So say I, EMINENT EMPEROR NIMROD THE FIRST AND LAST PARAMOUNT LEADER OF THE DIVINE NATION OF NIMRODUS, EXECUTIVE CARER OF THE PEOPLE, LORD AND MASTER OF THE DIVINELY APPOINTED, CONQUERER OF ALL SPECIES, KING OF DANCE.

Lights fade. Music.

SCENE 3

Light on IMBONGI.

IMBONGI: This is our beginning and your end. Ha! You thought that you'd get away with it forever. Hahaaaa. I warned you. I told you. Let it not be said. I warned you. Let it not be said. "Let it not be said Precious Child arrived during their time but was neglected, taken for granted, dishonoured. What about those whose spears fell on the battlefield? Their mission to end centuries of nights of terror? And give birth to golden dawn Child? Earth still choked on their blood. Too sacred to gulp down. Those whose blood was still travelling to and from the four chambers as Precious Child landed on their lap, started finger playing thumb twiddling, lopsided leisure, their sport, priorities upside down their undoing. Neglected Precious Child wept. Finally gave up, knowing such mission unaccomplished, is opportunity lost. Those mandated with cradling Precious, Child of promise, their new name became Iscariot. Child named Precious, orphaned, teeth chattering, kwashiorkor-ed slipped unnoticed between custodian's porous fingers; slid in the space between the wobbly legs of the carelessly mindless role abdicators, drunk with cheap wine labelled, 'Me me mine, people last.' Mistook this poison for best wine. Their followers raised hands in the air angry disappointed asking one another, 'How can Moses be a Pharaoh and mock the burning bush that tasked him midwife of Precious, Child of Promise?' Precious Child crashed onto hard rock and wailed into little pieces. And those charged with nurturing, mother of all duties, didn't even notice loss of Precious, Freedom Child, born in their lifetime. Let it not be said a hundred years from today they hoped for a second chance to get it right this time. How can the same child be conceived and born twice? And, so it was with Precious, Freedom Child."

　　Black out

END

---

[2]*Let it not be said, Upon These Ashes.* Copyright © 2018 Lynette Hlongwane.

A tragi-comedy about friendship,
racism and decolonization
(as well as reading)

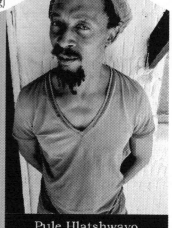

BOOK MARKS

with Luversan Gerard
Campbell Meas

Pule Hlatshwayo
Craig Morris

Written and
directed by
Allan Kolski
Horwitz

Soweto Theatre
cnr Bolani Link &
Bolani Rd
Jabulani, Soweto

NATIONAL ARTS COUNCIL
OF SOUTH AFRICA

DATE & TIME
23,24 February
7pm

PLAYWRIGHT'S NOTE

The debate on decolonization and racism which started in earnest at several universities in 2015 was initially focused on the University of Cape Town regarding the commanding presence of a statue of Cecil John Rhodes. Rhodes was the arch British imperialist who colonized the country now known as Zimbabwe and set in motion the Anglo-Boer War in order to control the Witwatersrand gold-fields and cement European rule over southern Africa.

The protests, dubbed 'Rhodes must Fall', provoked wide attention in all sectors of South African society and showed how the surface unity of a 'Rainbow Nation' is cracking under the weight of an ever-widening economic divide between the majority of black people and the white population and how institutions such as universities and the corporate sector which had formerly been reserved for whites had still not undergone sufficient transformation for black academics and professionals to feel accepted and respected. As such, the movement, inspired by the radical critiques of Frantz Fanon and Stephen Bantu Biko, was an expression of the rage of a new post-apartheid generation that feels cheated of change despite the 1994 handover of political power. Its desire for an Afro-centric South Africa that defines itself without apology or regret to Europe and the United States is challenging the assumption that the status quo of implicit white control can continue forever.

BOOK MARKS is set in this current period of intense ideological contestation and examines the reactions to it of three comrades from the 1980's 'Struggle'. They come together on a summer evening at the house of one of their number in Melville, a middle class suburb of Johannesburg, to launch a book club. There they are joined by a young woman whose life experience is essentially only that of the post-Apartheid period but who is very aware of the recent and historical past.

The host for the evening is Stanton de Villiers, a white, gay man of Afrikaner ancestry who is a consultant to the new government. The first to arrive is his old comrade, Vish Naidoo, who is agitated because a big business deal is scheduled to be sealed later that evening but he cannot locate the Saudi business man involved. Stanton and Vish talk about many things including the fate and present identity of Mncedisi *[aka Julius]* Matanzima – the third member of the NGO they had worked in, and resident of the communal house they had shared during the late 1980's in Yeoville, a more working class suburb. Thereafter, Cornelia, the daughter of a female comrade from the Eighties, arrives and begins the process of 'contestation' over the past and its truths. These interactions begin to wear away at appearances and become sharper and more exposing by the time Mncedisi finally makes his entrance and the play moves to its violent conclusion.

Correctly described as a tragi-comedy, BOOK MARKS looks at the delusions of erstwhile South African revolutionaries whose current life choices and life styles are shown to be hollow and self-defeating. It is an epitaph for the vibrant and hopeful mass movement that promised so much but which has, over the past two decades, dissolved into the corruption and mismanagement of a black-led neo-colonial regime manipulated by persistent white racism and economic control. The only hopeful aspect is the clarity of thought and courage of Cornelia, voice of a new generation, who is prepared to take on the burnt-out remnants of the old Struggle and forge a new path.

The first performance of BOOK MARKS was at POPart, Johannesburg on 26 January 2017 with the following cast:

VISH NAIDOO [*middle-aged Indian man*] Luversan   Gerard

STANTON DE VILLIERS [*middle-aged White man*]   Craig Morris

CORNELIA HENDRICKS [*young Coloured woman*]   Campbell Meas

MNCEDISI JULIUS MATANZIMA [*middle-aged Black man*] Pule Hlatswayo

SETTING

Evening. Stanton's house. A garden patio: pot plants; a deckchair, garden chairs, a table, a braai stand. A garden hose, connected to a tap, lies coiled up in a corner of the patio. The general stage lighting is muted on the sides as would be on an outside patio on a summer's evening.

AUDIO COMPONENT

The three songs [*STILL NO HOUR OF LIBERATION, NO VIPs and THE REVOLUTION NEEDS*] used as a soundtrack are from the author's albums *No VIPs* and *Look in the Mirror*. These can be accessed online at soundcloud under the name 'All Clear official'.

ACT 1

Play in with the song STILL NO HOUR OF LIBERATION. STANTON enters mid-way through the song; fusses around, preparing for the book club. He is followed by MNCEDISI who checks out the books in the book case. As the song is playing out, VISH enters.

VISH: The key question isn't whether the working class has the ability to change society so as to do away with violence, inequality and injustice. But whether human beings as a whole, as a species, have the ability to achieve this. We don't want to throw away years of our lives trapped in mindless jobs that may or may not pay well. We don't want to waste hours stuck in traffic jams or crammed in overcrowded trains. We don't want to have to read about endless corruption in government and the big corporations. Or have to tolerate dirty neighbourhoods and broken sewerage pipes. No, we most definitely want our shit to float as far away from us as possible. But what about what we do want? *[Slight pause]* After the houses and the cars and the private schools and the luxury trips and the latest smart phones and . . . and . . . and . . . we want romantic as well as comforting relationships. But above all, at a humbling 'number one', we want safe drugs. Ja, drugs. But in this case, I'm talking about mind-expanding, body-enhancing drugs that are cool. In other words, and, boy, this is really utopian, drugs that don't fuck us up even when we abuse them. Ja. *[Slight pause]* Alright, alright . . . stop laughing.

MNCEDISI: I won't start with the usual spiel about where I was born and my very humble origins in the desolate dongas of the Transkei, and how I pulled myself up by my bootstraps and got a varsity education despite the fact that my mom and dad were illiterate. I'll leave that to my official biographer whom I've already appointed. And would you believe it, she's a . . . no, no, not an umlungu princess with peach skin and tits like Charlize but a Korean. Yebo, a real live, genuine North Korean journalist who cut her teeth and her nails as an army correspondent in Matabeleland with Uncle Bob's 5th Brigade when they put down the Nkomo revolt leaving behind just a few casualties. Ja, I've always wanted to do 'stand up'. My heroes were comedians. I won't rattle off all their names but Idi Amin, Big Dada, was number one together with the emperor of the Central African

Republic, old Jean Bedel Bokassa, right, who built a fucking cathedral to rival Rome in the bush. Ja, 'Your Excellency, the President; Your Honour the Judge'. They and their natural-born get on board with the whites and smile for their supper. As long as they're around, we South Africans, and by South Africans I mean real Blacks, will never be allowed to have the power to do what we have to do.

CORNELIA enters. She moves as if she is in another 'zone', is a visitor to the one which the three men inhabit during this scene. She 'glides' around listening, observing them and the environment. When she speaks, she must signify that she is breaking into the audience's space, and then signify her exit in a similar manner.

STANTON: If you've wondered what kind of a name 'Stanton' is, well, that's my English side, from my mother. Came here in the 1860's – diamonds, my great-grandfather was a prospector round Barkly West. Made a bit of money, not that much mind you, and bought a farm in the area near where my dad's family had a place. Of course on his side we've been here a lot longer. As you'll know, de Villiers is a pretty typical Huguenot name, the first one came out to the Cape in the late 1600's. And then, not too long before my folks were born, there was that piece of trouble, the Boer War. In fact, quite a few of my dad's family were in the English concentration camps – something he never forgave nor forgot despite his crossing over and marrying my mother. So here I am, an only child who never took over the family farm – a great betrayal: wat is 'n volk sonder sy land?

VISH: My mom died after my youngest sister was born. My dad was a cop. Ja, you heard right. And for my sins I grew up in Verulam. You know where that is? Just north of Durban, or should I say, Ethekwini. And who lived in this little sugar town? Indians, man. Indians and more Indians and more Indians and quite a few Zulus and a handful of bloody umlungus. Now my Old Man had a low rank all his life because that was as high as a coolie could go. At school half the class hated me because I came from the family of a sell out and the other half thought my dad was smart because any job is a good job and six kids ain't easy to feed. Shit, he told me to also become a cop but after my two elder brothers, who were arseholes, went and joined up, I said, fuck this, who the hell do they think they are? I'm not going to wipe any white man's arse for a miserable pay packet. So I left

144

home, went to Durbs, got a job in a clothes shop. The owner, old Moosa Ebrahim, was a UDF type. I got roped in. Ja, I learnt a lot from old Moosa. Then his cousin said he needed someone to run a shop in Joburg, and I said what the hell, and I took the job and went to Joburg. And I carried on with the Struggle stuff and soon I was one of the leaders in the branch. And after six months I met Stannie and Julius at a meeting. Didn't take long and they asked me to join this NGO they started. *[Slight pause]* And that's where I wrote those bloody useless poems.

MNCEDISI: Izwe lethu! Our brothers in Zanzibar – they kicked out the Arabs. In Uganda they kicked out the Asians. In Kenya and Algeria and Mocambique and Zimbabwe, they kicked out the Whites. The time has come for Azania to turn inwards, to draw a line so that in our minds we can go back to where we were before slavery, before colonization, before the missionaries and the mines and the factories – before they took what we had. We have to go back to that time before we believed them when they said we were a dark continent. *[Slight pause]* Ag, don't worry. I won't eat you. I've got a little bit of Rasta in me. I'm a vegetarian.

CORNELIA: Once I arrive I'll have to live up to what Stanton wants. I'll have to play a certain role. *[Laughs]* Not that it's a particularly negative one but, all the same, it's annoying. I mean he hardly knows me but he's going to project all sorts of stuff about my supposed intelligence and spunkiness and my representing the 'born frees' and all that jazz. He'll demand that whoever is there likes me and at the same time, because he's a sly bastard – or so I've heard from my mom – he'll dare them to challenge whatever I say. And why is he doing this? Does his being gay make a difference? For so long he had to hide who he really is. He knows what it's like to be on the outside and have a massive chunk of your life seen as a sickness. Who knows, maybe that's why he wanted to join the Struggle. As for straight Afrikaners, they're scared of us, bruinmense. They think we're the bruised fruit of their loins, the living shame of their randiness. Just look at our names. I mean, mine is Hendricks!

STANTON: I was about fourteen and like most farm boys I went to boarding school, this was in Kimberly. And it was there that I realised that . . . I liked men. Of course, there was no one to talk to, so it stayed a secret apart from one, no, actually two men who I could be very open with. *[Slight pause]*

The first was . . . *[Laughs]* . . . the gym teacher. And where did it start? *[Mimes showering; laughs again]* And then around the same time there was the handyman, in those days, the handy '*boy*'. Yes, the two of them, a good South African combination. *[Slight pause]* And needless to say, the latter introduced me to ganja. Ja, it was as typical and obvious as that. *[Slight pause]* Hey, stick around – I'll roll you one later.

VISH: There was a funny incident at the NGO that made me leave. Some cash went missing. Not a hellava lot but enough for one of our biggest overseas funders to get pissed off. And when we went through the paper trail, all fingers pointed in one direction. But Stannie, who was the head honcho at the time, didn't want to make a case of it, so the whole thing was dropped. Maybe I'm wrong but it seemed like a fucking cover up. *[Slight pause]* The cash was gone and no prizes for guessing who was responsible. You hear me? No bloody prizes.

MNCEDISI: My father was a miner. You know, one of those men who left his village to go and work in the old Transvaal gold mines and came back once a year and didn't recognise his own kids. I mean, how the hell could he recognise me when I was shooting up like a mielie on Red Bull. And my mother was a . . . yes, a maid, in East London for a Jewish family. We got the clothes their kids couldn't wear and chocolates that were too hard to eat. *[Laughs]* Ja, there were five of us, only my brothers are still alive and one of them was crippled in a car accident. My eldest sister died of TB and the middle one was shot by a jealous boy-friend. And what do you know? They left behind kids, plenty kids. Sound like a story, a bad story? So I had to help out, had to find the extra bucks. And sometimes take a few chances. Yes, but I'm ready to go on. *[Slight pause]* I'm still ready to struggle.

STANTON: At the time the three of us were working together, we actually believed people, all people, but especially the poor, can work together for the common good. *[Slight pause]* Ah, 'the common good'. Just be a good boereseun, my seun. And don't talk about everyone having rights. And why don't you play rugby instead of chess? And why don't you take sweet little Hester out, she's such a beautiful girl and her family has five farms?" *[Slight pause]* Why can't people deal with reality? Take Mbeki's refusal to provide anti-retrovirals. Hundreds of thousands of people . . . If Mbeki had been white he would have been accused of genocide. But to defend what he called 'black pride' and prove that Blacks aren't sex maniacs, he thought he had to take the view that HIV isn't transmitted by . . . *[Makes the indecent sign of fucking]* . . . and that these drugs are a fraud, a western conspiracy. *[Slight pause]* But I was saved. I was saved because I had the money to pay for ARVs. I was saved because I was privileged.

CORNELIA: You know, we *Kullids*, a lot of the time we've been caught between blacks and whites, and depending which way the wind was blowing, we've changed sides. Hell, that has caused some problems. As for the new Khoisan movement, well, it's important but how do we revive dead languages and an ancient way of living that right now doesn't apply to ninety-nine percent of us? Apart from that, there are so many different dialects and shades of coloured. But I teach in a very mixed school and my friends swing all ways. Underneath the tans and the false eyelashes and the weaves, we're all relatives of the same chimpanzee. So don't get clever, brother. It's the luck of the draw. Having said that, I'm not here to give you a first year lecture on the do's and don'ts of racial togetherness, so I won't pretend it's not sometimes difficult. The old ways are still stuck in our heads although the reasons for any retreat into the tribe, or whatever you want to call it, are all too clear and, quite frankly, bloody pathetic. *[Slight pause.]* Ja, Stanton. Am I supposed to give him hope?

MNCEDISI: When I look around and see the buildings and the telephone poles and the electricity lines and the cars and shops and all the stuff that makes this a city, I feel more and more cut off, and at the same time totally trapped, like I've been kidnapped and thrown into a bubble on another planet. Ja, this white city our people were forced to build while those who designed it wanted to make it look like the cities they'd left in Europe. They stole our gold, our diamonds, to pay for everything. So how can I belong here? People running past each other: no time to greet, no time to look deep into the eyes, no respect, just boom-boom, using and abusing each other. *[Slight pause]* And for what?

STANTON: Sure, I was involved but I don't want to give the impression that I was a hero. During the Second State of Emergency, the Boers cast the net wide, they took in thousands of people. I certainly wasn't involved in anything underground in a military sense and I don't think Julius or

Vish were either. But, ja, being held at John Vorster *was* an experience. Also, we'd been close, a good team, and those two weeks inside really strengthened our bond. *[Slight pause]* Relationships. I've been involved in quite a number over the years but only lived with four of those guys. Take the last. Andile and I were together for seven years. It ended about six months ago. I miss him terribly but I know we can't work it out. He's just too . . . what can I say . . . adventurous? Thing is I'm past all the clubbing, the parties, so it's not so easy to meet people. Tonight I just want to see some familiar faces, bring in a few new ones . . . talk, drink, think. Just hang out, with intelligent folk. *[Slight pause]* You get it?

CORNELIA: I love reading. Ever since I was a kid. And I've got my mom to thank for that. She always made me aware of the power of imagination and the need to learn. Especially when your circumstances are pretty shit. After all, it's up to each of us to decide what we want to believe. She was growing up in Cape Town and went through all the forced removals and being dumped in nomansland. And she was the youngest and brightest but she wasn't able to finish school 'cause they all had to go out and work, the whole bloody lot of them. For years she was a machinist in a clothes factory until something happened, something that changed her life big time. *[Slight pause]* The neighbour's son.

MNCEDISI: They say we should go back to the bush if we don't like it, as if we never had villages and towns. They say we must be grateful for their civilization. *[Laughs]* Hitler, Stalin, Hiroshima, the Crusades, the Hundred Years War, the not-so holy Roman Empire . . . have I left anything out? Our *masters* . . . we had so much before they came. So many languages and so many stories; so many medicines, so many foods, so many drinks; so many tools and materials; so many ways to count the stars and predict the rain. *[Slight pause]* But now I'm walking in their city and I turn round and go home, and pour myself a beer, and pick up my old guitar and write a love song, a good old love song to good old . . . Mama Afrika.

CORNELIA: He was a student and he started to give her all sorts of things to read – novels, poetry and then political stuff which really got her going. And soon she was invited to join his study group, that's how these Marxists operate. And she found it tough at first, all that fancy language but she didn't give up and after a while it started to make sense. And when they

formally recruited her, she was ready for action. Fuck, she was the star
of that group. Always the first to volunteer for placing pamphlet bombs
and then the real thing. But not too much of that. She said she was scared
shitless of the grenades. And she didn't want to admit she was frightened.
Apart from that she couldn't take the home situation. Like her dad was
unemployed and expecting the girls to do everything. It was driving her
crazy so she came to Joburg. Her mom's sister was up here, in Riverlea,
and that's where she's stayed ever since. Except for that time in Yeoville.
With these guys. *[Slight pause]* So books saved her life. And they're saving
mine. Better than the nonsense the laaities are now using to run away from
themselves.

VISH: Sex! Sex is a sensitive subject: we either have an obsession and overdo
it or we stay starved of it. The thing about feminists is that they won't
accept certain biological imperatives. *[Mimes these actions]* Hunt, hunt –
gather, gather! *[Stops]* You were expecting me to come up with that facile
shit? *[Slight pause]* The real reasons why men struggle with monogamy
are as follows. *[Whispers conspiratorially]* a. With our small brains we get
easily bored and crave constant stimulation. *[Sexily]* b. We're susceptible
to most women who will make themselves available. *[Lecturing tone]* c.
We're democratic and don't believe in not giving everyone a chance to
enjoy it to the hilt. All the way, baby, all the way. *[Coughs]* Now this tool
called rationality, it's a new thing. We're struggling. And that's why for the
foreseeable future, `there's only . . . the Master's way to enlightenment . . . *[Sways
his hips, belly-dance style]* . . . Kundalini, my bra, that shivering down the
spine.

STANTON: Yes, it's true. My consultancy is starting to go down. Things
are looking quite tight and I may have to sell this house. The department
of Public Works is so shambolic that nothing gets done and you have to
fight like crazy to get paid, never mind being paid on time. I draw up
plans, check the costings, have dozens of site meetings, consultations with
communities but to get authorization for anything to actually happen . . .
And then there's all the black/white niggle. That's why I left the NGOs. At
the last one there was this one guy, very ambitious, who wanted me out.
So he came up with this story about my insulting black culture. When I
asked him to prove this, he said I never went to funerals, the funerals of

family members of staff, sometimes even of staff themselves. I told him that was because I thought funerals were a sentimental luxury, people were spending fortunes on the dead when there was so little for the living. *[Slight pause]* After he organised his coup, the organisation became his private business. He brought in his girl-friend and other family members. He killed off projects we had fought so hard to make happen. Gone. All gone because of the *baas* with a black skin. *[Slight pause]* But you know something. He had a point regarding the funerals. *[Slight pause]* He had a point. *[Slight pause]* Was I being racist or . . . was I just being plain fucking stupid?

MNCEDISI: Vish left first. He said the Struggle was dead, nothing much was going to change. After Stanton also bailed out, I decided to make a break. I didn't really know what I wanted to do so I left Jozi, went to my cousin's place. She had a small run-down house in Cala that needed fixing. I cut myself off from everybody. Sometimes I wouldn't even get out of bed. I would just lay there half dead with depression. And then, by total chance, I found a book, a history of the Eastern Cape. It was all about the Frontier Wars. And I was reminded how much 'divide and rule' destroyed us – as much as superstition. I mean how could the elders have thought that sacrificing our cattle would help the ancestors give us the power to destroy the enemy? *[Slight pause]* But aren't I blaming the victim rather than the conqueror? *[Laughs]* To be fair, I must admit that what Shaka did to his neighbours wasn't very neighbourly either.

CORNELIA: Two days ago while I was driving home after work I got a message. The school was broken into, they went straight for the computer centre . . . everything was taken, every single damn computer, every single last computer the kids need so desperately. And you know what? It must have been an inside job – no doors broken, no windows smashed. The thieves had the keys to the main gate and to all the doors that led to the computer centre. *[Slight pause]* And tomorrow at school assembly when the principal makes the announcement, the person who gave them the keys will be there and he or she will be shaking his or her head and crying krokodil trane, and saying what I'm saying now: that the bastards should be shot.

MNCEDISI: Almost to the end of high school I still didn't really know how to read English. I had the basics but I didn't have the patience to start and finish a book. I mean, school was damn boring. I wasn't in the Struggle then so there wasn't anything else to do except skip class and hide in the toilets and smoke zol. Now we weren't given real toilet paper, just scraps of old newspaper. So to pass the time I used to sit there and read the toilet paper, I mean the newspaper. And that's how I got into it – I got into reading the shit.

STANTON: Wragtig, liefie? Just look at us. Whatever he's become, he did some good work at that time. God, he was thin. And he had quite a scar under his bottom lip. Old knife wound. Bloody lucky not to have had his whole jaw sliced. Not that he was the violent type. But why I am saying this? Maybe because Julius was always a fierce arguer, the type of person who once he started a discussion was never going to leave you the last word. Though I must say he backed up what he said with some solid reading. We understood what we were fighting for. *[Slight pause]* Speaking of which, I made an avocado salad this afternoon with onion. You spice it with a touch of mayonnaise, lemon, salt and pepper. I sometimes cut in a boiled egg though today I didn't. When we three lived together we also ate a lot of pilchards. Julius liked them in chilli tomato sauce, I liked the plain, so there had to be a compromise. At first, neither of us was very happy. But after a while we found the blend so tasty we didn't want it any other way. *[Slight pause]* Can it still work today?

CORNELIA: That's a good question. *[Takes a journal out of her bag]* Listen to this. It's from someone's journal. *[Starts reading]* "I want a world of open borders, of open minds, of horizons that are never clouded. I want to be able to eat biltong in Beijing and sushi in Somalia, mopane worms in Mumbai and lasagne in Lagos. I want to walk alone at night and feel no fear. I want to choose any path and try it without being told I'm too weak or brainless or don't have the right. I want love to be the natural expression of the soul and not an emotion for sale. And I want what I want for everyone." *[Slight pause]* Quite a mouthful, hey? Almost religious. And does it matter who wrote it? Is the writer's age important? Do we only reach understanding of the world after a lifetime of experience? Well, let me tell you, it was a sixteen year old girl who wrote this passage. And it wasn't for a competition, it wasn't an assignment. It was an ideal, a pledge made to herself. Now has she achieved this? Has she remained true to her vision? You'll have a chance to answer that question this evening because that girl was ... *[Smiles]*

The song, NO VIPs, plays. CORNELIA dances. Black out. Music fades. They all exit.

ACT 2

VISH enters. Using his smart-phone as a torch, he walks around, examining the pot plants.

STANTON: *[OFF]* I won't be long, Vish. Make yourself at home.

VISH: *[In a loud voice which is sustained every time he answers STANTON]* Don't worry, pal. I'll find the perfect spot. *[Takes off his jacket]* Hell, you've always been cheap. I've brought my own booze. *[Takes out a hip flask and swigs. Starts walking around again examining the plants]* You know, I'm a great admirer of this type of grille work, the little side corners, the mass of plants.

STANTON: *[OFF]* But, darling, that's because it isn't a veranda. *[Sticks his head out]* It's a high class *patio*.

VISH: Patio? No, man, it's a good old South Effrican stoep which looks out onto the last dagga plantation of a doomed white man.

STANTON: *[Half his body visible. Wears a head torch]* Are you sure you want coffee? Not a beer.

VISH: Black coffee. Strong. And bring some candles.

STANTON: Ok. *[Withdraws off stage]* This last week we've been load-shed three times. *[Enters. Places a tray with the coffee and some other drinks on the table]* Here we are. I hope there's enough sugar. *[VISH opens the hip flask and pours into the coffee.]* Ooh, stylish! That flask must have cost a packet.

VISH: It did. As to what's in it, I don't stint either.

STANTON: Nonsense– since when do *churrahs* drink *expensive* whiskey?

VISH: We have to thank the bloody Brits for this most excellent habit. *[In a 'posh' English accent]* On the other hand, when it comes to genius, we lot came up with something even more important – the world's first, most exact and most comprehensive . . . sex manual . . . le karma sutra.

STANTON: If you spent half the money you throw at women on shrinks, maybe you'd get somewhere. *[Rising]* Let's face it Vish, you're a very horny and very pushy dealer who underneath it all is still fucking BC.

VISH: You want the truth? The first two – it's not happening like it used to, my brother. As for the BC label, I'll leave that to Julius.

STANTON: Julius? He wasn't that hard core.

VISH: *[Slight pause]* To be honest, I'm not sure I'm looking forward to seeing him again. He was a real bull-shitter, always looking for the limelight.

The lights come on.

STANTON: Hallelujah! But isn't that the way to become a successful brand? *[Sits again]* No, he was committed.

VISH: *[Sips his coffee. Makes a face]* Shit, where's the sugar? *[Starts to rise]*

STANTON: On the side board. *[VISH exits]* He was better than me at most things.

VISH: *[OFF]* True.

STANTON: And from the sound of it he's still a reader. And to prove it, when I spoke to him on the phone about the book club, he said he's long had enough of his slave name. He now insists on being called Mnce . . . Mn . . . Mn . . . *[Mangles the correct isiXhosa pronounciation]* . . . Damn, I just can't get it.

VISH: *[Enters]* Hey, shape up, bru. It's Mncedisi *[Uses the correct pronounciation]* But he was so proud to be called after Nyerere. Slave name or not, to me he'll always be Julius. *[Sits]* I bet he's in one of those really small Africanist groups that's constantly splitting.

STANTON: He mustn't bring that nonsense into my house. *[Drains his beer]* Ag, don't ride him too hard. He's apparently running some quite successful Youth Fund, one of those private/public job creation projects.

VISH: And no doubt also gives *motivational* courses.

STANTON: Don't be so cynical.

VISH: Why not? It's just identity politics. NGO's sponging off guilt-ridden funders. *[Stands. Looks at his smart-phone]* What! Nine o'clock! Where the hell are they, comrade? What's up with your miserable list of bookworms? *[Yawns; takes another hit from the hip flask]* I'm getting bored and dozy.

STANTON: That's what comes from potting since you've arrived. And, if I'm not mistaken, potting before you arrived. *[Standing]* Let me put something in your stomach before you pass out. *[He takes out his cellphone to check a message]* Now, who's this from? *[Exits. OFF]* Oh, no! He may not make it!

VISH: What's that?

STANTON: *[OFF]* Julius! He's in a meeting. He may not make it.

VISH: I'll guarantee it's not work that's holding him up. *[Begins to walk around examining the plants]*

STANTON: *[OFF]* Can't hear you.

VISH: He can't make it because he's busy trying to pick up some juicy underage number.

STANTON: *[OFF]* Ha, ha. Who doesn't want to enjoy fruit with firm flesh? *[Returns with a bowl]* Here some nuts to nibble. The real snacks are in the oven. I never put samooses in the microwave. They get soggy. *[Sits]* It's been lekker to see you these last few months.

VISH: Enjoy it while it lasts, brother.

STANTON: Now give me one of your famous back rubs. The memory of the bliss they leave is indelibly indented in my shoulder blades. *[Squats down next to VISH. Indicates his back]* Come on, just here. Dig those fingers deep.

VISH: *[Touching STANTON'S shoulders]* Hell, you are tense. *[Starts massaging his back]* But you've always been a manic type.

STANTON: Ouch! Don't rub it in. Not so hard!

VISH: *[In an Afrikaans accent]* Of course, not! Ons sal things *nice and soft* let bly. Won't we, skatie? *[Continues massaging]* You'd think you wouldn't have to deal with much stress in that cushy job of yours.

STANTON: Cushy?

VISH: Didn't the government spend thirty-four fucking billion rand on consultants?

STANTON: Not all on me!

VISH: Come on – you got your fair share, right? *[Stops massaging. Looks at his cellphone]* Yo, I've got to split. I really must. *[Slight pause]* Business, pal.

STANTON: Don't talk nonsense.

VISH: 'Strues God.

STANTON: What business?

VISH: With some guy . . . from Saudi.

STANTON: A bloody Saudi prince . . .

VISH: Just because they're homophobic, misogynistic, corrupt, hypocrite bastards doesn't mean . . .

STANTON: *[In an Afrikaans accent]* You can't do business with these people.

VISH: I really must leave.

STANTON: But everyone's on their way. *[Slight pause]* Except for . . . Cornelia. She was supposed to be a surprise. But she'll come to the next one.

VISH: Who the hell is Cornelia?

STANTON: Ah, she's . . . Nettie's daughter.

VISH: Nettie? Nettie Hendricks! I don't believe it!

STANTON: She's a teacher, history and science, and very dedicated.

VISH: Tell me more about Nettie.

STANTON: I know as much as you do. I met Cornelia by chance.

VISH: Well, if she's anything like Nettie I hope she'll give me a chance. Ha, ha.

STANTON: *[Laughing]* From what I've seen she's just a little bit too independent for the likes of Vish Naidoo.

VISH: *[Slight pause]* Who else is supposed to be coming?

STANTON: Just relax. There are quite a few people . . .

VISH: And the few are few and far between. *[Takes another shot from his hip-flask. Puts on his jacket]* No, man, I've done my time on colonial patios.

STANTON: *[Holds out his hand to VISH]* Please, Vish, just another half an hour. I suppose I could have organised it a bit better but, you know how . . .

VISH: You've always been totally fucking deurmekaar.

STANTON: See your Saudi tomorrow! How's the flask doing? I'll bring some Red Label. Just sit down and chill. *[His cellphone rings]* At last! And I'll bet this is . . . yes, it's got to be . . . *[Answering the phone]* Julius! *[Slight pause]* Julius, is that you? *[Shocked]* Cornelia! *[Slight pause]* No, just surprised. I'm really sorry you can't make it. We're having such a lovely . . . *[Slight pause]* No, no, you're not too late.

VISH: *[Calling out]* Come on in, baby. Come rollin' in.

STANTON: *[To CORNELIA]* Yes, things are getting a little rowdy. *[Slight pause]* You're five minutes away! That's wonderful! *[To VISH]* You see! I knew things were going to pick up. *[To CORNELIA]* I'm so excited! See you now-now. *[To VISH]* Let me check on those snacks. *[Exits]*

VISH: Jesus. Nettie's daughter. *[In a self-mocking voice]* No, we're not drunk and we're not high. *[Blackout]* Oh, damn! Not again! *[Calls out]* Hey, Stannie, don't forget to bring candles. *[Phone rings. Answers]* Hello, hello . . . *[Slight pause]* Ah, Mr Feisal! I was just about to phone you. I've got good news. My other appoint-ment's already over. *[Slight pause]* I can be with you in twenty minutes. *[Very disappointed]* Oh, I see. *[Slight pause]* I'm sorry to hear that.

STANTON: *[Running in]* God, I'm so please she's made it, and you won't believe it . . .

VISH: *[Gesticulates to STANTON to keep quiet]* Sorry, say that again Mr Feisal . . .

STANTON: Julius has just phoned. He's also . . . on the way.

VISH: *[Still on the phone]* But it won't take long. There just a few things to wrap up. Can we not possibly . . .

STANTON: Did you hear me?

VISH: *[Covers the phone. To STANTON]* Shut the fuck up! *[Waves STANTON away]* Not at all? *[STANTON exits]* Not even for half an hour? *[Slight pause]* You leave first thing in the morning? *[Slight pause.]* You really don't have any . . . *[Slight pause]* It's been a pleasure. I understand, Mr Feisal. I understand. *[Slight pause]* Yes, have a safe trip. *[Puts the phone back in his pocket]* Have a safe fucking trip.

STANTON: *[Enters with a tray of snacks. Puts them down. The lights come on]* Thank God!

VISH: Don't you know when to shut up? Fuck you, Stanton! If I hadn't come here first I could have met him earlier and sealed the deal. *[Slight pause]* He's going back to Saudi tonight.

STANTON: *[Puts an arm round VISH]* Don't give up, man! Drive out to the airport. Make a bloody commotion.

VISH: *[Mockingly]* In front of the twenty armed guards doing laps round his private jet. *[Slight pause]* Actually, he did sound quite . . . stressed.

STANTON: I'm sorry, Vish. *[Puts an arm round him]* Could it be that . . . his favourite wife's escaped the harem and he's personally taking charge of the search but as we speak, Princess Fatima, dressed in a zebra skin bikini is about to join Sheikh Feisal's half-brother in his palace on the Island of Jozi . . .

CORNELIA: *[Enters.]* Hello!

STANTON: And here she is!

CORNELIA: So sorry I'm late but I had a mountain of marking, it was crazy.

STANTON: Say no more, my darling! You're here – that's all that counts. *[Kisses her]* This is absolutely historic! But how rude of me! Cornelia, Vish, my old buddy, Vish. Your mom also . . .

CORNELIA: Yes, I've heard a lot about you.

VISH: You have? From Stannie? *[Takes off his jacket]*

CORNELIA: No, from my . . .

STANTON: Vish knows lots about your mom. We were just talking about her.

VISH: Nettie – what a woman! *[Stands up, extends a hand]* Lovely to meet you. You're her spitting image.

CORNELIA: *[She thrusts a bottle of wine into his hand – giving the impression that she doesn't want to make physical contact with him. STANTON takes her bag. Sits her down]* Oh, thanks. *[To VISH]* My mom says that apart from your Struggle reputation you have an artistic side. And in recruiting me, *Oom* Stanton told me you're very well read.

VISH: No, not at all. Oom Stannie is the big reader. I concentrate on other things. But . . . God, your mom was a beauty . . . how come you're here?

CORNELIA: Why? You think I'm not up to your intellectual standard?

VISH: It's just that Stannie told me you'd cancelled.

CORNELIA: What nonsense! I've been looking forward to this evening the whole month.

STANTON: *[Light-heartedly]* Liar! You said you couldn't make it tonight. But then you swore on your Maiden's Honour you'd make the next one.

CORNELIA: Oh, I've had to swear on other things for quite a while now.

VISH: Wonderful how the apple doesn't fall far from the tree.

STANTON: Hey, Vishnu, behave.

VISH: *[To CORNELIA]* But don't worry, my dear. I'll protect you from myself *by myself.*

CORNELIA: Why, thank you Mr Naidoo. It's lucky I do a good job all on my own. Anyway, here I am and I've got these *amazing* books to tell you about. *[To STANTON]* You said two very different books, right? And never the twain shall meet . . . though of course they usually do in one way or another.

VISH: That sounds too much like *reconciliation.*

CORNELIA: Don't worry. I'll give you in depth *contestation* if that's what you want.

VISH: With or without agendas?

CORNELIA: *[Pointing at STANTON]* Well, our host here is setting the agenda and from what he's told me he's a believer in the psychological interpretation of history, or should I say herstory. People *always* have agendas.

STANTON: Exactly. Strip away the rhetoric and what do you find?

CORNELIA: Men fighting over the biggest bone and . . . *the sexiest bitch?*

VISH: Oh, very insightful for one so young.

STANTON: *[Laughs]* You should publish a collection of wise sayings.

VISH: Wait a minute – getting published isn't be an easy thing. It's hard work to entice a complete stranger to fork out thousands to put your genius onto the market.

CORNELIA: *[Sarcastically.]* Is that what stopped you?

STANTON: Oh, no. Monsieur Naidoo here, as you know, is an authentic if self-published author who has never compromised his ideal of writing books for people who never read books.

CORNELIA: *[To VISH]* What did you publish?

STANTON: Don't be modest, Vish. You've published two collections.

CORNELIA: But that's cool.

STANTON: It was . . . very cool. That is – the reception.

CORNELIA: And what were the poems about?

VISH: That long distant time before the ink dried on the arms deal . . . and a few other . . . minor Mzansi 'wink-winks'.

CORNELIA: Meaning?

VISH: Forget it. I really am embarrassed.

CORNELIA: Were they that bad?

STANTON: No, they were very eloquent celebrations of the revolution . . . to-be.

CORNELIA: And Madiba was the hero or the sell out?

VISH: *[Crossing himself]* Saint Nelson, Father of the Fading Rainbow, accompanied by quite a few real kommunists, 'blink-blink'. And other banker gangsters. As for how they got away with the sell-out, well, there are very clear explanations.

CORNELIA: And that's why you've stopped working together and have . . .

STANTON: Yes, moved on and now recognise that . . .

CORNELIA: Only the rich have any brains and that the bigger the wage gap the more advanced a country is. What would we youngsters do without such penetrating analyses?

STANTON: Ja, we have failed you.

VISH: Go to hell, I've haven't failed nobody.

STANTON: We've fucked up, Vish. We all know the country's in trouble.

VISH: Well, here's more trouble! *[Holds his empty glass upside down]* This here is too damn empty. Mister Betrayal wants more damn fire water.

STANTON: *[Fake posh English accent]* A double, on the double, sir! But any refill on my part won't be up to the standard of your usual spirits. *[Fills his glass]*

CORNELIA: *[To VISH]* From here you smell of home brew.

VISH: Don't be too clever, my darling. In a short while we'll see how you handle someone who's a hundred percent proof. He's classy. His name is . . .

CORNELIA: Julius . . .

VISH: *[Picks up a glass from the table.]* To Julius!

> *Blackout.*

STANTON: Oh, fuck, not again. *[Starts Singing]* "We love you, Eishkom, oh yes we do . . . we love you, Eishkom, we're black and blue . . ." *[Exits]*

CORNELIA: *[Switches on her cellphone torch. Shines it in his face interrogation style.]* Why do you disown your poems?

VISH: I don't disown them – they disowned me.

CORNELIA: Because you got married and had a family and had to get some standards?

VISH: My ex certainly wanted standards. She insisted on leaving Yeoville. What could I do?

CORNELIA: Beat her. Bribe her.

VISH: Believe me I tried. I doubled her plastic surgery allowance.

STANTON: *[Entering with a lit candle on a tray and several others candles ready to be lit]* Sorry about that. I couldn't find all the candle holders but a boer will make a plan.

CORNELIA: Let me help. Only a klonkie can get the boer's plan to work.

STANTON: No, don't worry. I always find the right place in the dark. *[Sniggers. Starts setting the candles up around the patio. CORNELIA walks behind him and lights them]* And how did the two of you pass the time?

CORNELIA: We were talking about how men get rid of unwanted wives. Or should I say . . . side-chicks

VISH: You get the nyaope boys to do that shit.

STANTON: Nyaope? What do you know about the neighbourhood favourite? Wait a sec, I can smell burning! *[Exits]*

VISH: Where do you live?

CORNELIA: In Riverlea.

VISH: With your family?

CORNELIA: With my mom and her sister.

VISH: You're not married?

CORNELIA: No.

VISH: Why not?

CORNELIA: There must be about two thousand reasons.

VISH: So you're not looking for a boy-friend?

CORNELIA: No. I'm not looking for a boy-friend.

VISH: Are you looking for a girl-friend?

CORNELIA: No, I'm not looking for a girl-friend.

VISH: Then what the hell are you looking for?

STANTON: *[OFF]* For God's sake, give the lady a break, Vish.

VISH: But why? She's enjoying it. *[To CORNELIA]*And no kids I take it.

CORNELIA: *[Shakes her head]* I have more than enough of them in the classroom.

VISH: Ok, forget the kids. But let's talk about your mom. She was a lovely woman.

CORNELIA: She still is.

VISH: I'm sure she hasn't forgotten.

CORNELIA: What you did to her?

VISH: Of course not! I treated her very, very well.

CORNELIA: Like you do everyone.

> *Lights come on.*

STANTON: *[Enters with some eats]* Looks like it's going to be one of those bloody nights. *[Fusses, arranging the bowls]* Riverlea! God, I haven't been there in years.

VISH: *[To CORNELIA]* Has the grand liberation changed your lives?

CORNELIA: You really want to know? *[Slight pause]* There have been some changes. Some new housing, a new school, more tarred roads, there's a new light industrial zone nearby so there a few more jobs . . .

VISH: But mostly there's the usual stuff. You know, like . . . eh . . . child abuse, drug abuse, alcohol abuse, dog abuse, plant abuse . . .

> *STANTON's phone rings.*

STANTON: *[Answering the phone]* Hello. Julius? Hello. *[Slight pause]* Wrong number. I wonder where he is. *[Puts the phone back in his pocket]* But let me get the cocktail sausages before you burn the house down.

VISH: Wait! Quick question. *[To CORNELIA]* Do you eat pork sausages?

CORNELIA: No.

VISH: I thought so. Your mom wasn't very observant. But she did keep halaal.

CORNELIA: We still do.

VISH: Good. I don't touch pork myself. *[Slight pause]* And what about your dad?

CORNELIA: I don't know.

VISH: You don't know what?

CORNELIA: If he liked pork cocktail sausages.

VISH: Why? Did he leave before you were born? But of course you've met him since?

CORNELIA: No . . .

STANTON: *[Laughs]* For real?

VISH: *[Sniggering]* Do you know who he was?

CORNELIA: *[Sarcastically]* Is it important?

STANTON: Didn't your mom tell you?

CORNELIA: *[Sarcastically]* She just found herself pregnant. As you well know, she was a little wild at a certain point.

STANTON: But . . . she was a very valuable comrade.

CORNELIA: *[Cuttingly]* Yes, someone had to make food for the heroes and provide comfort when nights were cold.

VISH: But she wasn't a mattress, sweetie. No, no, not Nettie. She was a . . . blanket, a nice warm blanket.

STANTON: Jesus, Vish!

VISH: *[Drunkenly.]* 'Cause you know what, sweetie, we had a serious fucking system to overthrow and your mom seemed quite happy with her contribution. *[Walks towards her]* My, my, you've got her forehead. And maybe her hips . . . *[Tries to touch her hips]*

CORNELIA: How dare you!

VISH: You've definitely got her chin. Ja. Fortress chin with the faintest hint of her dimple. As a matter of fact . . . *[Opens his arms as if to hug her. She pushes him away]* Wait, this is stupid. Let's not fight. This is really an occasion. Why've I been so rude?

CORNELIA: Because this is your normal way of behaviour.

STANTON: *[Slaps VISH on the back.]* Especially after a few . . . *[Makes as if he is downing a drink]*

VISH: *[To CORNELIA.]* What's she doing these days? I must get in touch.

CORNELIA: I wonder what's kept you away for twenty-five years.

STANTON: Whoa, comrades! Cease fire! *[To CORNELIA]* Forgive him, my darling. Just see this as an initiation.

CORNELIA: *[To VISH]* Just keep your hands to yourself.

VISH: Hey, I said I'm sorry. Now get the halaal eats, Stannie. My stomach is voicing its utmost concern. *[Looks at his watch.]* And no wonder – it's already fucking ten o'clock. And bring another bottle. No water, no rocks. Just fucking straight.

STANTON: As always, sahib. Only the bent can procure. *[Bows. To Cornelia, in a staged whisper]* Don't worry. He'll get no more booze from me tonight. *[His phone rings. He answers]* Julius? *[Slight pause]* Oh, my God, at last! I'll buzz you in. *[Theatrically to VISH and CORNELIA]* Isn't this amazing! He's here! *[Pushes CORNELIA down on her seat]* Let me go get him. *[Exits]*

CORNELIA: *[Slight pause]* I'll give you one more chance.

VISH: *[Bows]* Best behaviour. *[Smiling]* You haven't known Stanton long, right?

CORNELIA: Just a few weeks.

VISH: Where did you meet?

CORNELIA: Where else but in a bookshop.

VISH: In the kiddies section.

CORNELIA: No, it was the drama . . .

STANTON: *[Running in]* Oh, my God, there's blood all over his shirt!

VISH: Blood?

STANTON: All over his shirt. He ran in like a madman. He's in the bathroom.

CORNELIA: Does he need help?

STANTON: I don't know. He wouldn't let me get close.

MNCEDISI: *[Shouts]* This country is totally insane! *[Entering]* Hello! Hello, everyone! Greetings! *[Bows and starts declaiming]*

> Another day in RSA
> eat your pap and eat your cake
> it's make or break
> secure your stake in RSA
> shoot first, that's the safest way
> or criminals will make you pay
>
> it's old and new taking what they think's their due
> and the colour's green no matter the dream

take it quick and take it neat
be the Chivas guy on your street
that's the way we play
that's the way we play in RSA

They all clap.

STANTON: [*Imitating MNCEDISI*] "From the moment I woke up – I knew there was going to be hell to pay."

CORNELIA: That was wonderful. Did you write it yourself?

VISH: Him! You want to hear a real poem, listen to this. [*Starts declaiming in an exaggerated manner*] "They came from the West sailing to the East with hatred and disease flowing from their flesh and a burden to harden our lives. They claimed to be friends when they found us friendly, and when foreigner met foreigner they fought for the reign, exploiters of Africa."

CORNELIA: Not even a clown can destroy a classic.

VISH: Hey, lady, I told you to watch that little tongue of yours.

STANTON: Peace, peace! You're all magnificent! [*Trying to embrace MNCEDISI*] Give me a hug. But . . . what the hell happened? Let me get you another shirt.

MNCEDISI: No, not yet, Stannie. Let me first see who's here. [*To VISH*] Well, I'll be damned, the all–powerful one who cools the hottest curry with his whisky breath. [*Holds out his hand*] Looking good, my friend. Not too much flab.

VISH: [*Taking his hand*] Ja, keeping fit.

MNCEDISI: Fit for what? Fit for what? [*Continues pumping VISH's hand aggressively*]

CORNELIA: [*To the audience*] Mister Naidoo, as I've heard from his very own mouth, is very, very fit. And he keeps so fit just by wagging his tongue. [*Laughs*] He's been telling me all about survival in the jungle. Especially how to survive bee stings. As in B.E.E.

MNCEDISI: And you don't support that idea?

CORNELIA: How could I? I'm Nettie Hendrick's daughter.

MNCEDISI: Nettie's daughter! What! How's your mama? I hope she's still a comrade.

CORNELIA: Well, we fight a bit about that these days. I know she did a lot but right now it's not enough to just have opinions. Ag, and I don't want to change the subject but seeing you're all here now, and I don't want to be rude, but from what I've heard, your famous NGO fell apart. Was that because of a lack of commitment? Or did you run out of money?

STANTON: To tell the truth, a bit of both. Everything was changing.

MNCEDISI: Yes, and the door we had opened was being shut in our faces.

CORNELIA: I heard Comrade Slovo, in his wisdom, was one of the gatekeepers. But he wasn't alone, hey. There plenty more of them to keep up the tradition. Take Msholozi – is he a comrade enemy or an enemy comrade?

VISH: *[TO MNCEDISI]* Never mind him. You're the one who always want to make an impression.

MNCEDISI: So these are . . . *[Points to the bloody marks on his shirt]* . . . just for show?

VISH: No, no, man. I'm referring to your poem, Julius. You're dead bloody right. RSA. It's either the 'bullet or the bribe'. And that shirt of yours – it's the blood of workers making a red flag. *[To CORNELIA]* You see, he's just come from moering a bunch of scabs. It was on CNN. Our bra here is going viral.

MNCEDISI: You've got quite a reputation yourself.

STANTON: For what?

MNCEDISI: Oh, you know, a bit of this and bit of that . . . *[To STANTON]* And you aren't far behind.

STANTON: Seriously, Julius, what happened? Let me get you a clean shirt. *[Is about to exit]*

MNCEDISI: Wait, don't go. You'll enjoy this story. *[Slight pause]* Like I'm coming off the highway at Empire Rd . . . and this fucking idiot tailgates me all the way to the robots. There's a red light. I stop. He pulls up next to me and starts shouting that I cut him off, you know, like I was switching lanes and almost forced him off the road. And then . . . before I know it, he's at my window, and he's got a fucking iron pipe in his hand, a fucking metre long iron pipe and he's swinging it around, screaming he's going to kill to me.

STANTON: Jesus!

MNCEDISI: *[Shouts out in a thick Boere accent]* "I'll teach you a lesson, you foking baboon! Where did you buy your licence? Go back to your foking township and stay there till you learn how to drive!"

VISH: You sure you didn't cut him off?

MNCEDISI: I didn't see this guy until he was up my arse on the off ramp.

VISH: Maybe he was in your blind spot?

MNCEDISI: You think I'm making this up?

VISH: It's just that I remember how shit a driver you used to be. *[To CORNELIA]* Like that time he went to Kimberley and he had more than one regmaker for breakfast and . . . *[To MNCEDISI]* . . . you almost rolled the car at fucking ten in the morning.

STANTON: Cool it, Vish! This sounds serious.

CORNELIA: Yes, it certainly does.

MNCEDISI: He nearly took my head off!

VISH: Maybe he was drunk.

MNCEDISI: Does that excuse him?

VISH: If it was a state of diminished responsibility then . . .

CORNELIA: Quiet! Let him finish.

MNCEDISI: If I hadn't put my foot down he would have killed me.

VISH: Did you go through a red light?

MNCEDISI: I would have gone through anything.

STANTON: *[Embracing MNCEDISI]* Thank God you're ok.

MNCEDISI: I don't remember seeing the guy at all.

VISH: What do you expect when you're wearing shades at night?

CORNELIA: God, stop making light of this.

MNCEDISI: *[Laughing]* Get me a whiskey, Stan.

STANTON: Now we talking! Don't let crazies knock you off your stride.

MNCEDISI: Pour the whole bottle, boertjie. Pay your fucking reparations. *[Slight pause]* Luckily after he smashed the mirror a few people started shouting at him.

CORNELIA: Only shouting? No one came to help you?

MNCEDISI: Actually one guy got out of his car and ran towards him.

VISH: I thought you said you pulled off straight after the mirror was smashed?

MNCEDISI: I did.

VISH: Then how do you know another guy got out of his car?

MNCEDISI: I saw him just as I was pulling off.

VISH: So just before you decided to burn your tires, you casually checked out the scene and . . .

MNCEDISI: What are you getting at?

VISH: Nothing, just that by getting out, the dude confused the Boer so you could get away.

MNCEDISI: And suppose he did?

VISH: Suppose, suppose . . . he fucking saved you, bro.

STANTON: Hey, Vish what's the point of all this?

MNCEDISI: The main thing was that I got out of there.

CORNELIA: And not a moment too soon.

VISH: I hope your rescuer was another wit ou.

STANTON: *[Loudly]* Enough! Comrades, where are your books? Let me make some room on this table.

VISH: Don't distract us from our contestation over a little situation. *[To MNCEDISI]* Umlungu saves darkie from umlungu.

STANTON: Here are mine. *[He places two books on the table. To VISH]* Hey, where yours? We've got work to do.

VISH: It's hard labour finding the potjie at the end of the rainbow. *[Takes two books out of his jacket pockets. Waves them in the air. Lays them on the table. To MNCEDISI]* And where are your books, bro? Did you manage to bring something other than your usual "Wretched of the Earth"?

MNCEDISI: Back off, Vishnu. Otherwise there'll be more blood on my shirt.

VISH: Yours or mine?

STANTON: Oh, come on, guys! *[Putting an arm round MNCEDISI]* You really can't sit here like that. *[Points to his shirt. Starts to exit]* I'll fetch you something. Then we'll start. *[Exits]*

VISH: *[To CORNELIA]* And you, Cornelia. What are you reading?

CORNELIA: *[Very cool and ironic]* I'm also reading "Wretched of the Earth."
    Blackout – strobe effect for just a few seconds.

VISH: Ah! Just what we need – a power surge!

STANTON: *[Running in]* Here you are! Nice and fresh and chosen with care. *[Displays the t-shirt; it bears Bob Marley's face]* Your poem wasn't quite rasta but I if I remember you loved the man's music. *[Hands MNCEDISI the T-shirt. Clears his throat]* Comrades . . .

CORNELIA: God, how you love the Word!

STANTON: How I love the word . . . As you know I've wanted to get this off the ground for quite a while and it's overwhelming that it's finally happening. And by way of opening, I'd like to raise a few observations that came to me while I was reading a fabulous novel, a relatively old one, as it is. Well, I picked it up and I must say I haven't put it down for the past three days. It's . . . well . . . 'Picture This'. *[Holds up the book]* By Joseph Heller – you know the guy who wrote 'Catch 22'. Well, this one's about Rembrandt painting Aristotle while Aristotle's contemplating a bust of Homer. And all the while he reminisces about Plato talking about Socrates.

CORNELIA: Socrates was put to death, right?

STANTON: Ja, for corrupting the youth.

CORNELIA: *[To the audience]* And they were right – it is corrupting to teach the young to think for themselves.

VISH: But they were reasonable in those days. They didn't necklace him. They gave him the choice of exile.

MNCEDISI: That's where you should go, my brother.

CORNELIA: A nice long lekker exile . . . maybe in . . . Orania?

STANTON: Listen! "Socrates did not like books, something that should have upset Plato who wrote so many. And he had a low regard for people who read them. He mistrusted books because, as he said, they neither ask nor answer questions and are apt to be swallowed whole. He said that readers of books read much and learn nothing, that they appear full of knowledge, but for the most part are without it, and have the show of wisdom without its reality."

MNCEDISI: *[To VISH]* Vish, that shouldn't bother you. You don't read. You never used to.

VISH: And you, my bra? You were so busy reading you forgot how to fight back? Why did you just drive off?

CORNELIA: You expect him to take a chance with a drunken Boer?

VISH: I don't remember him saying the guy was drunk.

CORNELIA: They usually are.

STANTON: *[To CORNELIA]* Don't get Vish wrong. Mr Action here walks the talk.

MNCEDISI: *[To VISH. Sneering]* Yeah, like in those days. *[To STANTON]* And you? What are you doing that's so involved?

STANTON: I didn't say I was *involved.*

MNCEDISI: Of course you aren't. How can you be? You always have it easy.

STANTON: What do you mean?

MNCEDISI: Even in detention. But I can't blame you, can I?

VISH: No, you can't blame him. This . . . *[Rubs STANTON's arm, referencing his white skin]* . . . gives them better chow, clean clothes and less of the nasty stuff. *[Grabs his throat and pretends to be hitting himself]*

MNCEDISI: *[To STANTON]* You got out after only one week. How did you manage that?

STANTON: I didn't decide when to release myself.

MNCEDISI: Why was I stuck in that shithole for almost three months?

STANTON: How am I supposed to know? I did what I could. I want to be free of all the kak as much as you.

VISH: Then learn isiXhosa, man. No, learn Sepedi, it's much easier. Yeah, Sepedi, man, that's one helleva language. But what about Swahili? Jumbo! Even the fucking Black Panthers were learning Swahili. Why don't you be cool?

CORNELIA: Can I answer for him?

STANTON: That's not allowed.

CORNELIA: Why not?

VISH: *[In a mocking voice]* I suppose with your psychological training, you know this moffie better than he knows himself. *[Blows her a kiss]* Our little Ms Socrates.

CORNELIA: *[To VISH]* I don't envy you.

VISH: *[Points at STANTON]* Don't envy him either, sweetheart. *[Points at MNCEDISI]* Or him.

MNCEDISI: There you are being Vishnu again. *[Looks suggestively at CORNELIA]* Life's worth living so long there's an Angela Davis around. Let's drink to a beautiful black sistah. *[Knocks back a shot]*

VISH: Yeah, let's get down to basics.

CORNELIA: *[To MNCEDISI]* You also want to get down to basics?

MNCEDISI: And why not? Let me tell you another story. *[Dramatically]* It was hot like tonight. We'd been drinking. I fell asleep in my bedroom. I woke up. It was dark. *[Redout]* I just felt this hand moving up and down my body. It was so relaxing, I felt myself getting all . . . I closed my eyes then I felt a hand taking mine, and then I was touching something, this hard thing, and just before I . . . I realised I was fucking holding a stiff bloody cock in my hand and the man next to me was holding mine and it was . . . just . . . I felt so . . . *[Slight pause]* And then I remembered who I was with, who had been with me in my bedroom before I'd gone to sleep. *[Lights]* It was . . . .

VISH: *[Looks from MNCEDISI to STANTON]* I knew there was something going on between the two of you.

MNCEDISI: I didn't let him near me again. *[To STANTON]* Isn't that so?

STANTON: Stop talking nonsense, Julius. I never touched you.

VISH: You're lying.

STANTON: I did not.

MNCEDISI: Come now, Stannie, if you don't have your hands on the levers, you don't control production. And we blacks are here to give everyone pleasure. *[Turns to VISH]* And you guys, you're getting rich like the Jews. You and your families.

VISH: Rich? My family?

MNCEDISI: And who else? Corrupt bastard.

STANTON: Leave this, Julius. This is totally unnecessary.

MNCEDISI: *[To VISH]* You've come a long way from when me and Stannie found you in that pathetic clothes shop and gave you a real job . . . that you left.

VISH: Yes, I did. And you remember why?

MNCEDISI: What are you suggesting?

VISH: Anything on your conscience?

MNCEDISI: What would be on my conscience? *[Moves towards VISH]* Shut up already!

STANTON: *[Coming between them.]* Please, guys! Please!

VISH: You aren't on the winning side of any government grants, are you now, my bra?

MNCEDISI: Why shouldn't I take government funding?

CORNELIA: *[To VISH]* Don't you have dealings with government?

VISH: I didn't win any tenders.

CORNELIA: Because you're Indian?

VISH: No, because I wouldn't pay bribes.

MNCEDISI: Unlike Mr Shaik, and Mr Gupta and Mr Reddy and Mr . . .

STANTON: You serious, Vish? You wouldn't pay anyone?

VISH: No, I wouldn't.

CORNELIA: *[Sarcastically]* I'm sure he wouldn't.

MNCEDISI: *[To STANTON]* Man, that's too good to be true?

STANTON: Oh, Vish has a hot deal going with a Saudi – not a Zulu prince.

CORNELIA: A big, fat deal. Could his name be . . . Khulubuse?

VISH: Damn, you, Stannie.

STANTON: Yes, Sheik Khulubuse. You hear that, Julius. I mean, Minisi . . . minisi . . .

MNCEDISI: Come on, say it.

VISH: Give him a break – he can't pronounce these fucking . . .

MNCEDISI: Well, the least he can do is give me another shot. *[Holds out his glass and STANTON pours]* Fill it up, Mister Lazy Tongue. Or should I say, Mister Forked Tongue. *[Swallows the whiskey. Laughs]* Good. One more kick for the road. One more fucking kick. You lahnies must wake up.

STANTON: Let me finish what I had to say about Plato.

MNCEDISI: Yeah, finish with those Greeks. Then I'll go fetch my books from the car.

VISH: Hope they don't include . . . *[Mockingly]* . . ."I write what I like"?

MNCEDISI: No. It's *I mic what I like. [To STANTON]* As for your Socrates, he had a lot of interesting things to say and a clever way of going about it – pity he was a slave owner like the rest of you.

STANTON: Small scale, bro, only two or three to help round the house.

MNCEDISI: Only a maid, a gardener, a trainee or two . . .

CORNELIA: *[Laughs]* What do you expect? While half the country is telling baas to fuck off, the other half is begging him for a job.

STANTON: *[To audience]* God, I'm so sorry. I didn't think it would turn out like this.

CORNELIA: There's nothing like perfecting the art of listening. So listen up! I'll guarantee none of you have read my first book though you've probably heard about its author. *[Holds up a book]*

VISH: The Marquis de Sade? Quite tame stuff actually. Just a little whipping and cutting.

CORNELIA: Which he did to young women workers whom he kidnapped.

VISH: *[In a high-pitched voice]* He and/or she who is about to sell his/her body should first do a security check before going off with a client.

STANTON: You're drunker than I thought, Vish.

VISH: What's the book called?

CORNELIA: "Justine."

VISH: What a coincidence! That's my ex-wife's sister's name. She's certainly a whore.

CORNELIA: You know, I've waited a long time to meet you. I've heard so many stories. My mother really loved you. But what did you do with that love? You trashed it. And the stupid woman allowed you to walk all over her. No, you didn't blush. Even when you called it off and then after a few months demanded that she come back and serve you — serve your screwed up ego and your sexual . . .

VISH: Nonsense! I've never abused any woman. Least of all your mother.

MNCEDISI: *[Confronts VISH with a physically threatening gesture]* Don't lie, Vishnu. You played games with Nettie. We all saw it.

VISH: Games? How many women did you dump with kids? *[Laughs nastily]*

MNCEDISI: *[Grabs VISH]* I'll give you something to really laugh about.

STANTON: No, stop! Please stop! He doesn't know what he's saying!

MNCEDISI: Nothing new about that. Make him stop!

CORNELIA: That's right – stop his nonsense.

MNCEDISI twists VISH's arm.

STANTON: Don't hurt him!

CORNELIA: Why the hell not?

VISH: *[Shouting]* Let go of me! Are we already like every other fucking African country?

CORNELIA: Don't make things worse.

VISH: Worse? I can't make it worse. *[Points at MNCEDISI]* That's their job.

MNCEDISI: Now I'll really . . . *[Pushes VISH violently so he falls]*

STANTON: *[Coming between them]* Please guys!

MNCEDISI: *[Putting his foot on VISH's chest]* He must fuck off before I break his neck.

CORNELIA: *[To STANTON]* Get him out of here. It's not just that he's drunk.

STANTON: It's the divorce. He's all bloody twisted . . .

VISH suddenly goes into a spasm at the end of which his head rolls to one side; his mouth remains half open.

STANTON: Oh, my God? *[Rushes to VISH]* Vish! *[VISH doesn't respond]* Vish! *[To MNCEDISI and CORNELIA]* I'll get some water.

CORNELIA: He's too far gone. You won't sober him up.

STANTON: Vish! Can you stand? *[Struggling to lift him]* Damn, you've caused enough trouble. *[To MNCEDISI and CORNELIA]* I can't move him alone.

MNCEDISI: I'm not touching the bastard. Get him out of here.

CORNELIA: Yes, throw him out.

STANTON: I don't know how he could have . . . slipped up like this. *[Exits, dragging VISH along]*

MNCEDISI: *[Shouts out.]* Another little slip of the tongue and I'll ... *[Pause. To CORNELIA]* Let's get out of here. You want to go for a drink?

CORNELIA: Thanks but I've still got lots of marking to do.

MNCEDISI: This late?

CORNELIA: I take my kids seriously.

MNCEDISI: I'm just too wired to go home to sleep. Come, a quick night cap.

CORNELIA: No, I'll pass. You're a dangerous bunch.

STANTON: *[ENTERS]* I've never seen him like this before.

CORNELIA: Ja, it was a once-in-a-lifetime performance.

STANTON: It's just that he lost out on some mega deal tonight.

MNCEDISI: Is he in the shower?

STANTON: No, sleeping on the couch.

MNCEDISI: Why did you defend him?

STANTON: I didn't.

CORNELIA: Yes, you did.

STANTON: *[To MNCEDISI]* Don't tell me you've ever seen him like this before. Not like this.

MNCEDISI: You're lucky I didn't sort him out earlier the way I klapped that Boer on the highway.

STANTON: You what? You klapped the Boer?

MNCEDISI: Ja, I got back at that drunken bastard. It took just one shot and he was in no position to say another word.

CORNELIA: You actually shot him?

MNCEDISI: He got what he asked for. *[Slight pause]* No, I didn't shoot him. Just fucking smashed him in the face. If they can't behave, we have to teach them a lesson.

STANTON: So that blood on your shirt was his – not yours?

CORNELIA: He didn't attack you?

MNCEDISI: What do you call cutting me off and calling me a kaffir?

STANTON: But he didn't actually hit you?

MNCEDISI: You should have heard the filth that came out of his mouth. Let him be too fucking scared to insult a black man again.

STANTON: But there could be a charge.

MNCEDISI: So what! Even the whitest judge will understand it was self-defence.

VISH: *[Runs in half naked; grabs MNCEDISI's hand and lifts it up]* Bravo! Well done, my brother. That's the only language they understand. You did

172

what you had to do. Amandla! *[Takes his hand]* Man, I'm sorry about . . . I
was way out of line but . . .

MNCEDISI: Get out of here.

VISH: Truly, bro, my apologies, big-big apologies. *[Bows, indicating humility]*
The last few months have been a nightmare.

CORNELIA: And you haven't woken up yet. *[To STANTON]* I'm going to
have to leave now. Got work to finish.

STANTON: But you will come again?

VISH: Yes, yes, you must! I swear I won't . . . Hey, we've all taken strain. And
those who claim to know better, don't always act better.

CORNELIA: Write a better script, Mr Naidoo.

MNCEDISI: *[To VISH]* You looking for amnesty?

VISH: *[Pause.]* Kind of.

CORNELIA: *[To STANTON]* If I come again will I find you sticking to your
original agenda?

STANTON: What do you think, my darling? I just want to spend time
with some intelligent people and a few of these . . . *[Lifts up a book]* . . .
and try and understand this current . . . dispensation. And like tonight,
membership of Stanton de Villier's book club will be free though there
may be a price. *[MNCEDISI and CORNELIA start exiting]* Wait! Before
you leave, I want to give you all something. *[Takes three book marks out
of his pocket; holding two of them in one hand, one in the other, he waves
them around]* Here. Let them travel with you through many reads down
many roads. *[Slight pause]* For you. *[Offers one to CORNELIA. After some
hesitation, she accepts it]* And one for you . . . *[Offers one to MNCEDISI]* . . .
sir. *[MNCEDISI also hesitates but ultimately accepts]* They were all done by
an artist from Ghana. She lives next door. *[To VISH]* And for you. *[Offers
one to VISH who takes it with alacrity]*

CORNELIA: *[To Vish]* You'll certainly need one, comrade. You're lucky oom
Stannie's the generous type. It's so easy to lose your place.

They all freeze. Fade as the song 'The Revolution Needs' plays out.

END

YONELA TSIBOLANE   DILLAN MAART
JESSICA PYBUS   KABELO KHANYE

THE
COUCH

THEATRE PRODUCTION

by Sjaka Septembir

Date: 2-4 October 2017
Venue: 228 Lower Main Rd, Observatory
Time: 19:00
R60 Standard   R54 Students

CAPE TOWN
FRINGE
FESTIVAL '17

Book online: https://capetownfringe.co.za/events/the-couch/ or buy at the door

PLAYWRIGHT'S NOTES

The Couch is the second in my trilogy of Boland Gothic plays; the first being 'Nagwandelaars' [KKNK 2016] and the third 'The Night of the Raven' [performed in November 2018]. It came about when I was asked to step in and mentor four AFDA Honours students and assist them to write and perform a play. The process kicked off with them handing me a very weak rom-com script for which each had written a monologue. I suggested that we do a free writing exercise to see what we come up with. For this I selected pages from the English translation of a Reza De Wet play and cut them up; I also cut up their own play. We then conducted a 'ritual' which consisted of each participant drawing lines from a hat. As they were drawn, the lines were stuck under each other. In this way we created a loose idea of our future script. In addition, I incorporated the monologues they had written and after several sessions in which the students gave feedback, we ended up with *The Couch*.

I did not intend for it to be a horror story, yet looking back, if you throw Reza De Wet into the mix, what else do you expect? I have always had a love for this genre – being an avid Steven King reader when I was a teenager. I love how the genre can be bent to 'exorsize' human fears. *The Couch* looks at regret, fear, homophobia and coming out of the closet. Isn't overcoming our fears the biggest hurdle to future endeavours? In many instances the best way to know ourselves is through accepting and then standing up to these fears: the fear of hell; fear of pain; of discomfort, of hunger; the fear of being alone.

The Couch offers a glimpse into the lives of four housemates moving into new digs. They are confident that they will be happy in their new flat in Woodstock, Cape Town and have even found a new couch that will bring them together. However, once the couch enters their lives, they start getting strange lifelike dreams. The couch, initially seen as a place of relaxation and comfort, starts becoming a place which brings up their individual pasts. This raises the question: who has the most traumatic, haunting past and who will be sacrificed on the altar of their own guilt?

The Couch was first performed in September 2017 at the Cape Town Fringe Festival.

CAST:

EDWARD	Dillan Maart
LUCY	Jess Pybus
SEVEN	Kabelo Khanye
SIMPHIWE	Yonela Tsibolane

Light dims up slowly on the couch. Eerie music. Strobe light and fog. Figures in masks [that reflect the couch] crawl insect-like around the couch. EDWARDS sits on the couch. They start banging a threatening rhythm around him. Lights go out, Lights up. The couch has moved and the masked figures drum more threateningly. EDWARD becomes aware of them. Lights out. Couch moves; lights up. EDWARD is now aware and fearful as the threatening masked figures start closing in on him. He jumps up.

EDWARD: Noooo!

> *Darkness.*
>
> *Three students moving the couch into an apartment. There are boxes all over.*
>
> *A little kitchen stage right, the front door stage left. They put the couch down.*

LUCY: Is it straight?

SEVEN: Yes, it is straight.

SIMPHIWE: *[Sarcastic]* How would you know what straight looks like?

> *SEVEN throws a playful stabbing stare at her then turns back to the couch. They move it and step away to see if it's in the right place.*

SEVEN: This couch is a beaut.

LUCY: It's hideous.

SIMPHIWE: Well, at least it was cheap.

SEVEN: Ah guys, it was a great buy. You'll see – it will bring us together.

> *They all freeze except SEVEN.*

SEVEN: *[Addressing the AUDIENCE]* I was so excited. I was on my way to grabbing the psychological treasure, Outliers, written by Malcolm Gladwell – the book that details how putting ten thousand hours into something can ensure your success . . . This may be off the topic, but I'd like to put ten thousand hours into having sex . . . but what does that make me? *[Sits down on the couch]* Anyhow, you see, at the bookstore I ran into Jared. Yes, Jared . . . Don't ask me to talk about love. He broke my heart that man. It was such a pure love. We fitted together perfectly. A pity that he had a wife and kids. She doesn't deserve him. It ripped the heart out of my chest seeing him again. We used to meet at his office, after hours. Fucking on the couch . . . After him, I promised never to love again but never mind that. I was wanting to tell you about the Malcolm Gladwell book and psychology and how my executive producer of an aunt promised she would get me my own TV show after university. Fuck Jared. I don't need him. I am going to be famous – the South African Dr. Phil.

Back to the 4th wall. The three start moving the couch again.

LUCY: I really don't think it should be here.

SIMPHIWE: But it's close to the kitchen.

SEVEN: I think Lucy may have a point.

They start to argue, pulling the couch this way and that; at the height of the fight, SEVEN angrily shoves the couch.

SEVEN: Better?

The cushions have been disturbed and there is a stain under one cushion that could be blood.

LUCY: Eeaagh! It looks like someone was murdered on this thing.

SIMPHIWE: Or had their period!

SEVEN: Don't be ridiculous! And remember it was a bargain. Just turn the cushion upside down, as it was …

Freeze.

SIMPHIWE: *[Addressing the AUDIENCE]* So you know those revelations that you have at least once in your life? Those life changing moments when maybe you realized that you're actually a moffie, but oops you're still married to a woman. *[Throws herself on the couch]* Whatever it is, it usually comes after some tragic event or before menopause. Well, I had one of those the other day. So there I was sitting on the couch, minding my own business, trying to figure out where I was last night and how the hell I got this massive hangover, when all of a sudden, it hit me. Why hadn't I seen it before? No, no, I'm not going to share it. Not with you. Not now, not ever. And if you think it's got something to do with my drinking, you're wrong.

Back to 4th wall and they start to argue over where the couch should stand again.

LUCY: Let's just get it in its place. We have a lot more unpacking to do.

SEVEN: Right here in the middle.

LUCY: Seven, you're being stupid.

She pushes the couch back to stage left.

LUCY: It needs to be here.

SIMPHIWE: *[Pulling it stage right]* No.

SEVEN: *[Pulling it down stage]* More back.

> *They are all pulling in different directions.*

EDWARD: *[Entering with a huge load of suitcases and bags]* Fighting again, really guys?

> *Freeze.*

EDWARD: *[Addressing the AUDIENCE]* Isn't it beautiful. The little family I never wanted. And here we are moving into this new flat, bigger than the last one. Yes, this is our second year of living together. God knows how I made it through the first! I guess these guys aren't as bad as my actual family though. *[He comes to sit on the couch]* I was an only child. Just me and my parents in a big house. In that situation both parents see you as some kind of hope for mankind, constantly putting pressure on you to do something with your life, while at the same time assuring you that you can keep all your options open. "You can do anything, darling, just make sure you really want it and that it can give you a living." I still don't even know what that means, it sounds contradictory to me . . . unless they expect me to be the best at everything I do. Which is probably what they expect from me since I clearly displayed my abilities at school and even at university. How can you be the best at everything? Not sleep? The best part of all of this is I still don't really know what I want to do . . . Ag, it's not that bad. There is this thing that happened. This thing that keeps coming up. I don't feel good about it. But it's no biggie . . . I'm taking pills for that. *[He gets up from the couch after stroking it and goes back to his bags and boxes]*

> *Back to the 4th wall. LUCY is taking the lead in putting the couch where she sees fit. The others see there is no use in arguing and stand back. EDWARD, with his suitcases and bags in hand, moves across the stage and enters the door [upstage] that leads to their rooms.*

SEVEN: *[Laughs as he begins opening a box with PRIVATE! and DON'T TOUCH written on it. He fishes out some sex toys and discovers a huge vibrator]* Oh, no, look what's slipped out! The deacon and all the elders are praying tonight! Put it back, put it back! There's a good girl.

> *He shows it to SIMPHIWE while hiding it from LUCY who is engrossed in moving the couch so as to find the exact 'right spot'. EDWARD re-enters and watches. One can see it excites him. SEVEN sees this and starts singing a sexy Prince song using the vibrator as his mic, and dances*

around the shy EDWARD. EDWARD, in a very tentative way, starts to sing and move along with SEVEN.

SEVEN: *[SEVEN teasing EDWARD by putting it in his mouth]* Oh, no, it's slipped out again! Put it back, put it back, there's a good boy.

SEVEN again singing, moving away from EDWARD, still hiding it from LUCY.

SIMPHIWE: I don't think you're using it right. And I wouldn't put it in my mouth if I was you.

LUCY: *[Pushing the couch in place, oblivious to the commotion]* There we go. Freeze.

LUCY: *[Sits down on the couch, exhales and grins. A part of the couch's front panel falls off. She looks at it but tries to ignore it]* Hi, I don't think I've actually introduced myself yet, sorry. But, I'm sure you've noticed how busy I've been. *[Looks at the fallen piece of the couch again]* You won't mind if I just . . . *[She gets up and pushes the piece back so that it sticks]* That's better. Oh, I'm Lucy by the way. The others didn't do the best job at introducing themselves, did they? Leave it to me, always ready to clean up or clarify . . . Well, this is Edward. *[She goes over to him]* And always a bit somber, dark, mysterious . . . this is Seven. *[Goes over to him]* Always the soul of the party and overly sexed *[Points at the vibrator]* if you ask me. And this is Siphiwe. *[Goes to her]* Well, she can maybe lay off the booze a bit and focus on her studies . . . As you can see we are moving into a new digs. Isn't this is a hideous couch? The others seemed to love it but I don't always want to be the party pooper. They seemed excited about it. It was cheap. I guess that was the main reason. I did see my dream couch the other day. But it costs thousands. Oh, yes, me. I think I would describe myself as your typical, fun-loving student, here for the best years of my life. You know, drinks, parties, boys, maybe some varsity work here and there. *[Beat]* I guess I haven't gone out in a while though – now that I think about it, I haven't actually gone out for a whole year. *[Sits back down on the couch]*

Back to the 4th wall. LUCY notices what SEVEN has.

SEVEN: *[Realizing LUCY has seen, knows the game is on and tries to put the couch between him and her]* Come on, sing with . . . you know you want to!

LUCY: Seven!

SIMPHIWE: Seven!

LUCY: Give it back!

SEVEN: *[Still teasing EDWARD]* Come on, you know you want to! Look, Edward will sing.

> *EDWARD tentatively starts to sing and move along with SEVEN.*

LUCY: Seven!

SEVEN: What?

LUCY: That's not yours.

SEVEN: Share and share alike . . .

> *Disturbing sound. The other lights dim and a light goes on above the couch.*

EDWARD: Shhht! I heard something . . . *[Everyone listens, long pause]* It's probably just the wind. Just branches scratching on the roof, that's all . . .

SIMPHIWE: Are you crazy? That didn't sound like a branch.

EDWARD: You heard it?

SEVEN: It was a branch. My big branch.

> *He puts the vibrator to his crotch and flaunts it about. Lucy lunges at him. They touch at the vibrator. SIMPHIWE and EDWARD try and pull them apart. It turns into a playful fight and they all land on top of each other on the couch, laughing.*

EDWARD: *[Getting up]* We better get a move on or we'll never finish all this unpacking.

> *SEVEN get's up tentatively. He's got an eye on EDWARD.*

LUCY: I'm enjoying just sitting down for a bit.

SIMPHIWE: *[Making herself comfortable on the couch]* Wicked! Let's have some beers.

SEVEN: *[Falling down among them]* Yes!

EDWARD: Come on guys!

SEVEN: Aaah, just come for a teensy sit down.

> *EDWARD comes forward hesitantly and SEVEN pulls him down between them.*

SIMPHIWE: Someone get us some drinks!

> *Light on the couch. Strange loud sound in the distance. They all look about.*

EDWARD: Something . . . unholy. Something hungry. Something roaming around, driven by the Devil's own lust that can never be satisfied. Something filled with the power of hell. That's what the old man said.

LUCY: Which old man?

SIMPHIWE: The guy who sold us the couch?

SEVEN: *[Dismissive]* That's what you get for buying an old couch from an old looney. That and a good dosage of a poorly crafted conspiracy theory. Remember how he went on . . .

SEVEN & SIMPHIWE: "They are coming! They are coming!"

They laugh. LUCY seems uncomfortable and tries to laugh. EDWARD just stares.

SIMPHIWE: Lucy, can you move up? You're taking up all the space.

LUCY: It's not me, it's Seven. Seven, move up!

EDWARD: There? Did you hear it?. . . Tonight's definitely a night for keeping ears open. And eyes.

Pause. They look at him.

SIMPHIWE: You're scaring me. I told you guy's I don't want to move into lower Woodstock. There are still gangs and crime . . .

SEVEN: Are you believing all that stuff on the news?

LUCY: So much fake news out there, one doesn't know what to believe. Nothing has happened. Christine stays a few houses away. Nothing big has ever happened to her. A few car break-ins, that's all.

SEVEN: And we're not on the streets, we're all safe inside.

EDWARD: Everywhere is dangerous. That's what he said. He kept muttering, things, about something . . . supernatural. Yet his eyes where so kind.

LUCY: Aah, snap out of it Edward. I don't like all this talk. I've had enough of your spirits and ritual mambo jumbo. Face up to the real world.

SEVEN: *[Again bringing vibrator out and pointing it at LUCY]* Ooo, someone's a bit stressed. Perhaps you should go and play with this. Relieve your tension. Should I rinse it for you?

SIMPHIWE: You should maybe use it Seven. It's better than sleeping with your ex all the time.

SEVEN: Ex-es.

LUCY: *[Grabs the vibrator; she and SEVEN scuffle]* It's mine.

SEVEN: Auoow! *[Sucks his finger]*

LUCY: Serves you right. Come on Edward, you were the one who said we need to get everything done tonight. Now you're sitting there like a stone.

EDWARD: This couch . . .

SEVEN: It's a fucking great couch.

SIMPHIWE: Must be thirty years old … and that stain.

SEVEN gives her a look, wanting to keep the knowledge of the stain away from EDWARD.

SEVEN: She means it's full of stains.

SIMPHIWE: I'm getting us some drinks.

EDWARD: It's just that . . . when I looked into that old man's eyes, it felt as if I knew the man . . . I don't know . . . it's probably nothing.

SEVEN: Yes, let's celebrate. Just think of the great parties we are going to have here.

SIMPHIWE: We can all drink to that!

SIMPHIWE pours wine into mugs and SEVEN hands them out.

LUCY: *[Turning down the wine]* I've got to study. Have to be up at 7 to revise Hesiod's Theogony.

SEVEN: Come on. One glass.

LUCY: *[Getting up]* No thank you.

SIMPHIWE: Urgh. Enjoy studying people who died thousands of years ago.

LUCY exits.

SIMPHIWE: Sure, 'study'. Why did she take her vibrator with?

SEVEN: *[Putting his arm around EDWARD and holding the wine in front of him]* Now we just need a TV.

EDWARD: *[Standing at the couch staring out in front of him and not taking the wine]* I'm going to turn in.

He turns and stares at the couch for a while then exits.

SIMPHIWE: *[Slight pause]* Ed seems a bit stressed.

SEVEN: I agree. He definitely shows signs of anxiety. Maybe he just needs to get out of the closet and get a bit of my ass?

SIMPHIWE: Hey, do you always reduce all peoples' complex emotions down to sex?

SEVEN: Yes.

SIMPHIWE: Great Dr. Phil you're going to make. *[Slight pause]* Moving's a big thing, it affects people. Next year we're going out into the big bad world. The uncertainty is disturbing.

SEVEN: It is a Big Bad World and I'm going to be bad to him, so bad.

SIMPHIWE: You're always making light of everything. Two people have disappeared in this area. I Googled it. There are stories of rituals, rape, murder. People do tik and then their minds go . . .

SEVEN: Focus on the bad and you will attract the bad. We are safe and secure inside.

She pours more wine. EDWARD enters slowly: light on couch and strange sounds in the background.

EDWARD: *[He looks dazed]* On his forehead, right between his eyes, he's got a carbuncle horn. The next one is the 'Midget'. He is only knee-high, and is wearing a tailcoat and a black top hat.

SIMPHIWE: Stop acting weird.

SEVEN: Edward? Are you okay?

SIMPHIWE: Lucy! Lucy!

EDWARD is frozen. LUCY storms in.

LUCY: I'd be very grate . . .

They all watch EDWARD who is frozen.

EDWARD: *[Suddenly normal]* I was thinking of travelling to be honest – not for long. What? What are you looking at?

The other three watch him.

LUCY: I'm going to go back to my studies.

LUCY remains hovering.

EDWARD: What?

SEVEN: Edward, are you okay?

EDWARD: I'm okay . . . I just feel a bit odd. Probably the medication.

LUCY: *[Leaving]* Classical Studies, the most prestigious and celebrated degree that one can have.

SIMPHIWE: *[Mockingly]* "Classical Studies, the most prestigious and celebrated degree that one can have". *[Handing EDWARD wine]* Have some. It will make you feel better.

SEVEN: Where did that come from? You need to sort yourself out Ed.

SIMPHIWE: Maybe you should take some sleeping pills or something?

EDWARD: Sure, fine. I don't know . . . I'm tired. I'm just gonna curl up on the couch if you don't mind.

SEVEN: Mind? I thought the couch creeped you out?

EDWARD: Tired . . . can't move.

SIMPHIWE: Enough fun for one night. And I'm locking my door, so no mother fucker comes to surprise me.

SEVEN: You'd be so lucky.

The others leave. EDWARD on the couch alone. Lights fade.
Lights change drastically. Thunder. Circus music in the distance.
The three – LUCY, SEVEN and SIMPHIWE – appear.
Each looks dazed; they put on black cloaks and 'couch' masks. They mumble strange chants.
They tie EDWARD up, sprawling his body over the couch in a dark ritual.

It has a cruel yet sexual feel. A noose is brought and put around his neck.
They begin to chant.

THE THREE: Muttered voices, muffled laughter, sweaty palms, heavy breath,
entranced eyes, blurry figures, fixated stare. Excited. He longed for you,
he wanted you. Closer, closer, closer. His breath on your face, his hand on
your heart, his lips so close, so close. *[Pause]* Broken! Broken! Faded eye,
hanging head. How can you escape this dread? *[Pause]* Regret! Regret!
[Chorus breaks up repeating words e.g. regret, shame, failed, your fault, I
don't know, think – until lighting changes]
    THE THREE *vanish. Everything goes dark.*
    Lights suddenly come up as EDWARD *gasps and sits up.*
    LUCY *enters.*

LUCY: Hey! Are you okay?

EDWARD: Jeez . . . just had a dream.

LUCY: I made myself some coffee. Do you want?

EDWARD: There were these masked . . .

LUCY: Masked?

EDWARD: Eerie, couch masks . . .

LUCY: That's what you get for believing stories from crazy old men.
    She exits to her room.

EDWARD: *[Addressing* AUDIENCE. *One by one,* THE THREE *enter with*
masks. They stand echoing a surreal image, then disappear again] It's Jesse,
isn't it? That is what must be happening. Who is Jesse, you ask? Jesse . .
. So I told you I was the only child, that I lived in that house and how it
was just continuous pressure from my parents, always showing me off to
their friends, always telling me how other parents talk about me to their
children. And then suddenly, nothing. Halfway through high school I went
from hero to zero. A friend of mine, Jesse, was exiled from the cool kids
when he came out of the closet, but I never stopped talking to him. I guess
people just thought that I was talking to him out of sympathy, which was
half true, but at the same time I really like Jesse, he was the one I bonded
with more than the others. Even more than Kyle who was something like
my right hand man. Anyway, at one party Jesse came to me while I was
getting punch from the table. We went to sit down on this comfy couch
– one of those in which one flops back like a bed – and started talking. It
was really enjoyable. At one point he said he wished the couch could grow

wings and we could fly out the room. Just the two of us. I secretly hoped the same. And then he kissed me, and though in that moment I didn't hate the idea, I saw that Kyle was watching so I looked back at Jesse and pushed him away. He fell to the floor. Everyone laughed at him and humiliated him. Kicking and screaming at him. Kyle even came to pat me on the back, I didn't react. I just kinda stood there. Jesse ran out. I wanted to go after him . . . Then the party went on as normal. Monday, back at school, Jesse was nowhere to be found. It was only at the end of the week that the teacher came in and said Jesse had committed suicide.

LUCY enters with her bag.

LUCY: Sorry, I didn't mean to be brash. Did you want to tell me something?

EDWARD: Nothing. It was just a dream.

LUCY: Edward, can you maybe give the couch a . . . rubdown . . . you know, freshen it up after sleeping on it.

EDWARD: You know Lucy, sometimes I feel like strangling you.

LUCY: That's uncalled for Edward!

SIMPHIWE: *[Walking in, in her pyjamas]* Hold on there, my brother. What's with all this violence before breakfast, jeez.

LUCY: But I don't blame him. The energy in this flat is strange. I feel tense for no reason.

SIMPHIWE: I'm getting a beer.

LUCY: *[Turning to the AUDIENCE; the other actors freeze]* I also had a strange dream last night. It freaked me out. We were doing this ritual . . . but I don't want to go there. I'm starting to think the real nightmare is living with these guys though it's the only way I can afford rent. Yeah, we don't really hang out or go out together that much. But why would we? We live together. We already spend more than enough time as housemates, plus I don't think that I'm interested in the same things as them. I mean, I know how to have a good time but I don't think I could ever keep up with Simphiwe's drinking. If we went out I'd probably just spend the night taking care of her and holding her hair back while she throws up. I already clean up after her enough at home, so no thanks. Edward's idea of hanging out would probably involve going to some cult gathering and performing a sacrifice to the gods of darkness – okay, now my dream is coming back . . . it was a bit strange – but Edward is a bit of a weirdo. Don't even get me started on Seven. Anyone who has that much sex and makes that much noise, is someone I'd rather not associate myself with. That's the main reason I'd never bring a guy home. I would never inflict the horror of my sex noises on the rest of the housemates like Seven does. That, together with the fact that boys are not really high on my list of priorities at the moment. I've been in relationships before, well, just one relationship technically, but I know how time-consuming and draining they can be. Besides, I've got a much better replacement, and for the rest, I'm focused on my studies this year. Just push through. Only one more year.

SIMPHIWE comes between LUCY and EDWARD, and holds the beer in front of them.

SEVEN enters, buttoning his shirt, late for class.

LUCY notices the time and hurriedly packs the books on the table into her bag.

SIMPHIWE: I think it's time for a house meeting.

EDWARD: That's my beer. Drink your own damn beer. When have any of you ever cared?

SEVEN: Calm down, my big boy. Let's get to class guys and we'll have a meeting tonight?

LUCY: Agreed.

SIMPHIWE: There's some strange shit going down and I know it's going to sound odd, but I've been having these dreams.

SEVEN: Look, I have to get to class. Simphiwe, you too! Down your beer and come.

All four look at her. They freeze.

SIMPHIWE: There's stuff going on inside me. You really want to know, don't you? You're quite curious, hey? Now let me give you a clue. The other day I overheard my housemates talking about how inconsiderate I am. The other week I heard my tutorial group members say how selfish I am – apparently I'm the only student that has ever handed in a group project late. Oh! And last month my little sister told me I'm rude. So you know what my revelation is? You wanna fucking know? I realized that the whole world hates Simphiwe! And furthermore? Simphiwe doesn't give a damn about the whole world either! Yes. I. Don't. Care. If people want to boil tea and have sister circles about the one or two times I didn't wash dishes, then fuck it! I don't care. I don't care about any of it. I don't care about my housemates, I don't care about my stupid classmates. Bro, I don't care

[Strange murmurs; room darkens] What is that sound? *[Slight pause]* That's another thing, and I'm not going to look stupid and admit it to the others, but something about this couch freaks me out . . . I think I need a tequila. And don't judge me. The whole damn world can hate me for all I care. Because I don't care. I don't care.

    SEVEN, EDWARD and LUCY still looking at her, unfreeze.

SIMPHIWE: What about coffee? I need a coffee. I had these dreams.

SEVEN: What dreams?

LUCY: *[Makes for the door]* I'm going to be late.

EDWARD: Dreams? Or drunken hallucinations? I'm going to shower.

    EDWARD'S phone starts ringing.

SEVEN: *[To EDWARD]* If I wasn't on my way to a lecture, I would have joined you.

EDWARD: Arrgh! My parents.

    He walks out as he answers.

SIMPHIWE: Fine just ignore me. I'll have some coffee.

    Freeze.

SEVEN: Hmm, my dad. I wonder how he enjoyed his Father's Day. I wonder if he misses the malva pudding my mom used to make for him. Sheila, the new woman, probably ordered in something tacky. Not like my mother. My mother has grace and elegance. My mother can cook. The new wife and my dad have twins. For the life of me I don't know why this bothers me. I saw the messages. On his phone. I told my mom. It was ugly . . . And now I miss Jared. I always miss Jared. I had no part at all or value to play in his life. But he was intellectual and he said things to me that his old wife would never get. We'd fuck and make love all at once and it almost never mattered where: the parking lot, movie theatre, and a few times at his law firm on his couch. I can still smell the leather. Our first time was on that couch. Interesting how he carried on with me like he didn't care if someone was to see and out him. We'd go on weekend getaways – for fucks sake – and he just blocked me and all of that like it was nothing.

    Lights change; ritual chanting in the background.

OFF STAGE: *[Chanting]* "Half-sitting, half-laying, we crawled up, tying him with rope. There's a blood lust in us all. Naked to his waist, he is half-sitting, half-lying, on a pile of cushions. His tiny eyes swollen closed, his breath heavy, he smells dreadful. In the dream Edward kept saying it's a magic couch, we can fly out of this room.

Suddenly the stage lights up. They are again getting ready for their day.

SEVEN: *[To SIMPHIWE]* But you're right – there is something strange. I think we are all suffering from parataxic distortion – a psychiatric term first used by Harry S. Sullivan to describe the inclination to skew perceptions of others based on fantasy. This "distortion" leads to a faulty perception of others and of situations.

SIMPHIWE: Thank you Dr. Freud. You're full of shit.

SEVEN: Oh, I can see we must have a house meeting tonight. Now let me tell you my other findings. Parataxic disorder . . .

SIMPHIWE: Why don't you psychoanalyze your projected fantasies onto Edward?

She leaves to get dressed. Lights fade as SEVEN finishes up and leaves. Late afternoon, evening. Lights up. EDWARD on the couch. SEVEN enters.

SEVEN: Have you been here all day?

EDWARD: Yes, that's a perfect . . . sensation.

SEVEN: What is?

EDWARD: Seven . . . come here. *[Slight pause]* What is he busy with?

SEVEN joins EDWARD on the couch.

SEVEN: Who?

EDWARD: You think you know what you want and when you study the subject, for the wrong reasons, even it turns out to be something different.

SEVEN: Ed, who are you talking to? Look, did you check our WhatsApp group? The girls should be here soon. Lucy's still at varsity. Simphiwe is probably in some bar, but she said she's on her way. Yes, we've agreed to have a house meeting.

EDWARD turns to him.

EDWARD: But you've risen above it. I can't tell you how much I respect you. I've always liked you. I use to watch you dance a lot.

SEVEN: Yes, we can go dancing. I mean we have to have a house warming.

EDWARD: Yes, I use to watch you dance a lot.

EDWARD becomes sensual and focuses on SEVEN.

SEVEN: Well, I was the best dancer at our school.

EDWARD: The way you turn your hips. Your skin chocolate brown, your
eyes half closed. Your feet moving with lightness. You always laugh.

SEVEN: That's right, no one can keep up when I start.

EDWARD: I couldn't keep up. You would spin and spin. *[Advancing on
SEVEN with a dreamy expression]* It's just the two of us. I have seen you
so many times, coming in. I watch when you don't know. Loosening the
buttons of your shirt.

SEVEN: Lifting my arm. Letting the material fall away from my warm skin.

EDWARD strokes him, starting to undress SEVEN.

EDWARD: My eyes going over your neck, your shoulders, down your back.

SEVEN: I stand up. Parade in front of you. You watch me.

EDWARD: Yes. Slow steps. Your fingers stroking over your face, down.

SEVEN: I loosen my belt.

EDWARD: You loosen your belt. You're in no hurry.

SEVEN: Slowly pulling the leather through the first loop, pulling it so that
the metal pin comes out of the hole.

EDWARD pulls off SEVEN's pants. They get ready to kiss.

EDWARD: I want you. I can never be satisfied. Something filled with the
power of hell. I have waited so long for this moment, Jesse.

SEVEN: Jesse?

The sound of a woman screaming from outside the front door.
*EDWARD jumps up, going to the door. SEVEN grabs his clothes and darts
back. LUCY enters, noticeably shaken.*

LUCY: Edward! Thank god!

EDWARD: It's alright. Was it one of them?

LUCY: Who? What's wrong with you? I was attacked. Call the police.

EDWARD: Was it the old man? Or his friend the midget? Did the three
friends come out with the coarse rope? Did he have a horn?

LUCY: Edward what are you talking about? I don't know. I couldn't see.

SEVEN: *[Entering, still pulling his cloths straight]* Are you okay? What
happened?

SIMPHIWE: *[Entering from the front door]* What's happening? On my way
home I saw a policeman with a big dogs on chains.

SEVEN: The town is full of them. It's the opening of Parliament.

SIMPHIWE: Then I heard screaming.

SEVEN: Lucy was attacked.

SIMPHIWE: No, Lucy? Are you okay.

EDWARD: I need to sit down. So heavy.

LUCY: I think I actually just got a fright. It was just a drunk bergie. The
whole day was strange.

SIMPHIWE: Why is it so dark tonight? It seems so much darker than usual.

EDWARD: It's a new moon!

SEVEN: The streetlights are probably out. Lucy, are you okay? This is what
we get for moving into this fucking dodgy area.

LUCY: *[Sitting down on the couch]* Pour me a drink. I have to sleep. *[Takes a
sip from the wine glass SIMPHIWE gives her]* I've been having such awful
dreams.

EDWARD: *[Desperately]* Have you been having them too?

The other three freeze. Then they turn to EDWARD.

SEVEN: Sounds like a good note to open our meeting with?

ALL THREE: Come on Edward, tell us.

EDWARD: Yes, and then you Lucy, Seven and Simphiwe, will tell me too.
We will all spill our guts. Open ourselves on the couch, to 'The Great
Listening'.

From here on the chaotic sounds from outside become louder.
SEVEN, LUCY and SIMPHIWE gradually get affected, their movements
become odd, possessed; the light throws focus on the couch as images are
projected onto it.

SEVEN: What's going on out there?

LUCY: It's not out there.

SIMPHIWE: It's in here. *[Pointing at the couch]*

SEVEN: Is this our house meeting?

The lights change. Eerie sounds.

EDWARD: See?

SEVEN: But we can still leave.

SIMPHIWE: Can't you hear the voice?

LUCY: I hear the voice. The old man. Everywhere is dangerous tonight.

SEVEN: I hear the voice.

EDWARD: Something . . . unholy. Something hungry.

ALL FOUR: Roaming around, driven by the Devil's own lust that can never
be satisfied.

THE THREE sit on the couch.

THE THREE: We know you never say anything. You don't need to. We can see.

THREE: Come on Edward, tell us.

THREE: The Great Listening.

EDWARD: In dark nights and dark days. Everywhere is dangerous tonight.

THREE: Ssshh . . . did you hear that?

EDWARD: What a mess I've made. It's all my fault. It's all my fault.

He looks at the other three. They start to chant – a chant that is just audible and keeps going underneath everything else. They lift the couch.

EDWARD: On his forehead, right between his eyes, he's got a carbuncle horn. The next one is the 'Midget'. He is only knee-high, and is wearing a tailcoat and a black top hat.

They place the couch stage centre.

THE THREE: Failed! Failed! Regret! Regret! It's all your fault, regret! It's all your fault, you've failed! It's all your fault, regret! It's all your fault, repent! An eye for an eye, a tooth for a tooth, repent! Come to me, join me – regret, repent! Come to me, join me – regret, repent! Come to me, join me – regret, repent! Make it right! *[Chorus echo]* Come to me, join me. REPENT!

A cloak is donned around EDWARD's shoulders. The others put their masks on.
They circle EDWARD. They chant. Sometimes echoing words he says.
They put a noose around his neck.

EDWARD: That is what must be happening. It's Jesse, isn't it? It's dark. There are torches in the corner. I peep through the curtain. There the monsters are. There's a little hole. I've been in relationships before, well, just one relationship, technically. But I know how time-consuming and draining they can be. Besides, I've got a much better replacement, and for the rest, I'm focused on my studies this year. I told you that I was an only child. Jesse was exiled from the cool kids when he came out of the closet, but I never stopped talking to him, Bro, I don't care. What is that sound? *[Slight pause]* The whole damn world can hate me for all I care. Because I don't care. I don't care. I was peeping, as if I could see into hell. Half-sitting, half-lying on a pile of cushions. His tiny eyes swollen closed and his breath heavy. Jesse. He smelled dreadfully. Naked to his waist. He has a horn between his eyes. I didn't care for these roommates. It's affordable. Sshhh. What was that? What was that? It couldn't just be a branch on the roof? I don't care. I don't care about any of it. I mean, Simphiwe's always drinking. Don't even get me started on Seven! And Lucy is stuck up. And old Edward's idea of hanging out would probably involve going to come cult gathering. I would never inflict horror. So I looked back at Jesse and pushed him away. Everyone laughed at him and humiliated him. Kyle even came to pat me on the back, I didn't react I just kinda stood there, you know. Then the party went on as normal. Monday back at school Jesse was nowhere to be found. It was only at the end of the week that the teacher came in and said Jesse had committed suicide. I want to sit on that great couch. Come sit with me, we can fly out of the room . . . just you and me . . . we can fly . . . we can fly . . .

THE THREE begin to pull the rope round his neck; EDWARD slowly convulses and slumps.
THE THREE, still wearing their masks, sit down on the couch and watch the audience.
Lights fade.

END

Iziyalo Zikamama

(My Mother's Teachings)

By The Botsotso Ensemble

Thandeka Shangase • Busi Radebe • Yandisa Khwakhwa
Mandelakhe Vilo• Nkanyiso Shezi • Allan Kolski Horwitz

SYNOPSIS

Iziyalo Zikamama is an ensemble created piece that was designed to promote the importance of reading and understanding what we read. Its five scenes show five different life situations that reflect the themes of family relations, peer pressure, false values, poor school performance, drug taking and teenage pregnancy.

In most working class black communities almost all young children/teenagers and their parents experience the same pressures and temptations. The play deals with these and points to solutions. Underlying its humour is a tragic vein that highlights the loss of human potential and satisfaction when a skill as basic to our current global world as reading is not perfected.

The play was created for the Botsotso performing arts program for schools that started in 2015 and stages plays, both those prescribed in the curriculum and new original workshopped pieces on specific themes that are relevant and of interest to young learners aged 12 to 17.

The first performance of *Iziyalo Zikamama* took place on 28 September 2017 at Lufereng Primary School, Gauteng.

LIFE WILL HUMBLE YOU

SCENE 1.1

Two chairs are placed on stage; Thando's home. Thando enters; she is jubilant, jumping around the stage as she interacts with the audience.

THANDO: Chomza, chomza . . . Unjani chomza!! Yabona chomza, iPride never got me anywhere. I don't know if it has helped you in anyway. Now when I was growing up, I had this idea of levels. Yabona futhi mina ngangingezwa mshini *[I never listened to anyone/anything]* Ngangi banjwa ngapha nangapha ngingakhuzeki *[I was all over the place and careless]* I was part of the popular clique. I had this thing of amaLevels. I knew everything and everyone knew me. I would go to every party on Fridays and hang out with people that I thought were the best. I probably had the biggest head in school and the mouth to match. Life was great nje. Kodwake kwasa ngokunye mhla ngifeyila uMatric. *[But everything changed the day I failed matric]* Ngangingazi nokuthi ngenze njani. *[I didn't even know what to do]* See, I came from a very small group of students. Sasibancane nje mhlampe la ko 50 sesiphelele Sisonke. *[We were a very small group, maybe fifty]* So you can imagine a whole grade made up of just fifty students. Everyone knew everyone very well, at least that what they thought. *[Starts getting irritated with herself]* Mina Ngabe angifeyilanga nje yazi. *[I didn't even know what to do]* Ilento yami yokuzenza into eyazi yonke into ngibe ngangingazi twa *[It's this thing of mine of acting like I know everything but at that moment I know nothing]* I never asked for help because I really never wanted to lower my guard. Eish, I remember my afternoons with ma-oledi *[Mom]* She would literally try to drag the words out of me when it came to reading isiZulu.

SCENE 1.2

THANDO is at home doing her homework with her mother. She is sitting on one chair, her mother on the other.

THANDO: *[She struggles to pronounce each word]* U-ma-ma u-ya-li-the-la . . . eish ma . . . *[She looks at her mother]* . . . I-ban-de . . .

MA: Hayi, Thando – you can't be in matric and still be reading like this! *[Correcting her]* "Umama uyalithela ibhande." *[My mother gives me a good hiding with the belt]* And that is exactly what I will do because you think I've got time to play. Thando, you are very confident when you are with your friends, are you not? Ulibele ukuphapha Koda awazi lutho eskoleni *[At school you are busy acting like you know it all, meanwhile you know nothing]* "Unyanya uyanyanya." Read it again!

THANDO: But mama, ngyazama *[But Mom, I'm trying]*

MA: Don't come to me with "but ma I'm trying" nonsense. That is not good enough. You are already on your final exams, Thando . . . but nothing says 'I'm final exam ready' with this reading of yours. You don't have a problem with reading your fashion magazines, you read those very clearly. You read that English very clearly and fluently. I want you to do the same with isiZulu.

THANDO: Mom, the English teacher makes it easier to understand. Unlike laba abanye bayazelisa nje futhi bayabhora. *[Unlike the others they make us sleepy and they are boring]*

MA: Are you trying to tell me that each and every teacher that is teaching you the other subjects is boring and that's why you are failing? My girl, you cannot depend on just Math and English to get you through matric since those are the only subjects you are actually passing. You have to balance everything.

THANDO: Easier said than done!

MA: And that's your other problem, Thando – that big head of yours. My girl, pride will never get you anywhere I promise you. I don't even know ukuthi ufuze bani ngoba mina I used to pass with flying colors. *[I don't even know who you got this from because I used to pass with flying colors]*

THANDO: Ma iskole sinzima manje *[Mom, school is hard these days]* and mina I'm not you. Times have changed and so has education.

MA: Yes, you are right, Thando, times have changed. But language never changes. The English you are learning your set-work is the same English we used many years ago.

THANDO: Ma, I really don't think you will ever understand my case.

MA: Try me!

THANDO: Ma ngeke ngikwazi ukutshela vele you never want to listen and understand my side of the story vele. *[Ma, I can't explain, I can't tell you]*

MA: Wena ke, *[And as for you]* do you ever understand anything anyone says? Or do you only want people to listen to what you've got to say?

Maybe if you started listening to other people, they would want to listen to you too. *[Picks up the book]* How little you know!

THANDO: Ma, most of everything I read doesn't make sense. It all just doesn't make sense.

MA: Thando, than why don't you ask for help? Your ego, my girl, will never get you anywhere.

THANDO: Ma, I told you wouldn't understand! I have a certain standard to maintain in school. Being popular is not an easy thing to keep up with. If I were to raise my hand all the time I didn't understand something, people will start thinking I'm not as smart as I act.

MA: My point exactly, Thando! Lower that guard of yours or before you know it, it will be too late and all these people that you are maintaining a standard in front of would have passed their tertiary level and be driving their cars to their nice big houses. And where will you be then?

THANDO: Ma, can I please go and clean my room now and ngzofunda *[Study]* later?

MA: Thando, the time is now. No one is here to watch you. Study now otherwise . . .

THANDO: Please ma . . . *[Runs off]*

SCENE 1. 3

An Actor crosses the stage with a board on which is written: TEN YEARS LATER.

THANDO enters as her mother is doing laundry. Her mom is complaining about all the laundry she has to do for both THANDO and her two children.

MA: *[Looks up at THANDO]* Wamuhle bo. *[You look beautiful]*

THANDO: Haw ngyabonga, Ma *[Thank you, mom]*. Ma sacela ungiboleke utwenty rand. *[Mom, can you please lend me twenty rand?]*

MA: Twenty rand wani? *[Twenty rand, for what?]*

THANDO: There is a cleaning agency that called me for an interview so ...

MA: Cleaning agency? Heh! Anginawo twenty rand mina. *[I don't have twenty rand]*

THANDO: Hau, Ma, uyithathe kweye grant ke. *[Mom, you can give me from the grant [SASSA] money]*

MA: Grant yani? *[Whose grant?]*

THANDO: Grant yezingsne. *[The kid's grant [SASSA]*

MA: Uyingane yini wena? *[Are you a kid?]*

THANDO: No.

MA: Remember when you were actually a kid and you were sitting right here, and I gave you a chance to study? And what did you say, "I have a standard to maintain". Where is your standard now? Now you are asking me for money to go to a cleaning agent? NEVER! Actually indlu yami ingcolile and nakhu ngiwasha washing yezigane zakho. Nansi ke I - interview awuke uwashe la ngzobona kuthi ngiyawuthola yin lo-twenty rand wakho. *[Actually, my house is dirty as well and here I am washing your kid's clothes. This is an interview – wash these clothes and I'll see if I can find that twenty rand]*

>   She exits

THANDO: *[Frustrated]* Eish yabona nje! Njalo mangicela imali Mel ngikhunjuzwe kuthi ngafeyila Matric *[Every time I ask for money I have to be reminded that I failed my matric]* *[To the AUDIENCE]* Yabona chomza *[My friends]*, life will humble you!

MA: *[Off stage]* Thando, hurry up! There's more than enough to keep you busy here!

THANDO: Coming ma! Coming . . . *[Exits]*

GLASSES

Scene 2.1

GOGO enters. She uses a walking stick. She sits down painfully. SIZWE enters: he is coming home from school.

SIZWE: Gogo, they gave us homework at school – about history, about Steve Biko.

GOGO: Ey, Mntanami, yini leyo mtanami?

SIZWE: The question is: what role did Steve Biko play in the black consciousness movement?

GOGO: *[Surprised]* Oh . . . Steve Biko, wayeliqhawe mntanami.

SIZWE: I know that Gogo, but I want details . . . like a history line Gogo.

GOGO: Pass me my glasses Mtanami. I want to read your question so I don't make a mistake. *[He passes her the glasses. She starts to 'read' but quickly takes off her glasses]* Ag, no, my child, these glasses are useless for reading! I need proper ones for that.

SIZWE: Are you sure Gogo? You've had these for years. It must be very frustrating not to be able to read comfortably.

GOGO is confused and they look into each others eyes.

SIZWE makes as if to leave but a thought hits him.

SIZWE: What did you want to be when you were growing up, Gogo?

GOGO: Ey, I wanted to be many things. A nurse, a doctor, a lawyer . . . Actually the thing I most wanted was to be a policewoman. Ah, that uniform, that cap! But it didn't work out, my grandson. Your mother was born and I had to take care of her. Then your grandfather died while she and her sisters were still very young. And then in her teens, you were also born so we both left our dreams to make sure that you become something in life – not like us. You know, we all make choices and we have to live with them.

SIZWE: That is very sad Gogo. I know you have had a hard life. But let us go back to Steve Biko.

GOGO: Yes, my child I was already a mother when he was murdered by the Boers. A great leader, make no mistake, if only we had people like him leading us today, if only. But don't make these ones who steal our money an excuse for sitting on your backside. Study hard, my son – that is the only way you will make something of yourself. And now let me go and make supper. You can't study on an empty stomach, can you?

SIZWE: *[Laughing]* No, I can't Gogo. And what's in the pot? It smells delicious!

GOGO: Your favourite – dombolo and beef stew.

SIZWE: *[Embracing her]* Oh, thank you Gogo – as a reward I swear I will save money for you to get new glasses – proper reading glasses then you can read all about Steve Biko and other heroes with me.

GOGO: You will? Oh, bless you, my child. I will make you dombolos every day if you do that! Come to the kitchen. Sit with me while I put the finishing touches to that stew.

Both exit

SCENE 2. 2

The graduation ceremony; the whole family gathers to celebrate SIZWE's appointment to the position of national media officer for the police service. SIZWE enters.

SIZWE: Thank you so much for gathering in celebration of my promotion.

As you know it has been a long and hard slog to reach this position. And to tell the truth, there were times I almost gave up. But then I was lucky to have the kind of family support that few people enjoy. And, of course, the main person standing behind me was uGogo, our dear Gogo who could only dream of what I have become today. How sad that she had to sacrifice herself for others! Truly, I feel blessed to have uGogo by my side. She has inspired me with her teachings and I am what I am today because of her encouragement. And now I would like to call uGogo on stage and ask her to read a short poem I have written in her honor.

GOGO: *[Shuffling forward till she stands next to him]* Eh, hau . . . ngyabonga ndodana *[She wipes her tears]* God is great . . .

Sizwe hands her a piece of paper on which the poem is written.

GOGO: Ag, where are my glasses? Child, you know I can't do nothing without them. Angiboni nokuthi kubhalweni la.

GOGO takes the paper, screws up her eyes but says nothing.

SIZWE: What's wrong, Gogo? Do you need better light? I'll bring a torch.

GOGO: Kahleni boh ayeseba mancane kanje lamagam. *[Clears throat]* Koda nisho kuthi nonke njoba nigcwele la nizolalelana nami nje ngihema . . . *[Audience response]* Hau, God is great. *[SIZWE looks puzzled]* What a beautiful poem you have written and all about your grandfather, such a strong man . . .

SIZWE: No, no, Gogo! It's all about you! Grandfather died when I was very young. You were the person who took everything on her shoulders. Please, read it Gogo, read how much I love and admire you. *[Moves close to her and holds the paper together with her]*

GOGO: Where are my glasses? Aish! *[She fumbles in her pocket; finds them; puts them on]* That's better, my son. *[Starts to scrutinize the page; puckers up her face in concentration]* Ag, no, these glasses they really let me down. You know I can't read properly with them, those letters are just so . . . so small. If only I could get proper glasses, yes, proper ones my life would be . . .

SIZWE: *[Laughing]* Gogo, I've heard your prayers. I remembered from when I was a little boy how you couldn't help me with my homework because your glasses weren't strong enough to read the letters. And all these years I swore that when I was earning more than peanuts, I would buy you the best reading glasses in the world. And you know what, Gogo? Here they are! *[With a flourish he takes out her new reading glasses and gently puts them on her face]* There you are, my dearest Gogo – the best present I could think of! *[Kisses her]* Now won't this make a difference! *[She looks very disturbed – not at all happy]* Read the poem now. I'm so excited. I spent hours getting it right.

GOGO: *[Squinting]* Eish, my son, I'm so proud of you and so thankful for these glasses but . . . I can't.

SIZWE: What do you mean you can't? Are these glasses also no good? But the optician swore they would be! Damn, you can't trust anyone these days.

GOGO: No, no, my son. Don't blame the optician. Blame me.

SIZWE: What are you talking about, Gogo?

GOGO: It's not the glasses. It's me. I should have told you a long time ago but I wanted to be an example to you. I didn't want you to be ashamed of me.

SIZWE: How could I be ashamed of you? You are the person I admire most in the world.

GOGO: But I can't read, my son. I never learnt to read and write.

SIZWE: Really? I can't believe this.

GOGO: I only went as far as grade 2 and then my mother needed me at home to look after the other little ones.

SIZWE: How come you never told me this before? Imagine what you could have been today if you'd had that chance.

GOGO: But you are my reward. You have made something of yourself. Good for you, my son. Give me a granddaughter soon.

SIZWE: Ungakhathazeki. *[Don't worry]* There will be children everywhere. *[To the AUDIENCE]* Oh, well, I'll read you the poem later. Let's go and have some refreshments now. There's still so much to celebrate. Come Gogo, let's go and sample those delicious vetkoek you've made. *[They both exit]*

GOGO: *[Rushing back; addresses the AUDIENCE]* But you know something, this thing of not being able to read and write, it's been the worst thing in my life. Yes, I'm strong and I have been there for so many people but when it comes to my own dreams? What have I been able to do? What? Reading, they call it a miracle that umuntu made alphabets and made books. If only I had been able to finish school and be part of that world. I wouldn't be this bitter old woman who finds fault with everyone . . . Ag, there's no point in crying over spilt milk. At least I have Sizwe. What a lovely boy!

Exits.

THE PASTOR'S TRICKS
SCENE 3.1

A church [Zionist] in a township somewhere in South Africa. We see Pastor KHOHLELA and his assistant XHATISA singing, dancing in a circle then standing before the congregation, preaching.

KHOHLELA: Watsho unyana womntu wathi ndimaxebanxeba nje ndima vithi, ngoba ndifele izono zenu ukuze nina niphile nigcamle ubo obungunaphakade. *[And the Son of God said, "My body is wounded and full of holes; I was on the cross, I made the ultimate sacrifice so all could be saved from the sins of the Earth, so all humans can experience eternal life]*

XHATHISA: *[Exaggerated gestures]* Mhhh!! . . . ewe kanty!?

A woman from the congregation shouts out, with one hand raised.

MAMIYA: Ewe ndiyakuva tata umfundisi,qha! Awusixelelange ukuba uvule ku verse bani apha ebhayibhileni? *[Yes, I hear all that you are saying pastor about Jesus and all that, but you did not inform us, the congregation, as to which verse and chapter you are reading from?]*

KHOHLELA: Mhhh! Eke' ndiyakuva Mamiya.ewe ay' ndiyakuva nyani. Ehh! mandithi wena ndisuke ndonyukwa ngumoya oyingcwele.Xhathisa lixelele ibandla. *[Oh, yes! The holy spirit just took over. My assistant Xhathisa will have to tell everybody].*

XHATHISA: Thixo! Yinto endizoyithini lena,kanene indawoni nale verse. Mfundisi ubufunda ndawoni kanene? *[God! How am I supposed to know which verse and chapter my pastor has been reading from?]*

> *KHOHLELA is staring straight into XHATHISA'S eyes hoping that XHATHISA will be intimidated and eventually save him from the embarrassment of the entire congregation, but XHATHISA is also caught off guard and is out of ideas as to how to save his pastor!*
> *They stare at each other for quite some time until XHATHISA starts a song, and a woman from the congregation takes over the singing.*
> *KHOHLELA raises a hand to interrupt the singing.*

KHOHLELA: Hallelujah! Ndicele uAmen!,Ndithi ndicela uAmen, Amen bazalwane. Ilizwi lethu silifumana phaya kwi-sigaba sesibini. Uthi Uyesu amen! bazalwene,uthi unyana womntu womntu! Mna ndiyindlela ndibubom.Unoyolo owo uthe weza elizweni l am ngoba yena . . .
[Hallelujah! Can I get an Amen! Can I get an Amen! Today's reading is from

Revelations, verse two, chapter two. And Jesus, the Son of God, says, "I am the Light, I am the Hope. All those who . . .]

NYAWO from the congregation interrupts by raising his hand while mumbling under his breath.

NYAWO: Uxolo Mfundisi kodwa andiyiboni mna le verse oyifundayo. Indawoni kanty tata umfundisi;futhi akuqali ukwenzeka lento apha ecaweni. *[Excuse me pastor, I don't mean to be rude or anything but I just cannot find the verse and chapter you said you are reading from. Worse part is that this is not the first time]*

The entire congregation mumbles in agreement with NYAWO.

Pastor KHOHLELA looks troubled and starts to sweat – his secret is finally being revealed.

Suddenly sis THEMBI shoots up from the congregation, her face filled with the excitement.

SIS THEMBI: Mfundisi ndinendaba ezimnnandi ebendingathanda ukuzitsho apha phambi kwebandla. *[Pastor, I have some great news that I would like to share here before the congregation]*

KHOHLELA: Ohh! Halleulujah, amen! Great news from a child of God! Speak child, let the Lord speak through you.

SIS THEMBI: God is great, indeed! I have just received the contract for selling my house. Here it is in my hand. But I need you, pastor, to help me with the reading of it and your advice would be highly appreciated as well.

KHOHLELA: Hallelujah! God is great! I would love to . . . in fact, I am going to help you with the contract. Come to the front sis Thembi. We need to pray for this blessing because we all know how long it took you to finally get a buyer. Hallelujah!

Sis THEMBI comes to the pulpit and kneels in front of Pastor KHOHLELA. With his urging and that of other congregants, she becomes hysterical and start praying in 'tongues'.

KHOHLELA: Let the contract come forth! I want to see it before the congregation!

Sis THEMBI produces the contract and Pastor KHOHLELA is in awe.

KHOHLELA: Yethixo yoh! uSis Thembi uzawuba rich! 5 million iza ezandleni zakhe, hallelujah! Malibongwe igama lenkosi, siyambulela uthixo!. Ndiyakucela Sis Thembi ze ubuye usixoxele ngomso emeeting ukuba izinto zihambe kanjani. *[God! Jesus! Sis Thembi is going is going to be rich! Five million is headed to her palms! Hallelujah! Let us thank the Lord our Savior, we thank God for this blessing. Please, Sis Thembi, you will have to give us feedback as to how things go in tomorrow's meeting]*

Sis THANDI exits with the contract in her hand.

Pastor KHOHLELA and his assistant XHATISA lead the congregation in singing and dancing.

SCENE 3.2

It is now the following day in church. Pastor KHOHLELA and XHATISA are standing on the pulpit before the congregants.

KHOHLELA: Iculo bazalwane, emveni koko sizawuthandaza sivule lomhlangano. *[I request a hymn, beautiful people of Christ, then we will pray]*

Sis THEMBI enters, the look on her face is that of a disgusted and furious person. She rushes past everyone straight to the pulpit and throws the contract into Pastor KHOHLELA'S face.

KHOHLELA: Yintoni ngoku. Kutheni Sis Thembi? *[What's wrong, Sis Thembi? What is troubling you?]*

SIS THEMBI: *[To the CONGREGATION]* This stinking Pastor of yours people is a crook! How could he tell me such nonsense? Since when is five hundred equal to five million? I want my house back, Pastor! How could you!

KHOHLELA: Ehh! uthetha ngantoni ngoku Sis Thembi? Andiyazi lento othethangayo uthi kutheni? *[What are you talking about, sister Thembi? I am totally lost]*

NYAWO shoots up from the congregation.

NYAWO: Okanye uPastor isn't working with these people, why would he lie?

MAMIYA: *[To Sis THEMBI]* No, no! There has to be a reason for this 'mistake'! I suspect that he did it on purpose just so his "friends" could rob you of your house.

KHOHLELA checks for a way to escape but when he eventually tries to run off, he gets caught by MAMIYA, and is brought back to explain himself to the congregation.

KHOHLELA: Bantu benkosi ndicela uxolo, I wasn't working with the people who robbed Sis Thembi of her house! This is a huge mistake! I want to clear the air and set the record straight. The real reason I tried to run away is because I was too proud to admit here before you people that I can't read. I am unable to fully understand what I read and I was too afraid that you people will lose all the respect you had for me if I admitted my flaws. I just hope and pray that one day you will find it in your hearts to forgive me.

XHATHISA: *[Addresses the AUDIENCE]* Beautiful people of the Lord, what Pastor Khohlela has done all these years, pretending here on the pulpit before the entire congregation, is appalling and was uncalled for. Therefore I want to say to you, don't lose hope and your faith because from now on, moving forward, I will be the head Pastor of the church. I will lead you to the promised Gates of Heaven! Amen, hallelujah!

SIS THEMBI: Haai, man! Suga! I want my money! Where is that crook? What is this church all about? I want justice!

She runs past XHATHISA and tries to attack KHOHLELA but he manages to break free and run off – the entire congregation in pursuit.

MAGHOST

SCENE 4

Narrator [a young woman] enters and starts addressing the audience.

NARRATOR: Do you know the saying, "You can take a donkey to the river but you can't make it drink"? I used to have a friend by the name of Maghost who lived back opposite my house. We didn't go to the same primary school though. She went to a laerskool where the learners were taught to write in cursive while I went to a Roman Catholic school with some learners reflecting the Yizo Yizo Tv series back in the day. *[Slight pause]* The thing about my friend was that she was hot, a le lepyatla *[she was hot]* with juicy . . . according many boys . . . juicy lips, a thin waist and half ripe pear shape curves. Nna ke le sdudlanyana sa maditamati *[While I was just the fat girl of the lady that sells tomatoes]* Mara byanong *[But now]* as much as she was physically hot, she was also hot headed, and whenever anyone said or did something that did not make sense in her own head, na tlago ghosta *[She will fight you – holding up fists for a fight]* whether o ngwanyana or moshimane *[Whether you're boy or girl]* So anyway, time for high school came and Maghost elevated to a more beautiful teenager and I remained sdudla sa maditamati. She now went to a school in town where she had to ride the bus everyday while I went to school not far from our home where I used a special taxi that picked me up at my gate. Heee *[Laughing]* I remember this one day in the morning waiting for my transport, people rushing to work and there comes my friend going to catch a bus. She bounces up and down the street wearing her short school skirt and tracksuit top.

MAGHOST enters.

MAGHOST: Chomiiii!

NARRATOR: Halawi friend of mine! *[MAGHOST unzips her top to reveal a bikini top underneath]* Bathong wena! *[Oh, my word!]* And then? Your books? School bag?

MAGHOST: What? Dibuka? A ke di tlhoke. *[Books? I don't need them]* She runs off.

NARRATOR: And there's my friend running off before I ask any further. Now that I think about it, I think she seriously misunderstood her status and thought she was popular. I say this because the many people who actually gave her attention were boys and those that didn't say much to her were those who were scared of her. So she did whatever she wanted, whenever she wanted, and in return she failed her 9th grade twice. So her parents decided to take her to a township school nearby in order to keep a closer eye on her. But now, because my friend was so hot na a gafisa bashimane thata thata and le yena na ba mo gafisa thata *[She drove the guys crazy and she was crazy about them]* while all the other children were busy studying books in class, she was studying the ceiling and got pregnant with her first child. Yo! But her parents were understanding and supportive and made an agreement with her that they will find a babysitter if she goes back to school and focuses on her school work. And as usual I was the motivating friend who was with her every day, talking about the subjects we enjoyed, the teachers that bored us or were funny, and, of course, the boys. This happened when I was in Grade 10 and then as I moved up to Grade 11 and 12, we started seeing less of each other because of the school work expanding and plus she said they have Saturday schools and holiday/winter school classes so we saw less of each other. Now one day I decided to visit her in her home and only found her cousin. I asked him what time she gets back from the extra classes. *[Laughs]* Yo, guys, I've never been laughed at o ka re ke stlela so. *[As if I'm a fool]* Her cousin was like: Maghost? Saturday school? Hee, what has your friend been telling you because she dropped out of school a long time ago. She had a second baby and is now living with her boyfriend. Yoh, azanka ka tlabega so. *[I've never been so humiliated]* So as a child of my parents, I continued my schooling so as to get to tertiary. And I've succeeded. I have everything I set out to achieve. *[Slight pause]* You know what really hurts me is that every time I go back home, I find my friend walking around with one child in her hand, one on the back, and one on the way – all that, and no one else in her life but her unemployed boyfriend. Eish, her story reminds me that you can have all the support and assistance of your family, friends, and school, but if you don't take the responsibility on yourself to take your education seriously, no one else can make a difference. *[Slight pause]* Maghost . . . what a ripe peach gone to rot!

    Exits.

CLASSROOM MADNESS

SCENE 5.1

MFUNDO and SCELO are smoking cigarettes outside the classroom.

SCELO: Ekse kuhambani ntwana? *[Hey, how are you?]*

MFUNDO: Ayi ngigrand mfana. *[I am okay, boy]*

SCELO: Wee Mfundo uready for iclass ka Mam Tshangase. *[Mfundo, are you ready for Mrs Tshangase's class?]*

MFUNDO: Tjooo Ntwana Sine homework yini? *[Do we have homework?]*

SCELO: Hayi ntwana, we are continuing with leya novel ye Animal farm.
    [No, my friend, we are continuing with the novel, Animal Farm]

MFUNDO: Eish mina reading in class kuyang'bora, manje sekmele ngi accept ukuthi unkulunkulu akangigayanga dayidengi . . . ey Ntwana why uringa uyi one? *[I get bored easily in class especially when it comes to reading. I should accept that God didn't give me reading skills . . . Boy, why are you talking to yourself?]*

SCELO: Ntwana uthe eclassin kunjani? *[Boy, what did you say about class?]*

MFUNDO: Ngithi mina ngingenza noma yini mara ukufunda akusizo izinto zami. *[I can do anything except reading. Reading is not my thing]*

MANDLA: *[Entering]* Sho, sho, majita. *[Yes, yes, buddies]*

MFUNDO and SCELO: Sho ntwana. *[Yes, boy]*
    They exchange 'cool' hand and shoulder greetings with MANDLA.

MANDLA: Eyi bafethe ngiphethe this heavey stuff from Bra Sabza, he says he got the shit back in Cape Town and majita yooo les'stuff sikthatha sikubeke. *[Gents, I have this strong weed. Bra Sabza said he got it from Cape Town. This is the real stuff hitting up the streets]*

MFUNDO: *[Sniffing the stuff]* Ntwana . . . ntwana . . . ntwana! *[Boy . . . Oh, boy . . . Oh, boy!]*

MANDLA: Sikubamba ushaye ama get down. *[It makes you dance till you fall]*

SCELO: Eish sani phele vele Bra Sabza is one of the best dealer's la ekasi. *[Everyone knows he is one of the best dealers around]*

MANDLA: *[Anxious]* Manje are we going to smoke this shit or are we just going to praise Bra Sabza?

SCELO: *[Concerned]* Wena Mfundo, you shouldn't smoke, you know your situation. *[To MANDLA]* Ntwana, maybe after school, not before class.

MANDLA: Nooo! No boy, after school is too late, sifak'idata sphume kanje. *[Nooo! No, boy, after school is too late, lets recharge and go]*

MFUNDO: Uyazi ntwana. *[You know I can handle it]*

SCELO: *[To MFUNDO]* Dog, you know unenkinga namagama. *["You have a problem when it comes to reading." He says this looking back at them and shrugging/shaking his head so that he does not focus on the clouds]* If you smoke, I doubt you're going to see anything at all.

MFUNDO: Hai wena! Ungazozenza ityma lami. Mangfuna ukubhema ngizobhema. Khona manje ulokhu ubusy uringa wedwa, ubani okunakile wena? *[Hey, you! Don't behave as if you are my father. If I want to smoke I will smoke! Right now you busy talking to yourself and nobody said anything to you about it]*

MANDLA: Sho boy.

SCELO: At least mina I read properly . . . yazini, entlik awuthi ngiye e clasini. *[You know what? Let me go to class]* We are already late. Eish, I hope le mvula doesn't catch up with me after school.

MFUNDO: Nxaa vaya! *[You can go To MANDLA]* Mara Ntwana le iyeclassin shuth ntwana sesi late *[But boy, if this one's going to class that means we really are late]*

MANDLA: Shiya dayideng ntwana ngiphethe istuff saseVenda. *[Forget about him. I brought Venda stuff]*

> MFUNDO and MANDLA decide to follow him.

SCENE 5.2

MRS T enters the classroom to find just THANDI.

MRS T: Good morning, class.

THANDI: Good morning, Mam.

MRS T: Hawu, bakaye ba bangwe? *[Where are the others?]*

THANDI: Akitsibi mam. *[I don't know]*

MRS T: Okay Thandi, today we are continuing with the reading of the novel 'Animal Farm'. Last time we left it at page 37, right?

The boys sneak into the classroom and sit down – MFUNDO is last.

ALL: Askies, Mam. *[Sorry]*

SCELO starts to look out the window – facing upward to the audience as if looking at something interesting.

MRS T: Ayi wena Mfundo! *[No, Mfundo!]*

MFUNDO: Hau mam, ngenzeni? *[Mam, what did I do now?]*

MRS T: Wenzeni? You come late to my class uzangibuza ukuthi wenzeni? *[What did you do? You come late to my class to ask me, 'what did you do'?]* Okay, Mr Mfundo, because you were the last one to enter this class, you are going to stand up and read. Page 37. *(He does not respond)* Mfundo funda! *[Mfundo, read!]*

MFUNDO stands up.

MRS T: Some time today Mfundo.

MFUNDO: *[He starts to read, struggling with each syllable]* Ew-era-eht-naimasl-fo-eht-fram . . . *[The class starts to laugh; he clears his throat and continues seemingly unconcerned. But while he is reading, Scelo start to play with his pen. Sitting back on his chair, he taps his foot still looking outside, 'spaced' out in thought]* Ni eht tasl adys fo rou ilves ew . . .

MRS T: Mfundo, o nale nako ya go dlala ne? *[Mfundo, I don't have time for games]*

MFUNDO: No, Mam, angazi why bahleka Mam. *[I don't know why they are laughing]*

MRS T: Byanong yini le uyifundayo? *[What are you reading?]*

MFUNDO: Hau, Mam, I am reading the book. The chapter on page 37, right? *[He starts reading again while pointing to the words and does so with confidence]* Ew era eht naimasl fo eht fram. Ni eht tasl adys fo rou ilves –

MRS T: Mfundo udakiwe yini? *[Mfundo are you drunk?]* Udleni before class? *[What did you eat before class?]* Scelo!

SCELO: Yes, mam. *[Looks sharply at the teacher then stands to read]* "We are the animals of the farm. In the last days of our lives we . . ."

MRS T: Scelo! *[He looks at her]* I didn't ask you to read, stop disrupting my class.

SCELO: Kodwa Mam iskhathi sami se class siyahamba wena no Mfundo niya khuluma kodwa we are not getting anywhere, I was just . . . *[You are wasting my time in class . . .]*

MRS T: Scelo, I am busy with a learner and you disturbing my class. Don't start that tone with me. I will take you to the principal.

SCELO: I am sorry Mam, I was not doing any tone. All I am saying is that uMfundo . . .

MFUNDO: *[To SCELO]* Hey, ungangifaki mina, uqalile uyaphapha. *[Hey, don't include my name, you have started with your forwardness]*

SCELO: Mfundo, you know angiz'enzi. *[You know I can't control myself]*

MFUNDO: Usho kanje. *[If you say so]*

MRS T: Scelo! Mfundo! This is not a fighting zone!

MANDLA: *[Standing up to stop them from fighting]* Mamzo! Mina ngine solution kule situation uMfundo wena Mamzo une Lexus *[Mam! I have a solution to this situation. Mam Mfundo has Lexus]*

MRS T: Ini? *[What?]*

MANDLA: Yebo, Mam uMfundo uphethwe iLexus, lona ufika la eklasini ezosifundela isi China, uphethwe iLexus . . . *[Yes, mam, Mfundo has Lexus, he comes here and reads like he is reading Chinese]*

MFUNDO: *[Grabbing MANDLA by the neck; they tussle with each other]* He wena san! Ubiza bani nge Lexus, ngi Lexus mina *[You buddy! Who you calling 'Lexus'?]*

MRS T: Hey! Hey! Hey! Not in my classroom! Mfundo!
      The principal enters.

MRS T: Principal! Ay ay ay! Yabona your children . . . *[Principal, you see your children]*
      Everyone settles down quietly.

PRINCIPAL: And what seems to be the problem?

MRS T: Principal, these three are disrupting my class. Firstly they came late, and then this one . . . *[Points at MFUNDO]* . . . is making jokes while reading. He reads a language I don't understand while this one . . . *[Points at SCELO]* . . . plays his spokesperson and provokes a fight. *[Points at MANDLA]* Lona, he is a headache I wish I never had in my life. He is

212

always sleeping in class I don't even know why he bothers to come. I am tired principal.

MFUNDO: Kodwa principal . . .

PRICIPAL: Kodwa principal kwani? Angikuficanga ulwa lana wena?

SCELO: Principal . . .

He starts to make agitated movements, moving back and forth in one place, but not saying anything.

PRINCIPAL: I have already given you several warnings and now, unfortunately, I will have to suspend you until I see both your parents and . . .

SCELO: *[He bursts out]* Mara Principal you people don't understand! If you would just listen to me – I have so many voices in my head!

PRINCIPAL: Scelo my boy! You are in no position to request to be listened to when you can't listen to others. Until . . .

MANDLA: *[Stands up]* Wooo! Principal! Nginesolution kulesituation. *[Wait, principal! I have a solution to this situation]*

MRS T: Mr Solution! He always has a solution, I don't know how because he is always sleeping.

MANDLA: uMfundo uphethwe iLexus. *[Mfundo has Lexus]*

PRINCIPAL: Yini leyo? *[What is that?]*

MANDLA: Uyafa avueke, afike la eklasini ezosifundela isi China wena Mamzo, uphethwe. iLexus wena mazmo. *[He dies and come back to life again and then he comes to class and reads like he is reading Chinese. He has 'lexus' mam]*

MRS T: Mina I don't understand because Lexus kikoloyi. *[I don't understand because Lexus is a car]*

PRINCIPAL: Dyslexia, it could be dyslexia which means Mfundo has trouble recognizing sounds in words and matching them with the right letters and symbols and then bringing together them to make words.

MFUNDO: Yes, mam, and then they say I am playing games.

PRINCIPAL: So, my boy, have you ever been tested for dyslexia?

MFUNDO: Dyslexia? Mam, yin dyslexia? *[Mam, what is dyslexia?]*

PRINCIPAL: I've just explained, Mfundo. It is a problem that your brain has in recognizing the right sounds that every letter stands for. It doesn't mean you are unintelligent or brain damaged. It just means you need special lessons to help you remember the right sounds. And you, Scelo?

SCELO: Mam . . .

MRS T: Scelo, sit down Scelo!

MANDLA: Principal uScelo ufike abeka da uScelo, asuke abeka da, aphinde abeka da, uScelo u out of focus, uphethwe I ABC.

The PRINCIPAL and SCELO move from one spot to another and then another.

MANDLA: He is out of focus, mamzo. He has ABC.

PRINCIPAL: What?

MANDLA: ABC...

PRINCIPAL: Oh, you mean 'ADHD'. That stands for 'Attention Deficit Hyperactivity Disorder'.

MFUNDO: Yo, that's a lot to remember!

PRINCIPAL: It means he has difficulty paying attention. Also that he likes to move around a lot, not be the same place for too long and does things very quickly without thinking about where they will land him.

SCELO: Hey, mam you are right, I've been trying to tell them this thing always disturbs the functioning of my mind. I have five thought at the same time and all of them want to come out and ...

MRS T: Hai mam, umsangano lo wonke. *[This is ridiculous]* Principal, there is no such thing! These children are just disrespectful.

PRINCIPAL: No dear, we have similar situations in other classrooms.

MRS T: We have?

PRINCIPAL: Yes, we have similar situations in other classes. There is treatment for such cases. And after treatment, uMfundo will be able to read properly and uScelo will be hlalaphansi. He will be able to control his energy. I will arrange a meeting with the counsellor and we will take it from there. Scelo noMfundo come.

MFUNDO: *[To MANDLA]* Wena, after school is after school.

PRINCIPAL: After school eskoleni sokabani? *[After school at which school?]* Out!

MRS T: *[To MFUNDO]* Thwara handbook yahayo. *[Take your book]* *[To SCELO]* If you leave your books who do think is going to take them for you? *[SCELO goes back and takes his book]* Oh, do you have a slave to carry your school bag? *[He returns to fetch his school bag]*.

SCELO: I'm sorry mamzo.

MRS T: Alright Scelo.

SCELO: Mamzo I said I'm sorry.

MRS T: Scelo I heard you. I said its fine.

The PRINCIPAL, SCELO and MFUNDO exit. MANDLA has fallen asleep.

MRS T: Mandla! Mandla!

MANDLA: *[Waking in a disoriented state]* Sure, sure . . .

MRS T: *[Furious]* Sure? Sure? Sure to me?

MANDLA: Hade hare mamzo. *[I'm sorry mam]*

PRINCIPAL: What is wrong with this child? Do you ever learn anything in class?

MANDLA: Ja. *[Yes]*

MRS T: Wena? Tell us ufundeni namhlanje? Tell us ukuthi what stood out for you today Mandla. *[You? Tell us, what did you learn today? Tell us what stood out for you today Mandla]* Tell us! Share.

MANDLA stands up and, after a few moments, starts singing.

MANDLA: Umama wami, wayengiyala, ethi mtanami ubofunda njalo.

Iyo, iyo, iyo ubofunda njalo.

Sengiyazisola, Sengiyazisola.

Iyo, iyo, iyo ubofunda njalo.

[My mother used to advise me; my child, you must always read.

Oh, yeah, oh, yeah, oh, yeah, always read.

I regret, I regret.

Oh, yeah, oh, yeah, oh, yeah, always read]

END

FINDING ME

MOEKETSI KGOTLE

Written and directed by Moeketsi Kgotle [mentored by Robert Colman with the support of the Sibikwa Art Centre], the play takes place in and round a taxi rank. Two street vendors witness the lives of people as they relate to issues of gender. They then interrogate the issues themselves and allow people to voice out what they think about their opinions. As such, the title of the show, Finding Me, is directed to the audience in that each audience member ought to find him/herself in the characters and reflect critically on the content of their views.

In general, the story is about the relations between men and women. It is a physical theatre piece that expresses the imbalances of power that create differences in societies – revision of the gender roles prescribed by various religious ideologies that curtail equality being an urgent task vital.

The process of ensemble making was based on exploring popular conceptions of gender relations held by working class Black people and how they explain it. We created scenes out of the information we gleaned from discussions with a wide range of men and women, as well as including our own conditioning and experience. Later, in order to get the show to a point of performance, I started writing up the script in order to add new insights and make the work even more accurate with regard to social relations.

The show was first performed at the Sibikwa Art Center on 25 August 2009. The most recent performance was at the Wits Nunnery in 2016. It was also performed at various school festivals organized by Botsotso in 2016.

NUNNERY CAST

SUGAR DADDY and FISH	Luckey Gxubane
MAZ	Melissa Hlahele
JONES	Thepo Lecholo
SCHOOL GIRL	Khabonina Riba
MINGAS	Michael Nkoe
SECOND GIRL	Recheal Makatile
TSUMA	Sandile Zikhali

SCENE 1

Two STREET VENDORS are standing at their stalls down center stage: a shoemaker and a cosmetics seller.

Opening song

While the audience is coming in, the vendors are busy selling. They leave their stalls and move over to a fire place [imbaola] on the street. MAZ comes in and greets them. THE VENDORS see a successful woman's car and excitedly point at one of the lady's in the theatre. Then they freeze as MINGAS comes on stage and sits. MAZ greets him then moves over to the stall.

MAZ: Hello, Mingas.

MINGAS: Hi.

MAZ: How is your day?

MINGAS: Good.

MAZ: And how is business?

MINGAS: Also good. I've managed to fix five pairs of shoes. These two are R10.00 jobs and this one is R5.00. How is your day?

MAZ: Ag, very slow. It's a day for look-and touch, touch-look-and-touch. No sales.

> *MAZ and MINGAS minimize the action while TBOOS, FISH and SPIDER play a game.*
> *TBOOS observes a passing woman.*

TBOOS: Majimbos, you do the listening and I'll do the talking. You see that woman, that's exactly what a man needs. Gorgeous!!!

FISH: Yo, imagine walking with her at the mall.

SPIDER: Let me tell you about women. A woman's breast is man's pillow yet a man's slave is a woman. Truly speaking a female's word is an insult to us gents yet our word is a command.

TBOOS: Hey spider, skatlo re baezisa hieso me laitie. You watch too much TV sani.

SPIDER: No, man. A male's belief is always to lead a female yet a female's destiny is to lead males.

FISH: Hey wena, I cannot be controlled by a woman. All this 'gender' equality talk is rubbish.

SPIDER: Do we always have to fight? Does it always have to be a challenge? Gender. What is gender, guy?

218

FISH: Gender means a man should be on top of a woman like when . . .
     [Makes the motions of the sex act] Imagine it hlokoloza!
       They sing hlokoloza and dance.

SPIDER: Ya! . . . when I think of it, my tongue runs out of words because of
     the mirror I stand in front of. But it is not about who is going to win. It's
     about everyone winning.

TBOOS: Come on, you're going soft! It's about who is going to win. Check
     hieso madala, you have a man and woman who are about to run a race,
     they run fast like their heads are cut off. Then who is going to win at the
     end? Madala, let that play in your mind.

SPIDER: Gents, will we ever survive the storm?

FISH: OK spider, stop taking us to school. Let's play.
       They start selling.

MAZ: Hey those men have got a lot to say about woman. Maybe they should
     look for work and . . .

MINGAS: But work is scarce these days, Maz.

MAZ: True, but look at you. You have found a way to make a living, just like
     me. At least we are trying. They should do the same – get off the street
     and take some responsibility in life. I wonder how many of them have run
     away leaving some poor woman to raise their children.

SCENE 2

TSUMA enters.

MINGAS: Ja, but not all men are the same.
       The three men continue playing. JONES enters.

TSUMA: Hello, Jones, can I speak to you?

JONES: Eish, Tsuma, man.

FISH: Setabane.

TSUMA: Voetsak. Don't call me that, don't insult me. You don't even know
     the meaning of the word. Setabane.ntho empe e kareng machenclos a
     poho.
       JONES and TSUMA speak away from the three.

TSUMA: I'm sick and tired of how these buddies of yours insult me. It seems
     as if they don't like our friendship.

JONES: What are you doing here? I told you more than once that when I am

with my friends you must stop acting like a girl, act like a man, man. What
do you want them to say?

TSUMA: I don't care.

JONES: But I do. I told you, phone me instead. Don't just come around when
I'm with the guys.

TSUMA: Oh, well, it seems you are no longer interested in our friendship.

JONES: I am baby, I am.

TSUMA: When are you going to tell them about us?

JONES: When the time is right. *[Slight pause]* I will tell them soon but go
before they start suspecting.

    TSUMA leaves; JONES joins the guys.

SCENE 3

*A teenage GIRL enters at one side of the stage; a SUGAR DADDY enters from
the opposite wing.*

SUGAR DADDY: I thought seeing as it's lunch time, I'll bring you a treat.
Also I can't pick you up you at four o'clock – I've got a board meeting – so
a quickie in the car? *[Laughs]* Just joking! Anything you need, sweetie? You
have enough airtime?

GIRL: Yes, yes everything is fine . . . I've . . . it`s just I must tell you
something . . . *[Slight pause]* Promise you won't be upset.

SUGAR DADDY: I promise. Nothing you do will upset me. *[Gives her a kiss]*

GIRL: No, no . . . forget it, forget it. Anyway, how's . . .

SUGAR DADDY: Come on, babe – what are you talking about?

GIRL: Eish . . . remember about five weeks ago? The weekend your wife went
home with your children to visit her mother . . . and I stayed over at your
house . . .

SUGAR DADDY: Of course, how could I forget such a beautiful weekend!
Just me and my baby . . .

GIRL: I'm pregnant.

SUGAR DADDY: Pregnant?

GIRL: Yes.

SUGAR DADDY: Who's the father?

GIRL: What do you mean? It's YOU.

SUGAR DADDY: Impossible – I use a condom all time.

GIRL: You've forgotten? That weekend we didn't.

SUGAR DADDY: You should have known better! Anyway, maybe I'm not the father. How do you know?

GIRL: I only sleep with you.

SUGAR DADDY: Why are you doing this? What do you want? No, don't tell me. *[Slight pause]* More money.

GIRL: Baby, I love you, I want this child.

SUGAR DADDY: Do you think I have time for such nonsense.

GIRL: So what are we going to do now? This is your child.

SUGAR DADDY: How can I have a child with you? You are a child of sixteen years – I am a man of thirty-six.

ALL: EYO . . .

GIRL: Baby you should have thought about that when you said you loved me.
She walks away, he follows her.

SUGAR DADDY: I am a respected man, a married man with a good reputation in the community; you want to drag my good name in the mud.

GIRL: But you said you loved me.

SUGAR DADDY: No, you must have an abortion.

GIRL: Never!

SUGAR DADDY: So this was your plan all along?

GIRL: *[Crying]* It's not my plan .You are also responsible, you happened to date a sixteen year old kid.

SUGAR DADDY: Who is old enough to tell me to use a condom.

GIRL: And you're old enough to know to use a condom.

SUGAR DADDY: Suga! Why you doing this to me? All I am asking is that you have an abortion. *[Puts his arms round her]* Come on, baby, I love you, I'll give you the money for the clinic. We'll sort it out and then we can carry on just as we were . . . before . . . this.

GIRL: No!
They freeze.

MINGAS: Look at that kid, she should be in the school yard but she's on the pavement with a man old enough to be her father. These young girls, all they want is the moola.

MAZ: Not all girls are the same
VENDORS freeze.

SUGAR DADDY: You are ungrateful. I have given you everything you want

– cell phones, clothes, jewelry, a holiday in a game reserve, a weekend away in Mauritius. I take you to the best pubs, clubs and restaurants . . . come on, be reasonable . . . think about my reputation.

He walks away, passing the VENDORS.

SUGAR DADDY: What are you looking at – mind your own business.

MINGAS: Eish, you see men like that, they'll never bring their shoes for repairs, they just chuck them out and buy new ones.

MAZ: Exactly and they treat their teenage girlfriends the same way.

SCENE 4

All the women characters come together to sing a protest song.

TV PRESENTER: Hi viewers at home, we are here at Tumahole where women are protesting. Let us find out from the leader, Thandi Mofurotsi.

THANDI MOFUROTSI: Ntate, we say 'no' to woman and child abuse. Back then women protested the Government's first attempts to force women to carry passes. In 1913 officials in the Orange Free State declared that each month women living in the urban townships would be required to buy new entry permits. In response, the women sent deputations to the Government, collected thousands of signatures in petitions and organized massive demonstrations. Unrest spread throughout the province and hundreds of women were sent to prison. Ntate, if woman managed to stop that injustice, what can stop us now?

TV PRESENTER: Wow, women are taking a stand in Teboho, in Makau, in Tumahole, in Parys.

SUSAN SHABANGU, the minister for Gender Relations, is interviewed.

SUSAN SHABANGU: The New Africa Agenda provides for 50% women representation in decision-making by 2020. This vision of gender parity requires both public and private sector to work together in ensuring equality and women empowerment in all spheres of the economy. The successful implementation of this strategic framework will go a long way in destroying the economic and political glass ceiling that restricts women's progress and integration into the economic mainstream. And in order to achieve this, the development of the Girl Child should be at the center of our work. The Cell C Take a Girl Child to Work programme is a step in the right direction because our investment in the Girl Child of

today means a better Africa and a better world in the future. Amandla!
Forward with the woman's struggle, forward!

TV PRESENTER: That was Minister Relations of Gender Susan Shabangu.
Now it's time for the weather report.

SCENE 5

*Back to the taxi rank. A woman customer approaches MAZ. LERATO is clearly
a person with a good job and plenty of money.*

LERATO: How much are these?

MAZ: R 6.00.

LERATO: So reasonable! That's why I like to shop here in e`kasi instead of
the mall. Thanks, I'll take three.

MAZ: Dankie, sisi. It`s a good color for you. Make no mistake – a classy
color for a classy lady.

    She approaches MINGAS.

LERATO: Can you fix these for me? The heel has come off.

MINGAS: No problem, my dear. Come back in an hour.

LERATO: Thanks, my brother.

    LERATO walks away. MAZ watches as MINGAS stares after her.

MAZ: Ah, you like her Mingas!

MINGAS: Just because I'm looking at her?

MAZ: Your eyes tell me you're interested.

MINGAS: I was looking at her shoes!!!

MAZ: Hey, come on, she doesn't wear her shoes on her bum.

MINGAS: Hau, Maz! Can't I look at a beautiful woman? Must I always
discipline my eyes?

MAZ: That's why I asked if you liked her.

    MINGAS stares down at the shoes the customer had given him.

MINGAS: [To MAZ] Stop looking at me! I haven't committed a crime! I
think you're going overboard.

MAZ: No, no! I am just LOOKING OUT FOR YOU! You're new here in
Tumahole. I don't want you to get in trouble. I know this place well. You
can't judge the book by its cover.

MINGAS: Don't worry. I know people. I can tell what a person is like from
their shoes [He holds up one of the successful woman's shoes] You see, this is

the shoe of a lucky woman, a successful woman, a woman with everything she wants in life.

MAZ: Yes, that`s why you must be careful my friend. Maybe she wants a plaything on the side. Though I must say a woman like that is usually sorted.

MINGAS: What are you talking about! She's just a customer.

SCENE 6

A man and a woman are alone at home.

GUY: Baby, can we . . .

WOMAN: Can we what?

GUY: It's been six weeks without . . .

WOMAN: Patrick, I am tired. You know how exhausting my work is!

GUY: He! Bana I also work.

WOMAN: GEEZ !! Typical! All you men think about is sex, sex, sex, ahi soka!

GUY: Sala le ntho eo ya hao Nca!!

WOMAN: Ntho e ya gender equality, I really don't understand

Switch across to the vendors.

MAZ: Mmmmmmmmm *[Slight pause]* Can you ever imagine what it would be like to put yourself in a woman's shoes, Mingas?

MINGAS: I have never thought about it.

MAZ: Well, just think what would it be like if men fell pregnant?

MINGAS: That would be something! But what about the other way around? We, men, are taught to never show our feelings though those are something you can't hold down. I think you women are lucky – you can let it out, talk about issues and still act strong.

MAZ: Ja, nee.

MINGAS: If we had to swop shoes maybe we would understand each other's pain. But some men are also abused by their wives.

MAZ: True but it's more the other way around.

   LERATO returns.

LERATO: Are my shoes ready?

Mingas: *[Clearly love struck]* I'm sorry, madam, I was talking to my friend, you woman talk too much. I am nearly finished.

LERATO: No problem . . . but be careful what you say about us, ne sister?

MAZ: Ja, watch it, Mingas.

LERATO leaves. MAZ looks at MINGAS as he stares infatuatedly at LERATO's shoe.

MINGAS: What?

MAZ: Nothing. You had better stop admiring her shoe and fix it. It looks as if you have already lost your heart but you might also lose a customer.

A little girl, THEMBI, comes to fetch her shoes.

THEMBI: Greetings, Malume. Are my shoes ready?

MINGAS: Yes, my sweetie, here they are. Did mommy give you money for Uncle Mingas?

THEMBI: Yes. Here it is. *[She pays MINGAS. To MAZ]* Hello ma.

MAZ: Hello my child, how are you today?

THEMBI: I am so happy. It's my birthday.

MAZ: That's wonderful! Come, you can choose one sweetie for your special day.

She takes a sweet and offers it to the girl.

THEMBI: Oh, thank you, thank you! *[She stands to one side, chewing her sweet]*

MINGAS: The little ones are lucky today, the born frees. Yah, born free time! Things are changing. Africa has got a woman President in the United Nations. Our own vice President was a woman and there are so many other women in powerful positions in parliament. For a little one like that... *[Gestures towards THEMBI]* ... the sky's the limit. She can have big dreams.

MAZ: It's true, Mingas. But it's one story for those in power and another for us working people. I've never had a proper education and I'm here next to you every day trying to sell cosmetics to earn a living. This isn't power.

MINGAS: Come on! You can make something out of the cosmetics business. Look on the bright side of it! At least you don't go to bed on an empty stomach. With the cosmetics money you could go back to school, there are bursaries, or BEE companies. It's even easier if you are a woman ... they are forced to help you.

MAZ: Ag, Mingas, everything with you is always simple and quick. But anyway at least I am next to you every day.

MINGAS: Ah Maz! You! What do you mean?

He is fixing the expensive shoes. MAZ looks at him fondly.

MAZ: Nothing, it's nothing. Just talking.

MINGAS: *[Points to THEMBI]* But this little one – at least she can dream big.

THEMBI: Yes, Malume. Like I said, today is my birthday.

MINGAS: Lovely, lovely! And how old you are.

THEMBI: I am ten years old.

MINGAS: A big girl, hey? So what do you want for your birthday?

THEMBI: Malume, I want a dolly. A big dolly. And a party and a big house for the dolly.

MINGAS: Okay, that's nice . . . and what about a cake?

THEMBI: Yes, also a cake, a big cake.

MINGAS: Okay, so mama is going to give a party.

THEMBI: She said she doesn't have money.

MINGAS: Don't worry, Malume will buy you some sweeties. But first tell Malume what would you like to do when you are big?

THEMBI: I want to be a social worker, like my auntie.

MINGAS: That's nice, but do you know what social workers do?

THEMBI: They help people, people that are hungry . . . and they help grannies, who are old and can't do things for themselves . . . and grandfathers, little children and mothers and I want a big house in the suburbs with my children.

MINGAS: Yo, that's a good idea, you are a good girl. Okay, since it's your birthday, you can you help Malume and go to the shop for loose draw and you can keep the change to buy some sweeties for your birthday.

THEMBI: Oh, thank you, Malume, thank you! *[Gives him a hug and exits]*

MAZ: I pray for the little children today – things are so dangerous. I pray they do not need to be fixed like your broken shoes.

MINGAS: Hai, soka ha ha ha.

They both freeze.

SCENE 7

On the other side of the stage, THEMBI enters with an old man.

MALUME: How you've grown, Thembi! Makes my heart jump up with joy to see such a big girl! But first uncle must give you a happy birthday kiss. *[He kisses her on the cheek]*

THEMBI: Why are you closing the door, Malume?

MALUME: It's cold.

THEMBI: But it's dark.

MALUME: Well, you know I don't have electricity here. But don't worry you are safe with Malume in the yard. Now what about that special kiss?

THEMBI: What's a special kiss?

MALUME: A special one, because now you're a big girl. *[He holds her face and tries to kiss her]*

THEMBI: No, Malume! That's for the old people.

MALUME: Come on, my darling.

THEMBI: No Malume, that's for old, old, old people. Please, open the door! *[She calls out]* Mama! Mama!

MALUME: Mama is at work. Stop it! *[Holding her tighter]*

THEMBI: No Malume! No!

Chorus shouts and screams, NO!

MINGAS: Hela, ho etsa hala eng moo, what is going on?

MAZ: Bathong ba Modimo

WOMAN: This rubbish is trying to rape this little girl.

MAN: Sies! He lives in the yard of the mother and this is how he repays.

WOMAN: Where are the police? We called them one hour ago.

They freeze.

MAZ: You see this is the problem Mingas. Everything is good on paper. In the constitution we are all equal but who protect our rights? Where are the police when you need them?

MINGAS holds up two shoes. One is LERATO's expensive shoe; the other is the broken shoe of a poor man.

MINGAS: Look at these shoes, Maz. How can they be equal? This is the shoe of a classy, sophisticated woman, a woman with everything she wants in life. And this is a poor man's shoe. I can tell this is the only pair he has and I am sure he wears it in rain, wind and sun while he works hard and all the salary goes to some woman. You see they can never be equal, no matter what they say in the courts.

MAZ: But we have to start somewhere. Today it's 50/50. You go left, I go right, and we meet at the front door. Gone are those days when you would tell me to keep quiet and just cook, clean and look after the children. Never again!

MINGAS: Haibo! This 50/50 thing – according to my culture there is no such thing. And today the world is upside down because of it. Let me tell you something. To me a woman will always be a woman, meaning you submit to your man as the Bible says. You may have more money than me, drive a luxury car . . . still I am the head of the house. This 50/50, it's all rubbish.

MAZ: Mingas, you mean to say the man who wears that shoe can tell the woman who wear this one what to do? Forget it!

MINGAS: So you agree mos we can never be equal!! Constitution . . . it's a constipation causing nothing but problems and who will protect your rights? These days everyone has got rights . . . it's all upside down. Even dogs and cats they got rights. Everyone is on top of someone else and every one want to exercise their rights without given others a chance to do so. Hai man soka.

LERATO arrives to fetch her shoes.

LERATO: Sanbonani, are my shoes ready?

MINGAS: Your shoes are ready my . . . madam.

LERATO: Thanks and how much do I owe you?

MINGAS: Never mind. It was my privilege to fix them.

LERATO: No, no, don't be silly I must pay you.

MINGAS: No, I insist.

MAZ: Mingas!

LERATO: I insist. *[To MAZ]* I must pay this man!!!

MINGAS: Okay, sorry, sorry. *[Slight pause]* R10.00.

LERATO: Here, thanks. And keep the change. I'm in such a good mood today. I got a promotion.

MAZ: Congratulations!

LERATO leaves. MINGAS looks longingly at her departing figure. He kisses the money she gave him.

MAZ: Yo, Mingas, you really like her.

MINGAS: What? *[Still looking at the money]* Why are looking at me funny all the time?

MAZ: Come on, Mingas! I am your friend. I am sitting here next to you every day. Where must I look?

MINGAS: Hei wena! Mind your own business!

MAZ: SHOO!!!

SCENE 8

GUY: Can we talk?

WOMAN: You are embarrassing me.

GUY: I've been waiting for you for an hour wena.

WOMAN: Get your hands of me *[She walks away]*

GUY: Come here!

WOMAN: What?

GUY: *[Running after her]* Where were you? *[Grabs her]*

WOMAN: If I am not talking, it means I'm fucken busy. *[Pushing him away]* Get your hands off me Patrick!

GUY: Who was that you were busy talking to? *[Grabbing her again]*

WOMAN: I said get your fucken hands of me!

GUY: Who was that? Tell me who? Are you making me a fool just because I'm unemployed? *(Pushes her)*

WOMAN: People are looking Patrick! Don't fuck with me in public *[He pulls her closer to him]* Shit, people are looking at us. Take your hands off me.
  The bystanders attack him, shouting, "Take the bastard!"

OTHER LADY: *[Approaching with a loud voice]* Hey, you man – what's wrong with you?

OTHER LADY: We will call the police if you do that to her again. *[To the WOMEN]* Don't worry, we'll see that this bastard doesn't touch you again.

GUY: Relax, relax . . . everything's ok, it's fine, man, fine . . .

MAZ: Don't worry my dear, we are with you. You don't have to put up with these nonsenses.
  Everyone freezes except the 'couple'.

WOMAN: What do you really want? I've been talking to you for the last five minutes and all you've done is give me shit.

GUY: You are crazy, babe.

WOMAN: Now listen here Patrick, listen to me. You have been fucken staying at my home eating my food, driving around in my car, spending my fucken money. You know what? All this shit ends now right here, right now. *[She pushes him]*

GUY: Wait! Wait a minute!

WOMAN: Don't tell me to wait! *[Pushes him harder]*

GUY: Don't push me!

WOMAN: You aren't listening to me! You are a piece of trash! Half a man and good for nothing, rubbish . . .

GUY: Stop this, please! You are embarrassing us.

WOMAN: Me, embarrassing? It's your behavior that's embarrassing. *[He starts walking away]* Don't fucken walk away from me!

　She grabs his head and pushes him then hits him on the chest.
　The bystanders do not intervene.

GUY: No, no! What's wrong with you!

WOMAN: Don't give me that shit! *[Hits him again]*

LADY: *[Laughing]* Sies, this guy can't control that woman. He really isn't a man o tla ipona. Ha ha ha ha ha.

　The bystanders all exit.

MINGAS: *[Admiring LERATO'S shoe]* The perfect woman with the perfect life – a perfect woman for me.

MAZ: You think everything is so simple? How do you know her life is perfect? Even a woman with everything can have problems.

MINGAS: Who would make problems for her?

MAZ: Some man.

MINGAS: *[Laughs]* But that's why she needs a man like me to help fix everything.

MAZ: Mmmmmmmm *[Slight pause]* Mingas, what if there is someone who needs a man to stand with her in her life and she is always around and sees you every day?

MINGAS: You mean she'll bring shoes to me every day?

MAZ: *[Picking up a pair of battered shoes]* Look at this shoe and look at that one. They are not the same but they need each other.

MINGAS: Too true! There's a left and a right but together they make a pair. I am happy you support my statement.

MAZ: *[Smiling]* And so? *[She kisses him]*

MINGAS: *[Returning her smile]* Okay Maz. I get it. We are both in the same shoes.

MAZ: Yes, mister – I'm glad you've finally got it.

　He kisses her. They embrace.

END

BIOGRAPHIES

Sipho Zakwe completed his undergraduate qualification at DUT [Durban University of Technology] where he studied Dramatic Arts – Script and Screenwriting being one of his specialisations. He prides himself on having been awarded numerous accolades at this institution which included awards for the 'Best Newcomer, Best Male Lead actor and the Best Script and Screen Writer. Sipho graduated [Cum Laude] in 2015 and completed his Honours degree at WITS University in Applied Drama.

Simphiwe Vikilahle is an award winning playwright who grew up in Kwazakhele, Nelson Mandela Bay. He started as an actor but found his calling to be rather in the composing of words. In this regard, he was mentored by Professor Roy Sergeant. His first playwrighting award was for *Two Eyes of The Bird* which was staged in the G.M Eastern Cape school theatre competition and was the overall winner and best script with Qaphelani High School. In addition, he was the 2012 Winner of the Zwakala Festival [Market Theatre, Johannesburg.]

Hans Pienaar writes novels, plays and poetry while earning his keep as a freelance journalist. He has won national awards for *The Third War against Mapoch,* his history of Kwandebele, *Three Dozen Roses,* a play about cultural clashes, and a short story, *My Dog Hitler.* He was news editor of Vrye Weekblad, and travelled through Africa and elsewhere over ten years as a journalist at Independent Newspapers.

Palesa Mazamisa is a satirist, writer, playwright and producer. She co-wrote the play *Bubbly Bosoms* [for the Thari Ya Arts group] which was staged at the State Theatre in Pretoria, South Africa in 2010, and at the National Arts Festival in 2011. The play included leading South African actresses Nakedi Ribane, Connie Chiume and Faith Kekana, among others. Her writings have been published in various publications, and include *Bad Ag* [Baobab Literary Journal], *Kadra's Decree* [Open: An anthology of writing by South African women writers) and *A Day in August* [Botsotso 17]. *Shoes and Coups* is her most recent work and its recent production was her directorial debut.

Allan Kolski Horwitz lives in Johannesburg where he directs the Botsotso Theatre Ensemble and co-ordinates Botsotso publications. Since 1996 he has published several volumes of poetry and short fiction [including *Saving Water* and *Meditations of a Non-White White]* as well as *Collected Plays: 2009-17,* consisting of *The Pump Room, Comrade Babble, Boykie and Girlie, Jerico* and *Book Marks.*

Sjaka S. Septembir has a MA in Theatre Making and 20 years of physical theatre experience. He is an actor, writer, director and producer. His Graphic Novel *Bal-Oog en Brommel — Moord in Ixiastraat* launched at the Open Book Festival in 2017. It opened as a theatre show at Woordfees in 2018 and proceeded to tour the country – www.bal-oog.co.za

The Botsotso Ensemble is a theatre group consisting of Thandeka Shangase, Nkanyiso Shezi, Yandisa Kwhakwha, Sibusiso Ncgobo, Buhle Sithole and Allan Kolski Horwitz. Founded in 2016 it has performed at dozens of schools around Gauteng, presenting both prescribed works [as set down by the Gauteng Department of Education] and more general dramatizations that it has itself created on subjects ranging from the need for a culture of reading to South African history and education on adolescence and its challenges.

Moeketsi Kgotle is from Tumahole, Parys. A performer, theatre maker, percussionist, facilitator and director, he has performed at The Market, The State and the Soweto Theatres. He underwent an internship at the Sibikwa Art Centre and has NGF level 4 and 5 in performing arts and facilitation, NQF level 4 in Arts Administration and an Advanced Diploma in Applied Drama. He is currently completing a B.Hons in Arts at the University of the Witwatersrand.

Printed in the United States
By Bookmasters